The Bionic Woman
and Feminist Ethics

ALSO BY DAVID GREVEN

*Gender and Sexuality in Star Trek:
Allegories of Desire in the Television Series and Films* (2009)

The Bionic Woman and Feminist Ethics

An Analysis of the 1970s Television Series

DAVID GREVEN

McFarland & Company, Inc., Publishers
Jefferson, North Carolina

LIBRARY OF CONGRESS CATALOGUING-IN-PUBLICATION DATA

Names: Greven, David, author.
Title: The Bionic woman and feminist ethics : an analysis of the 1970s television series / David Greven.
Description: Jefferson : McFarland & Company, Inc., Publishers, 2020. | Includes bibliographical references and index.
Identifiers: LCCN 2020013680 | ISBN 9781476674070 (paperback : acid free paper) ∞
ISBN 781476639482 (ebook)
Subjects: LCSH: Bionic Woman (Television program) | Feminism on television. | Women on television.
Classification: LCC PN1992.77.B523 G74 2020 | DDC 791.45/72—dc23
LC record available at https://lccn.loc.gov/2020013680

BRITISH LIBRARY CATALOGUING DATA ARE AVAILABLE

ISBN 978-1-4766-7407-0 (print)
ISBN 978-1-4766-3948-2 (ebook)

© 2020 David Greven. All rights reserved

No part of this book may be reproduced or transmitted in any form or by any means, electronic or mechanical, including photocopying or recording, or by any information storage and retrieval system, without permission in writing from the publisher.

Front cover image by Abramov Vsevolod (Shutterstock)

Printed in the United States of America

McFarland & Company, Inc., Publishers
 Box 611, Jefferson, North Carolina 28640
  www.mcfarlandpub.com

For my dear aunts,
who loved Jaime Sommers, too.

Table of Contents

Acknowledgments   ix

Introduction: Why The Bionic Woman *Matters*   1

Chapter 1: Mrs. Steve Austin   15

Chapter 2: Feminist Ethics   32

Chapter 3: In the Shadow of Sasquatch   62

Chapter 4: Bionic *Vertigo*   71

Chapter 5: Fembot Theory   101

Chapter 6: Mechaphobia and Self-Shattering   131

Chapter 7: Dogs and Sympathy   148

Epilogue: Awakenings   157

Notes   159

Bibliography   167

Index   171

Acknowledgments

When I was a child of five, my aunts showed me an episode of *The Six Million Dollar Man*. It was "The Bionic Woman, Part 2." My life was forever changed by this introduction to Jaime Sommers. My aunt Gina (as she was called at the time) often babysat me during the first season of *The Bionic Woman*. I have a clear memory of watching "The Ghosthunter" with her and us marveling at Jaime's smoking shoe after a bottle of telekinetically hurled acid falls on it. The shoe was vaporized, but Jaime's foot, as resilient as the rest of her, was fine. What was it about feet? I also remember us watching "Claws" and the gasp-inducing moment when the elephant Tusker placed his foot on Jaime's own. She was fine once again.

Over the years, I've talked about Jaime Sommers with just about every significant person in my life. In particular, I thank Marina Stenou, the old gang of chums from Film Forum back in the 90s (Marianne, JJ, Anna, and the rest) with whom I enjoyed marathon viewings of the series that we called "Bionic Breakdown Night," Chris Barreto and Rick Cole, and Viki Zavales for always being receptive to my Jaime-love. And I thank Allison De Fren profusely for teaching me so much about Fembots—and friendship. My thanks to Julie Grossman as well for friendship and film adaptation erudition. And always warm thanks to James Bogdanski for his friendship and passion for art.

In recent years, I have been delighted to share responses to the Bionic shows with other fans on Facebook. There are so many people to acknowledge. In particular, I want to thank Guy Allen for his Facebook fan group *Lindsay Wagner: Bionic & Beyond* and a regular contributor, Marko Krunic, for his always astonishing insights about *The Bionic Woman*. I also thank Matthew Hays for, with exceptional kindness, sending me a lovely reproduced image of Steve Austin and Jaime Sommers wearing their red and blue tracksuits, respectively, and sharing a loving embrace. (He originally sent the image out as Valentine's Day cards.)

Facebook routinely and probably deservedly comes under fire for its

Acknowledgments

practices. But I have stuck with it for the remarkable space it creates for intellectual and personal exchange. Without committing any of these folks to Bionic idolatry, I am so very grateful to Larry Frascella, Joe McElhaney, Corey Creekmur, Adrian Martin, Adrian Garvey, Jose Arroyo, Tania Modleski, Robert Lang, Kevin Bozelka, Elisabeth Karlin, Keri Walsh, George Toles, Lisa Ruddick, Matt Bell, Bob Gutowski, Ben Sampson, Murray Pomerance, Christopher Sharrett, Matthew Sorrento, Daniel Humphrey, Ina Rae Hark, and many others for always being up for movie and television and popular culture conversations. I rely on you all more than you know.

The friends who share one's love of movies and television are friends for life. In Columbia, South Carolina, I am especially grateful to Catherine Keyser, Paul Famolari, Hunter Gardner, Casey Catherine Moore, Scott West, Tom Lekan, and John Lane for sharing in the joys of collective viewing.

I thank my two younger brothers Mike and Ozzy Greven for having endured all of my endless *Bionic* repeat viewings in syndication and on VHS (meticulously taped without commercials, of course) when we were kids. My brother Mike died in 2019, the same year that I finished this book. He will always live in my memory and infinite love for him. I thank my mother and father, my aunts, and my illustrious cousins who kept the dream of Jaime Sommers alive all these years (and more than once performed key roles in childhood reenactments of key episodes).

If I have missed anyone, I humbly apologize. Thank you for taking this journey with me. Before I close out, I must thank, in particular, Kenneth Johnson and Lindsay Wagner for creating a character that has so profoundly enriched my life and that of so many others.

And, as ever, with love that can never be adequately described, I thank Alexander Beecroft for making everything possible. My love for you is like the Bay of Portugal—it hath no bottom.

Introduction:
Why *The Bionic Woman* Matters

The Bionic Woman (1976–1978) is a pivotal 1970s television text—pivotal for its legions of female fans; the study of feminism in the popular culture of the era; the representation of women in television, cinema, and other media forms of the decade; the development of science-fiction and genre shows of this time and after; and the LGBTQI fans that have so passionately loved the show as well.[1] *The Bionic Woman* can be simultaneously enjoyed as an action-adventure series and read as a feminist critique of dominant culture and a male-centered text. I argue that it can also be read as an allegory of transformation that has relevance for queer spectators and as an example of a popular culture text that engages critically with feminist ethics.

The series is a spin-off of *The Six Million Dollar Man*, a television series that ran from January of 1974 to March of 1978 on the ABC network. *The Six Million Dollar Man* was a 1970s juggernaut, a popular culture sensation that went far beyond weekly viewings of series episodes. The Sunday night episodes shown on ABC often paled alongside the merchandising's action-packed images and tactile accessibility. Steve Austin, ripping apart the bars of a jail cell in which he had been wrongly imprisoned; tearing down a concrete wall; battling some animal behemoth, a bear, a gorilla, a lion, et al: these iconic images dominated the 1970s childhood imaginary. The Bionic Man demonstrated his strength on lunch boxes and decals, in comic books, coloring books, dioramas that parents could assemble for avid child fans. The Steve Austin action figure was a must-have—an accurate mock-up of the character as played by Lee Majors, in a red running suit, with a bionic eye one could look through "bionically" and a bionic right arm with a panel on it that could be opened to reveal Steve's sizzling bionic circuitry.

The Six Million Dollar Man and *The Bionic Woman*, which I will refer

Introduction

to as *Six Million* and *Bionic*, respectively (and when referring to both shows, simply Bionic, unitalicized), had their original source material in Martin Caidin's unassuming novel *Cyborg* (1972). (Caidin wrote four novels in the *Cyborg* series.) Steve Austin, a former test pilot and astronaut, becomes the world's first bionic man after a near-fatal accident, which occurs while he is testing a new kind of plane developed by the United States government. The character was introduced in series of TV-movies that then got picked up as a series; the first of these telemovies was "The Moon and the Desert," which aired on March 7, 1973. Now bionic, the famous astronaut Steve Austin becomes a superspy for the secret government agency, the "OSI," or the Office of Scientific Intelligence, working for his OSI boss Oscar Goldman (played in the series by Richard Anderson). Dr. Rudy Wells, the inventor of Bionics, also became a series regular, beginning in *Six Million*'s third season (from this point played by Martin E. Brooks, who replaced Alan Oppenheimer; Martin Balsam was the original Rudy Wells). Oscar and Rudy were also series regulars on *Bionic*, establishing and maintaining both series' continuous universe.

In the two-part *Six Million* episode "The Bionic Woman" (original airdates, March 16 and 23, 1975), Steve returns to his hometown, Ojai, California, to buy and remodel a house. His mother Helen Elgin (Martha Scott) and stepfather Jim Elgin (Ford Rainey) still live there and welcome him back warmly, annoyed only that he did not tell them himself of his return. Steve maintains a loving relationship with Jim, whom he calls Dad, as well as Helen; neither yet know that he is bionic. While back in Ojai, he reencounters his childhood friend, Jaime Sommers (Lindsay Wagner), now a famous tennis player. (It is established in these episodes that Jaime's parents are dead. On *Bionic*, it is established that Steve's parents adopted the young Jaime after her parents died. Further, Jaime's mother was a spy herself. Early examples of retrocontinuity.)

Over the course of the first episode, Steve and Jaime, rekindling and intensifying their adolescent passions, fall in love and plan to marry. After a horrible sky-diving accident, Jaime, having lost both legs, right arm, and right ear, lies on the verge of death. Steve makes a desperate plea to Oscar, as Oscar Goldman is always called, to save Jaime's life by making her bionic.

Steve helps Jaime to accept her bionics, and their romance continues to bloom. When Helen sees, with palpable shock, Steve and Jaime using their bionics during an outdoor run, Steve explains to her the truth of his and Jaime's cybernetic transmogrification.

Steve and Jaime plan to marry. But Jaime's body begins to reject her

Why The Bionic Woman *Matters*

bionics, leading to excruciating pain that causes her to lose all control. At the end of part two, Jaime, suffering one of the seizures that define her bionic rejection-moments, bursts out of the hospital where she's being treated and runs into the dark, thunderstorm-swept night.

Running blindly in the rain, she stops to enter a rain-pounded telephone booth, shutting the metal folding door behind her. Jaime picks up the phone and begins talking into it without actually making a call. In her madness, she cries out for help to those who aren't there—"Steve? Oscar? STEEEEVE!" But her wrath has a mythic, Herculean edge. She smashes down the telephone booth door as she runs back out into the pounding deluge. Steve, running after her, eventually finds her and takes her back to the hospital. The doctor who made her bionic, Rudy Wells, and his team try to save her—but she dies.

"The Bionic Woman (Part 1)" aired on March 16, 1975. Part 2 aired on March 23, 1975. I was born in 1969, and by 1975 I was an avid connoisseur of all things televisual, bionic stuff most of all. Despite being indelibly imprinted on my consciousness, "The Bionic Woman" *Six Million* episodes always end in my memories with the image of Jaime knocking down that telephone booth door. As vividly as I remember watching the scenes of Jaime running madly in the second episode's first airing of, I retain no memory of her death scene at the end. (Most likely, I blocked out a memory too terrible to bear.)

The event of Jaime's death was apparently a collective trauma for the nation's children. The ratings for this *Six Million* two-parter were extremely high, providing the impetus for the spin-off. Concerned parents wrote to the ABC network, claiming their children had been severely affected by the death of Jaime. Psychiatrists wrote treatises about the impact the episode had on children, left bereft because they were too young to cope with the enormity of Jaime's death.

Some of this may be the stuff of legend—but then again, ABC did act decisively on the reaction to Jaime Sommers. The writer and producer of these episodes, Kenneth Johnson (who would go on to create *The Incredible Hulk* TV series for CBS, starring Bill Bixby, the first *V* miniseries for NBC, and the later *Alien Nation* for Fox), at the behest of ABC, decided that he had to bring Jaime Sommers back to life. Season 3 of *Six Million* opened with a two-part follow-up called "The Return of the Bionic Woman," which aired on September 14 (Part 1) and September 21 (Part 2), 1975.

Given the outrage over the death of the instantly popular Jaime, the producers decided to bring the character back to reassure audiences, chil-

Introduction

dren especially, that she had not died. Well, Jaime *had* died—but through revolutionary cryogenic technology, she was brought back to life. The success of these follow-up episodes led to the creation of the spin-off series, *The Bionic Woman*, starring Lindsay Wagner, reprising her role as Jaime Sommers (and being paid immense amounts of money to do so, much to Lee Major's highly public chagrin). The premiere episode of the series, "Welcome Home, Jaime," first of a two-parter, aired on January 14, 1976.

The staying power of Steve Austin and Jaime Sommers shows no signs of abating. Innumerable tributes adorn the pages of Facebook, where fan groups dedicated to both series abound as do groups devoted to each actor, such as Guy Allen's *Lindsay Wagner: Bionic and Beyond*; Facebook's fan group *The OSI Files* provides astute podcasts deconstructing entire episodes; websites such as *The Bionic Wiki* and *The Bionic Woman Files* and *Bionic Blonde* provide reams of useful information, and at times sharp commentary; Herbie J. Pilato wrote a lively history of both shows; *Bionic* was rebooted as a new television series on NBC in 2007 by the creators of the acclaimed *Battlestar Galactica* reboot; indie-film guru Kevin Smith authored a new series of *Six Million* comic books (the first appeared in 2011); in 2012, a new *Bionic Woman* comic book series from Dynamite also appeared; a six-issue comic book series (2016–17) from DC Comics, written by Andy Mangels and illustrated by Judit Tondora, paired The Bionic Woman and the 70s TV incarnation of the DC comics icon Wonder Woman. (Wonder Woman was given her own series starring Lynda Carter that aired from 1975 to 1979, first on ABC, then on CBS, and finally given her own blockbuster DC film starring Gal Gadot in 2017.) In 2019, a new comic book series pairing The Bionic Woman and Charlie's Angels (based on another iconic 1970s ABC series) hit the stands. And perhaps most dramatically of all, *Death Stranding*, a 2019 action game developed by director Hideo Kojima and Kojima Productions for PlayStation 4, reproduces the image of a Jaime Sommers–like Lindsay Wagner, successfully enlisted by Kojima—a passionate *Bionic Woman* fan—to be a member of the cast.

Popular Culture and Queer Possibility: Or, Coming Out with Jaime Sommers

I expand on the idea of feminist ethics later in the introduction. For now, I want to orient the reader in my approach to reading this popular culture text.

Why The Bionic Woman *Matters*

The cyborg has been voluminously read as a metaphor for both queer subjectivity and for race, especially mixed race, and the cyborg woman for the mulatta.[2] Long before I came to know critical theory, I knew Jaime Sommers in her screen guise as a woman undergoing an endless series of transformations. Long before I read the British psychoanalyst Joan Riviere on the female masquerade—femininity, following Riviere, understood as a masquerade, albeit one that causes the woman tremendous psychic distress—I *experienced* these masquerades as directly as I could through my identification with Jaime. This identification with Jaime has many facets, but arguably its central one is my recognition of the overlaps between the character's life and the dilemmas she faced and overcame and my experiences as a gay man, closeted in my youth, out since my early twenties. This identification found a metaphor within a metaphor in Jaime's various undercover identities (flight attendant, nun, a rodeo rider, a French artist's model, a tutor to an Arab prince, a gypsy, and so forth) and, most resonantly, her ultimate masquerade as ordinary human. Just as Jaime donned different identities, I played different roles throughout my life in the closet, in an effort to pass as straight—a mission assigned me by the culture at large.

Jaime's sustained and shifting disguises served as palpable indications to my younger self that identity itself was a mask people put on, some so much better than others (mine, insecurely fashioned during my closeted youth, always fell off). *Bionic* literalized what it suggested about the flimsiness and arbitrariness of identities, appearances, personal masks, and the female masquerade in its legendary race of villainous superwomen, the Fembots, Jaime Sommers' chief foe. "I call them *Fem*bots," announced John Houseman, in his plummiest Britishy tones, as the diabolical mad scientist Dr. Franklin, who creates the Fembots to infiltrate the OSI. "Programmable, obedient, and as beautiful—or deadly—as I choose to make them!" More on the Fembots soon.

To establish the subjects of this book: I treat *Bionic* as a popular culture myth of femininity that is specific to its time, reflecting the aspirations, limitations, and personality of its era, and timeless, if we understand timelessness to be one of the markers of myth. I discuss the series critically even though I am unable to do so in any kind of fully objective, distanced sense. The series has so seeped into my soul that it's part of my psychic DNA; my critical analysis of the series will be an attempt to work out its ideological muddles, to offer a critical account that is, indeed, critical even as it reflects ardent fan love. Which is to say that, to use Alexander Doty's term, I write always as a scholar-fan. I believe that working through

Introduction

Bionic's emotional impact on me, foregrounding the odd and specific ways in which that "me" got made, can shed light on the underexplored phenomenon of popular culture's impact on and influence over socialization—how we become subjects of a particular social order, how we come to understand ourselves as embodiments of our racial, ethnic, and social elements.

Like Unlikeness and Bad Others

In a two-part episode from *Bionic*'s second season, "Doomsday Is Tomorrow" (original airdates: January 19 and 26, 1977), Jaime must battle against a sentient supercomputer, the Alex 7000, which has been programmed to destroy the world. Alex's creator, Dr. Elijah Cooper (Lew Ayres), has attempted to blackmail the world into peace with the threat of total annihilation should any country in the world launch a nuclear weapon.

Dr. Cooper's warnings about the world-destroying Doomsday Device bombard the airwaves of every country; his voiceover commandments, translated into in different languages, suffuse the soundtrack over a montage of stock footage images of key world cities (Paris, Cairo, and so forth). Some skeptical officials somewhere in the Middle East, refusing to believe that Cooper's Doomsday weapon exists, continue to test their nuclear weapons, thereby triggering the Doomsday Device, which is activated just as the aged Dr. Cooper dies.

Jaime, sent in undercover as French scientist Dr. Marguerite Perry, begs the old dying scientist to dismantle the device, but to no avail. No army can storm his compound and deactivate the device, either, because the Alex 7000 has been specifically programmed to stop any such force or individual intruder from doing so. Jaime, with only a few hours until doomsday, must battle against Alex and all the defenses he has put into place. She must enter and make her way through Alex's labyrinthine maze of killing traps and bottomless deeps. "You will die if you make the attempt," the supercomputer informs Jaime in his cold, vaguely ironic robotic monotone. Alex's ominous disembodied voice pervades the complex, issuing forth from every corner and crevice. "You know how big I am," he taunts her when she threatens to "tear your brain apart."

The closest we get to an image of Alex is the trope of a security camera. Bearing his human/machine name, the security camera glows with one pinpoint yellow light, not the eye of God but an Orwellian all-seeing pitiless menace, a metallic miniature construction whose shape and position—oblong and suspended—connotes the non-human.

Like the Fembot episodes, "Doomsday" thematizes a key element in the series: the repulsion of like for like. I will theorize this phenomenon chiefly as "like unlikeness" and "mechaphobia." Alex, remarking that he regrets having to terrorize Jaime given how alike they are, pronounces them "Cousins." (He then emits a high-pitched mechanical screech that startles Jaime so much that she tumbles down a flight of stairs, leading her to pound away at a stationary computer, which he mock-sympathetically identifies as only one of his "remote modules.")

One of the chief ideological conflicts in the series is its consistent thematization of *the bad other*, who resembles the heroine but more importantly must be destroyed. This bad other contains all the qualities the heroine either fears or loathes. The Fembots look like human women, speak and act like the women in Jaime's world whom they replace. But their terrifying otherness is revealed when Jaime knocks off their facial covering to reveal the scary circuitry beneath.

Similarly, Alex 7000 is human-like, his voice bespeaking intelligence. Despite his monotone, unrelenting, and pitiless manner, he seems to like and care for Jaime even as he plots her destruction. But the goal of the episode is less about saving the world, in the end, and more about annihilating Alex, which Jaime climactically does by reactivating the sealed-off sprinklers and effectively drowning the supercomputer.

The repulsion of like for like has implications for feminist, queer, and historical readings of the series. The 1970s were the era in which second-wave feminism flourished. While the advances that feminism made in this era were significant, it is also true that organized feminism divorced itself from its lesbian community, gaining public legitimacy by doing so. Lesbians may have shared the same cause but were feminism's bad other. Similarly, in gay male communities at the time, the push to adopt a hypermasculine persona included a rejection of effeminacy, swishiness, and the sissy associated with the pre–Stonewall, pre–Gay Liberation era.[3]

I concede that *Bionic*'s frequent exploration of the bad other was a reactionary dimension of the series. This includes the character of Lisa Galloway (also played by Lindsay Wagner) introduced in the first season *Bionic* episode, "Mirror Image." Working with a group of criminals attempting to infiltrate and steal state secrets from the OSI, Lisa has been surgically altered to look and trained to sound like Jaime Sommers. The episode concludes with a final confrontation between heroine and evil doppelgänger. Lisa is clearly the inferior version—not only because she is

Introduction

evil but because she is white-trash; she is the class other, her original Southern twang a marked contrast to the mellifluously middle-class tones and manner of Jaime Sommers.

Yet it is precisely here that the radicalism of *The Bionic Woman* comes through: in the two-part second season episode "Deadly Ringer," Lisa Galloway returns, her criminal accomplice and handler Dr. Courtney engineering a swap between Jaime and the imprisoned Lisa, who gets to live in Jaime's house while impersonating her, leaving the real Jaime to endure life in jail. The horror of incarceration's dehumanizing effects confronts Jaime when she protests, "I am Jaime Sommers!" and receives cold, blank, unresponsive stares in return.

As part of the criminals' plot, Lisa, in prison, has intentionally given the impression that she really believes that she is Jaime so that the real Jaime's cries of protest when placed in the prison will seem like her double's feigned ones. As the episode proceeds, however, we see that Lisa's delusion is no ruse: she has come to believe that she *is* Jaime, descending into madness as she attempts to make Jaime's life her own. The episode does not end with the vanquished Lisa being discarded. Instead, Jaime reaches out to her and tries to help her, even as the OSI and law enforcement verge on apprehending and possibly killing her. This reconciliatory gesture, Jaime reaching out to a woman who has injured her and showing her compassion, literally cradling the damaged double in her arms, represents the achievement of the series' feminist, queer, ethical promise.

Feminist Ethics and Martha Nussbaum

As I elaborate in Chapter 2, my concept of feminist ethics is derived from feminist theory, first-wave feminism as it is represented by nineteenth-century women's writing (Sarah Orne Jewett being my chief example), second-wave feminist writing, the classical Hollywood woman's film, and works such as *The Bionic Woman* itself. My thinking on these matters has its foundations in the work of Martha Nussbaum, especially *Frontiers of Justice*. Several aspects of her argument are salient to this study.

As Nussbaum argues, today there exists "three unsolved problems of social justice." First, we need justice for those with "physical and mental impairments." Second, we face the "urgent problem of extending justice to all world citizens, showing theoretically how we might realize a world that is just as a whole." Third, we must "face issues of justice involved in our treatment of nonhuman animals."[4] The classical theorists of the social contract left outside of their utopian visions of a just society women, children, elderly people, and especially people with "severe and atypical physical and mental impairments."[5] The rights of nonhuman animals have been similarly neglected. What continues to exist is "the need to extend our theories of justice outside the realm of the human, to address issues of justice involving nonhuman animals."[6]

Part of my effort in this book is to take a popular culture text such as *Bionic* seriously. Though some might consider a text with an inherently lowbrow status unworthy of serious study, much less accede to the view that is a work of art with multivalent meanings, it is my contention that *Bionic* did, not consistently but often enough to qualify, rise to precisely this level of achievement. That the series and its protagonist were created by a genuine television auteur, Kenneth Johnson, and graced by Lindsay Wagner, an actor of extraordinary ability and committed humanist politics, count immeasurably toward making *Bionic* a text worthy of study.

The central concerns of Nussbaum in *Frontiers of Justice* resonate in *Bionic*. Though a series that, like the SF action show it was spun off from, foregrounded superhuman strength and the thrills of it seeing it in action, *Bionic* also never let one forget that these strengths and thrills had their foundation in almost unimaginable physical trauma, the loss of limbs and senses. In an article written by the queer director Jonathan Caouette, "Twenty-Five Things I Love," Lindsay Wagner is at the top of the list. The director opines:

> 1. Lindsay Wagner
> There's this Stepford-Wives–like "Bionic Woman" episode where Lindsay Wagner plays a dual role as Jaime Sommers and arch-enemy Lisa Galloway, who throws Jaime in an asylum then impersonates her doing evil in the world! Lindsay Wagner is astonishingly intense in this episode as she was in the entire series. I once read her explaining she played Jaime Sommers as a triple amputee in post-traumatic shock, and that motivation always comes across. *The Bionic Woman* is the only female action superwoman of the '70s that's as vulnerable, passionate and full with multifaceted grief as a Robert Altman heroine.

Caouette references the S2 two-parter "Deadly Ringer" in which Jaime Sommers confronts her double, Lisa Galloway. Caouette's description of Wagner's performance is especially apt: she played Jaime Sommers as "a triple amputee in post-traumatic shock." While Wagner's characterization certainly deepened and shifted over the course of the three seasons, that initial intensity was what made Jaime Sommers such a startling and unexpected character, particularly on a series such as *Six Million*, with a

Introduction

laconic lead who rarely went to emotional extremes (though the pilot episode certainly depicts Steve Austin's agonized early relationship to his bionics).

Several *Bionic* episodes eerily conduct a dialogue with Nussbaum's concerns. In season 2's "The Vega Influence," Jaime develops an initially difficult but ultimately meaningful alliance with a young deaf woman named Laurie Boylin (Jamie Smith Jackson), the daughter of a scientist overseeing a remote government scientific facility. When Jaime and Dr. Michael Marchetti of the OSI land on the island where the facility has been set up, they confront a strangely depopulated zone. As it turns out, the inhabitants have been transformed into zombies of sorts, wandering around with a collective mind controlled by a sentient meteorite.

Jaime initially experiences confusion when speaking to Laurie. And when she and Laurie race from a hangar to Laurie's car to escape the zombie horde, Laurie runs ahead and leaves Jaime, staggering to the ground and crying out for help, behind. Laurie, because she is deaf, is immune to the meteorite hum that enslaves the others; Jaime, because of her bionic ear, is partially but not fully immune. Picking herself up just before being grabbed by the zombies, Jaime bionically runs to Laurie's car and just barely manages to escape becoming a zombie herself. Laurie begins to drive away once Jaime is in the car, and Jaime stares at her in angry confusion. Back at Laurie's family home, Jaime once again experiences feelings of alienation and confusion when she speaks to Laurie and gets no response.

It is only after confronting Laurie about her behavior that Jaime realizes the problem—the impasse—has been her lack of understanding that Laurie is deaf. Jaime tells Laurie about her bionic ear. ("I have the granddaddy of all hearing aids. It's implanted in the ear; you can't see it.") The episode makes it clear that forming community is a difficult and hard-won but not impossible task. Jaime, apologetically and warmly saying, "Hi, again," gently, even sheepishly extends her hand for Laurie to shake it. The imperiled women can now forge an alliance built on the mutual recognition that each is differently abled. The women begin their relationship anew once they properly recognize one another.

As I discuss in Chapter 2, the S1 episode "Claws," written by a female screenwriter, significantly depicts Jaime's relationship to the animals she cares for when their female handler goes out of town. A strong correlation exists between feminist ethics and women's bonds with nonhuman animals, as the episode demonstrates. In Chapter 7, I discuss the S3 two-parter "The Bionic Dog," featuring Max, a bionic German Shepherd suffering from depression who is, almost literally, brought back to joyous life by Jaime. In her bonds with nonhuman animals, Jaime Sommers extends the compassion and empathy she exhibits in her interactions with other human beings, including the nebulous would-be villains she encounters over the course of the series, to vulnerable creatures that benefit from her intervention. They, in turn, allow Jaime to discover what is meaningful to her and not only to articulate her ethical positions but also put them into action.

Chapter Outline

1. Mrs. Steve Austin

This chapter discusses the four episodes of *The Six Million Dollar Man* that introduce the character of Jaime Sommers, Steve Austin's love interest and potential bride, and *The Bionic Woman*'s two-part pilot episode, "Welcome Home, Jaime." The contributions of Lindsay Wagner, an actress with a publicly expressed, personal humanist vision, and the television auteur Kenneth Johnson, creator of the Jaime Sommers character, were crucial in creating both a heroine and a television series that was self-aware and pursued a politics of feminist ethics. One of the ideological difficulties the series poses is that Jaime's ascendance as an autonomous character is directly linked to her commitment to the United States' Cold War–era geopolitical mission. While this aspect of the series is problematic, another significant aspect of the show, its retooling of tropes of the Hollywood woman's film, facilitates a more progressive vision, especially the idea of the independent woman's negotiation of her relationship with her mother or a maternal figure. Considering the series' engagement with the themes of female melodrama—the classical Hollywood genre of the woman's films—I frame it as an initially tragic and ultimately utopian myth of female autonomy that liberates the heroine from the conventional marriage plot.

2. Feminist Ethics

The Six Million Dollar Man emphasized Jaime Sommers as tragic figure, doomed to die even though given the bionic technology that saved the hero Steve Austin. While Jaime's suffering has a great deal of significance, *The Bionic Woman*'s first season worked to establish the heroine's auton-

Introduction

omy and maturation, to emphasize the possibilities available to her. The first season's depiction of Jaime's bonds with nonhuman animals evinces the series' engagement with feminist ethics, a concept that I elaborate here. Drawing on feminist theory, nineteenth century women's writings, Greek mythology, and the classical Hollywood woman's film, I argue that feminist ethics guides *Bionic* at its most progressive. In terms of the series' reimagining of female melodrama, I discuss the episode "Jaime's Mother." Both this episode and "Mirror Image" introduce a recurring theme of central importance to *Bionic*: the double.

3. In the Shadow of Sasquatch

This chapter discusses the two-part crossover episode "The Return of Bigfoot," focusing on the distinctions between *Bionic*'s and *Six Million*'s treatments of a similar theme. The Sasquatch/Bigfoot character was initially introduced on *Six Million* in a now-legendary two-part episode written by Kenneth Johnson that focused on a battle of cybernetic brawn between Steve Austin and Sasquatch, revealed to be a bionic creature, a kind of Golem for a community of deep-space explorers who live in a secret base deep within the California mountains. Though ultimately shown to be a benevolent being who works with Steve Austin to avert disaster, the Sasquatch is initially presented as a terrifying entity. In the crossover *Six Million/Bionic* sequel, Sasquatch is depicted from the start as an exploited and suffering creature. The relationship that Jaime Sommers develops with Sasquatch models the series' commitments to ethical treatment of the nonhuman animal. Moreover, the episode "The Return of Bigfoot, Part 2" emphasizes the strength of female relationships and the resourceful woman.

4. Bionic *Vertigo*

This chapter uses *The Bionic Woman*'s surprising affinities with classical Hollywood, the female melodrama in particular, as a foundation. Noting its parallels with Hitchcock's film *Vertigo* and Douglas Sirk's *Imitation of Life*, this chapter focuses on the extraordinary two-part episode "Deadly Ringer," for which Lindsay Wagner won a leading actress Emmy playing both Jaime Sommers and her mentally ill doppelgänger. The chapter explores the feminist, queer, and class politics of the double and the ambivalence toward the normative heroine that the doppelgänger plot facilitates.

5. Fembot Theory

Bionic's most iconic contribution to popular culture is the Fembot, robot women "programmable, obedient, and as beautiful or as deadly" as their creator Dr. Franklin chose to make them. Fembots and other kind of artificial women abound at present, in works ranging from *Ex Machina* to the *Battlestar Galactica* reboot and the HBO *Westworld*. Including commentary on the classic 1970s paranoid thriller *The Stepford Wives*, this chapter theorizes the Fembot as a contemporary manifestation of the Medusa myth. Topics include mechaphobia, early versions of nonbinary and gender nonconforming identity, and lesbian cruising.

6. Mechaphobia and Self-Shattering

Mechaphobia is a fear of the nonhuman in mechanical and technological forms that take the appearance of or in other ways simulate the human. The fearful encounter between Jaime Sommers and her machine double exemplifies mechaphobia. This chapter analyzes mechaphobia in three standout episodes, the two-parter "Doomsday Is Tomorrow" and the series finale "On the Run." All thematize Jaime's confrontations with her phobic hatred of the nonhuman, externalized and interiorized.

7. Dogs and Sympathy

In the third season, *Bionic* introduced Max, a bionic German Shepherd. Max was the first bionic being, but now suffers from a mysterious ailment. Rudy Wells insists that it is a new form of bionic rejection, one that comes with age; Jaime insists that Max is suffering from depression due to his grim, imprisoning surroundings and lack of affectionate interaction. Defying the orders of Rudy and Oscar Goldman, Jaime breaks Max out of his OSI prison and, through grueling trial, restores him to joyous life. Using the work of Alice Kuzniar as a foundation, I argue that this two-part episode draws on the sentimental tradition to make a resistant political point about the urgency of feminist activism on the part of nonhuman animals.

Chapter 1

Mrs. Steve Austin

The four *Six Million Dollar Man* episodes introducing the character of Jaime Sommers, "The Bionic Woman, Parts 1 and 2," and "The Return of the Bionic Woman, Parts 1 and 2," and *The Bionic Woman*'s two-part pilot episode "Welcome Home, Jaime," were all written by the television auteur Kenneth Johnson, *Bionic*'s creator. Over the course of the Jaime Sommers–focused episodes of *Six Million* Jaime is introduced as Steve Austin's love interest, nearly dies, is made bionic, almost marries Steve, dies, comes back to life, struggles with amnesia and the fact that she no longer remembers Steve, attempts to go on an OSI mission and fails despite being accompanied by Steve, struggles over her feelings for the scientist who successfully brought her back to life, and finally embarks on an uncertain future.

A few months later, Jaime's own spinoff series premiered. "Welcome Home, Jaime, Part 1" establishes that Jaime's worst health scares are finally over. Some, but not all, of her memory has been restored: she remembers growing up in Ojai, her adoptive parents Helen and Jim Elgin, her star career as a tennis player; she still does not remember being in love with Steve. Jaime returns to civilian life, moving into a loft-apartment above a barn on the Elgins' property and becoming a schoolteacher at the Ventura Air Force Base. Grateful to the government for having saved her life, Jaime tells Oscar Goldman, her OSI boss, that she wants to work for him and begins to go on secret missions.

Jaime remarks to Steve at one point after she has made peace with having been transformed into a bionic woman, "It might not be so bad being the Bride of Frankenstein." Jaime presumably refers to James Whale's sequel to his famous film adaptation of Mary Shelley's novel *Frankenstein*, but Kenneth Johnson has acknowledged Shelley's novel as an important

The Bionic Woman and Feminist Ethics

intertext for his creation of Jaime Sommers within the context of *Six Million*. Johnson reimagined *Frankenstein*, a male-centered work with a great deal of feminist significance, as an initially tragic and ultimately utopian myth of female autonomy.[1]

"You Can't Speak for Me"

> "The Bionic Woman: Part 1." Directed by Richard Moder.
> Written by Kenneth Johnson. Original Airdate: March 16, 1975.
>
> "The Bionic Woman: Part 2." Directed by Richard Moder.
> Written by Kenneth Johnson. Original Airdate: March 23, 1975.

The pre-credits sequence (or cold open) of "The Bionic Woman, Part 1" shows Steve Austin pursuing a plate used for counterfeiting money that has been acquired by the dapper, white-suited villain Joseph Ronaugh (Malachi Throne). In this thrilling sequence, Steve follows Ronaugh's speeding van at night, jumping on to it, tears off the back door, and grabs the plate. It's not clear why this subplot is attached to the introduction of Jaime Sommers and her transformation into a bionic woman until later, when Jaime's first mission, accompanied by Steve, involves Ronaugh.

In a telling ellipsis, the narrative proper begins with Steve driving to his hometown of Ojai, California, where he buys and renovates a house. (Adding a country and western jocundity to these scenes, Lee Majors sings, non-diegetically, his own songs about Steve's restless need for change.) The implication is that Steve is burnt out from dangerous missions such as the one to retrieve the plate. He wants to put down roots where they were initially planted. Soon, his parents Helen and Jim (Steve's stepfather, whom he calls Dad) are helping Steve redo the house. As Helen is making a batch of wallpaper paste that Steve accidentally mistakes for cake batter, she alerts him to the presence of another return visitor to Ojai—Jaime Sommers, Steve's former classmate and, as will be later revealed, Helen and Jim's adopted daughter after teenage Jaime's parents died.

Jaime is now a famous tennis star. Steve ventures downtown to meet up with her, discovering her playing tennis. They immediately engage in the snappy childhood banter they once enjoyed. Delighted to reconnect, Steve and Jaime take a walk around their old neighborhood, former residents returned as celebrities: the highway signpost for Ojai has the legend "Home of Steve Austin, astronaut," and a young girl (Dana Plato) watching Jaime play tennis tells Steve, "Jaime Sommers is the most famous person

1. Mrs. Steve Austin

ever to have come from Ojai, except for that astronaut guy." Despite their successes, Steve and Jaime each experience loneliness because of the professional lives that have made them famous. But Jaime remarks that in the time she and Steve have been strolling, arm in arm, around Ojai, "I haven't felt lonely at all." Steve concurs. After a few rough spots, and Helen Elgin's cheerful and sensitive matchmaking, Steve and Jaime realize that they are in love. (Steve remarks he's been in love with Jaime since they were children.) While expressing doubts about how their busy schedules will mesh, the two plan to marry.

It should be noted that it is Jaime, listing her looming international tournament dates, who verbalizes doubts about the life they will have together as two such overcommitted people. "What kind of a life are we going to have *without* each other?" Steve counters. In the next scene, the couple go skydiving. The pair engage for some time in the pleasures of this leisure sport. Then the episode turns its notes to tragic. Jaime's skydiving suit glitches and she falls nearly to her death, her right arm, legs, and right ear shattered.

Steve, desperate to save Jaime's life, begs his OSI boss Oscar Goldman to make Jaime bionic. Steve tries to persuade Oscar by promising Jaime's services to him as a spy. Oscar doesn't buy it: "Steve, you're in love with her. You'd sell your *soul* for her." After a very tense conversation in which Oscar makes it quite clear that he will indeed employ Jaime's bionic abilities in service to the OSI, Oscar makes the call to Rudy Wells. Jaime becomes the Bionic Woman.

In making a case for the progressive politics of *Bionic*, we are immediately confronted by some intractable problems posed by the premise. In our moment of heightened awareness of the misogynistic dimensions of American culture, a reading of *Bionic*'s premise as sexist is unavoidable. Steve and Oscar and by extension Rudy argue over the fate of a young woman denied agency to contribute to this discussion. There is an important moment when Steve talks to Jaime as she regains consciousness after the accident; looking down on his bionic hand, he realizes that bionics might save Jaime's life, too. He asks her, "Jaime, there may be a way—will you trust me?" And she nods yes. At least to a certain extent, Steve asks Jaime for consent.

But, as Wagner so exquisitely conveys, Jaime, once she wakes up from the procedure, is horrified to learn that she has been made bionic. Her eyes roll back, and she quietly cries, "Oh, my God ... why didn't you let me die?" The *Six Million* pilot amply documented Steve Austin's horror at his bionic transformation as well, so Jaime's reaction adheres to a tra-

The Bionic Woman and Feminist Ethics

dition of realistic depictions of this inevitable aftermath. Nevertheless, Jaime's body now belongs to the United States government and on some level belongs to the men who made her bionic—ideas made horrifyingly apparent in *Bionic*'s series finale "On the Run," when Jaime is explicitly told this and that she is not allowed to pursue an independent life free of government oversight.

We cannot, then, escape the fumes of old sexist forms. Jaime's bionic transformation signifies the traffic in women, the use of women as a means of exchange and figures of transaction between men, the patriarchal understanding of women as property. Gayle Rubin and Eve Kosofsky Sedgwick, expanding on as well as critiquing the work of structuralist theorists such as the anthropologist Claude Lévi-Strauss and the literary critic René Girard, have acutely taught us about these enduring patterns, governing not only male/female but also male/male relationships.[2]

We tend retroactively to read the four Jaime Sommers episodes on *Six Million*, despite being discrete from *Bionic*, as part of the later show. Nevertheless, it is important to distinguish the four *Six Million* episodes introducing Jaime from her own series. The series emphasizes Jaime's autonomy and ability to make decisions both strategic and personal. (Some commentators would disagree.) Her four initial *Six Million* appearances emphasize her lack of control and psychological and bodily unraveling.

There is, however, a striking moment in "The Bionic Woman, Part 2" when we are made aware of Jaime's subordinated gender position and the patriarchal power of the men deciding her fate. Jaime uses her admittedly compromised position as secret agent-draftee to articulate her autonomy. Steve and Jaime, back from a joyous bionic run, are surprised by a grim-faced Oscar, who asks Jaime if she will excuse Steve and him for a moment so that they can speak privately. Oscar and Steve walk into his kitchen and discuss the upcoming mission to stop Ronaugh from using a new counterfeit money-plate. Steve misapprehends Oscar's meaning—he's not here to assign Steve to this mission but, for the first time, Jaime. Steve protests this immediately, arguing that she is not ready for a mission, much less so dangerous a one. Clearly, Steve cannot imagine Jaime *ever* going on a mission despite having made the desperate case to Oscar that Jaime should be made bionic precisely because "she can get into places I could never get into."

While the men argue over Jaime, she suddenly appears, saying "I apologize for overhearing this conversation," but explains that "this bionic ear you both gave me" has allowed her access to their discussion. When Steve further protests that Jaime cannot take on this mission, Jaime says, "You can't speak for me." This is a highly significant moment for several reasons. First, it exposes the ongoing efforts to silence Jaime on the part of Steve and Oscar. Second, Jaime's articulation of her own position, using her voice both literally and symbolically, is a crucial feminist intervention in the steady traffic in women. Third, it introduces a different register when Jaime adds, "I've got to pay my own way." Jaime believes that she owes a debt, one that can never be repaid, to the United States government. She personally wants to repay the government for bringing her back to life. "On the Run" will offer a pointed, even lacerating critique of these core ideas in *Bionic*'s premise. But Jaime's initial sense of gratitude and good-American commitment to the Cold War effort are definitive aspects of much of the series.

Mrs. Steve Austin: Bionic Woman and the Woman's Film

As I will have several occasions to note, *Bionic* evokes the core themes of the woman's film, or female melodrama. In her study *A Woman's View*, Jeanine Basinger offers a persuasive description of what constitutes the classical Hollywood woman's film: it is one that "places at the center of its universe a female who is trying to deal with emotional, social, and psychological problems that are specifically connected to the fact that she is a woman."[3] The popularity of the Hollywood woman's film genre is generally believed to span from the 1930s to the early 1960s. The history of the woman's film, the evolution from "female weepie" to "chick-flick," needs a much more expansive historical account than I can provide here. Any proper analysis of this topic would need to account for the made-for-TV film from the 1970s to the 1990s; the Lifetime channel and its wide array of content ranging from the TV-movie genre it has kept alive to its various original and re-run TV series; cable TV series such as HBO's *Sex and the City*, which self-consciously and explicitly evoke the woman's film, and the more recent *Girls*; Netflix and the Hallmark Channel; and so forth. Moreover, the extraordinary cross-fertilization of the woman's film with other genres, such as noir, horror, science-fiction, biopic, screwball comedy, romantic comedy, spy thriller, rape-revenge film, et al, needs to be included in any analysis. As Basinger argues, the woman's film genre far exceeds the boundaries of melodrama; to limit the genre to melodrama would "eliminate more than half of the films that are concerned with women and their fates, among them Rosalind Russell's career comedies,

The Bionic Woman and Feminist Ethics

musical biographies of real-life women, combat films featuring brave nurses on *Bataan*, and westerns in which women drive cattle west and men over the brink."[4] For these reasons, I believe that a science-fiction narrative can share the woman's film paradigm.

What *Bionic* specifically shares with the woman's film is two of its central themes. As I have argued elsewhere, these two themes are the female protagonist's ambivalence over marriage and her significant, often fraught relationship with her mother.[5] I will discuss the latter in the next chapter's analysis of the S1 episode "Jaime's Mother." Here, I want to address the ways in which, from the character's inception, Jaime Sommers expresses an ambivalent attitude toward marriage.

At one point in "The Bionic Woman, Part 2," Steve, Helen, Jim, and Jaime all raise a glass at the breakfast table to "Mrs. Steve Austin." Tellingly, this family toast occurs over orange juice and in the morning, neither the beverage nor the time of day or meal one would normally associate with a wedding toast. As they all clink orange juice glasses, Jaime shatters her glass of juice in her right hand. Ostensibly, Jaime's ongoing hand tremors—evidence that her body is rejecting her bionics, which leads to her death at the end of the two-parter—cause her to shatter the glass. But we can interpret this moment as a symbolic expression of Jaime's resistance to marriage, even perhaps her anger at its inevitability.

Another key aspect of Jaime's personality that emerges here—and one that endures all the way up to her last appearance in the third crossover reunion movie, *Bionic Ever After?* (1994)—is her reluctance to divulge life-threatening physical illnesses related to her bionics, especially to Steve. One might also interpret this rather odd—both self-destructive and neurotic—stubborn streak as indicative of Jaime's ambivalence over marital vows, a sign that she does not trust her imminent spouse to be able to cope with and share her burdens.

I contend that *Bionic* represents a progressive political vision and foregrounds feminist ethics. For some critics, *Bionic* is a reactionary series that contains Jaime Sommers's independence and unregulated sexual agency, transforming her into a woman with much less autonomy than she had at the start of her narrative. When we first meet her, Jaime is a brash, energetic young woman who has made a considerable name for herself as a star tennis player. She turns down Steve's request for a date (technically, she postpones it because she already has a date that night). Jaime travels the world and socializes broadly, encountering a glittering assortment of venues and people; in the season 2 "Doomsday Is Tomorrow, Part 1" she explains that she has learned passable French through her tennis-pro travels. The episodes leading up to the series and the series itself transform Jaime into a relatively much more traditional young woman.[6]

In the season 1 *Bionic* episode "Jaime's Mother," Chris Stuart, the fugitive Cold War era double of Jaime's now-dead mother, is finally tracked down by the double agent-henchman who have been pursuing her. These henchmen are about to kill Jaime for having seen them abduct Chris to kill her as well. Chris, intending to save Jaime, protests, "She's a schoolteacher! In a hick town! Alive, she's no threat to you." Chris successfully convinces the men not to dispatch Jaime. While one would not put the matter as bluntly and harshly as Chris Stuart does, and with all due respect to the noble and vital role of schoolteachers, Jaime's transition from glamorous celebrity tennis star to local schoolteacher does seems like a containment of unlicensed female autonomy.

Interestingly, once the series transitions from the ABC network to NBC for its third and final season, *Bionic* will eschew much of the small town, local, familial trappings of the first two seasons, focusing on Jaime as an autonomous and sexually adventurous woman of the world, even as it gives her a convincing romance with a man other than Steve Austin. (Chris Williams, who works with Oscar and Rudy at the OSI, is Jaime's love interest in the third season. But Jaime is also depicted in this season as having numerous heterosexual relationships past and present.)

The major woman's films—such as *Alice Adams* (1935), *Now, Voyager* (1942), *Letter from an Unknown Woman* (Max Ophuls, 1948), *The Heiress* (William Wyler, 1949), *Beyond the Forest* (King Vidor, 1949), *Autumn Leaves* (Robert Aldrich, 1956), and, I would argue, many Hitchcock films—place a woman's desire at the center of their plots and themes, as Robert Lang argues.[7] *Bionic* will explore the nature of desire, but rarely in the form of a heterosexual romance. Instead, the series will consider desire in terms of class longing, as it does in the great two-parter "Deadly Ringer" from the second season, and in terms of the desire for family, community, and connection, also a vital aspect of "Deadly Ringer" and central to the season one episode "Jaime's Mother."

While there are numerous moments in "The Bionic Woman" *Six Million* two-parter that rapturously depict Jaime and Steve's love for one another—and I write as someone who responds to their mutual ardor as one of the great depictions of romantic love on television—increasingly the episodes featuring Jaime Sommers emphasize her fears about marriage and reluctance to reveal these fears. The parallels with great woman's films such as *Now, Voyager* emerge in this ambivalence over the marital union.

The Bionic Woman and Feminist Ethics

The series allegorizes these fears as Jaime's privately terrified responses to her malfunctioning bionics, which take the form of a trembling right hand, an effect augmented by quivery sound effects.

While one accepts the nature of the premise of both series, that we enjoy the demonstration of bionic superpowers and associate these powers with beloved heroes, it is also true that for these superheroes to come into being, an unimaginable amount of trauma must be inflicted on the body. Jaime Sommers is a "new woman, now," as these early episodes note, but in part because her body undergoes traumatic injury to achieve this ideal.

If Jaime is successfully, if only temporarily, normalized as dutiful wife-to-be and government agent in "The Bionic Woman" episodes, it is also true that she frequently explodes with rage, especially at the end of the two-parter. The series allegorizes this explosive female rage, a desire to break out of the mold of normative gender roles and compulsory heterosexuality, as somatic breakdown. The dual nature of bionics, its status as *pharmakon*, both illness and cure, emerges here as the cause of Jaime's suffering and precisely the means through which she expresses her anger and rejects her imposed confines.

At the end of "The Bionic Woman, Part 1," Jaime escapes the hospital where she is meant to undergo corrective, life-saving surgery. That Jaime undergoes this suffering and that her treatment is thus delayed are unpleasant outcomes. In terms of sexual allegory, however, Jaime's unstoppable fury and power as she forcibly exits the prison-like hospital reflects her intransigent rebellion against the male-dominated, patriarchal systems of government and institutionalized biomedical authority—always conjoined in both series—that seek to contain her.

Jaime's Question Mark

> "The Return of the Bionic Woman: Part 1."
> Directed by Richard Moder. Written by Kenneth Johnson.
> Original airdate: September 14, 1975.
> "The Return of the Bionic Woman: Part 2."
> Directed by Richard Moder. Written by Kenneth Johnson.
> Original airdate: September 21, 1975.

When I was a child and then adolescent viewer of the bionic shows in syndication, the only form in which they were, for decades, available, this two-part sequel to "The Bionic Woman" acquired a lost object's mythic status for me. I never saw it aired on *Six Million* repeats, but then again

1. Mrs. Steve Austin

I much more avidly watched and followed *Bionic* ones. And the four Jaime Sommers episodes made before *Bionic* began were not included as part of *Bionic*'s syndication package. So, for years, the only experience I had of the "Return of the Bionic Woman" episodes were the snippets shown, as flashbacks, in *Bionic*'s pilot episode "Welcome Home, Jaime." Now that the episodes have been available for years, first on the Syfy Channel and then on DVD (as well as networks like Me TV and Cosi), and having seen "Return" repeatedly, I think my initial impressions of it were quite fitting. It represents a liminal position in the myth of Jaime Sommers.

Believed dead, to the chagrin of the nation's children, at the end of "Bionic Woman, Part 2," Jaime returns to life in "Return," but her memories are gone, very much including those of Steve. And she has a new love interest, Dr. Michael Marchetti (Richard Lenz), who intervened after Jaime died on the operating table and applied his newly developed cryogenics to bring Jaime back to life.

"Return" has an eerie, unsettling atmosphere due in part to Jaime's unclassifiable nature here. Her signature mischievous wit and intelligence remain intact, but there's something else as well, a slyness that signifies a refusal to play by the rules; a distant quality that makes Jaime seem enigmatic. In part 2 of "Return," Steve and Jaime walk to the park where they were once childhood sweethearts and where they rekindled their romance before the skydiving accident. They stand in front of the tree where they had so many meaningful conversations. Steve thoughtfully places his hand over the heart carved into the tree with the inscription Steve + Jaime, hiding this emblem of their earlier romance. Given that flashbacks to the past, especially those involving Steve, cause Jaime tremendous pain, Steve's gesture is a sensitive one. But Jaime, with the air of a prankster, carves her own heart and inscription into the tree ("What every woman wants—bionic fingernails"). The inscription she carves says "Jaime +?"

"Return of the Bionic Woman" evokes women's films about amnesia, such as *Random Harvest* (1942), given a thorough analysis by the critic Alison L. McKee. In sympathy with her argument, I want to make the case that "Return of the Bionic Woman," like this key example of the woman's film, occupies "a multivalent organizing subjectivity that is occasionally positionless and bodiless."[8] While the first half of the two-parter focuses closely on Steve Austin's experiences, the two episodes gradually merge consciousnesses, being finally Steve's and Jaime's distilled experiences or neither of theirs, something distinct entirely.

The episode begins on a melancholy note in a scene between men. Steve looks wistfully from a helicopter at the ground below; Oscar is sitting

The Bionic Woman and Feminist Ethics

next to him. They are headed to the site where two mob families conduct a meeting that Steve will bionically foil. Oscar asks Steve how he's doing; Steve responds that he is thinking of someone. Oscar, pointedly, answers, "Anyone I know?" "Not anymore," Steve responds. This scene of emotional intimacy, however discreet, between Steve and Oscar is atypical. The intensity of Steve's love for and grief over Jaime allows the men to share common emotional ground. To my mind, the presence of Jaime/Lindsay Wagner also brings out an unexpected depth and complexity in Steve and Lee Majors' performance (and for that matter in Richard Anderson's as Oscar).

Steve suffers crippling injuries during the mob-assignment and is rushed to the closest medical facility. In a druggy haze on a gurney, Steve, using his bionic eye, suddenly sees Jaime in a hospital bed, and begins intoning her name. Much of the first episode of the two-parter focuses on Steve insisting that Jaime is still alive as Oscar and Rudy maintain the illusion of her death. Finally, the truth is revealed, an irate Steve threatening to punch the men's lights out if they do not tell him what's going on. They explain that Jaime *did* die, but that Michael Marchetti brought her back to life with his cryogenics. She has, however, suffered brain damage—the extent of which remains unknown—including memory loss.

Steve, understandably overcome with emotion, begs to see Jaime even if only briefly. He walks into her hospital room. She opens her eyes and looks at him warmly and kindly. "Who are you?" she asks. This is, without question, one of the most significant moments in the evolution of Jaime Sommers's character (and Steve Austin's, at least insofar as these episodes go). It is a shock, still, to hear Jaime say these words. The soaring romance between the two; the shared bionic pain and wonder; the tragic denouement: all explode into a shocking and unforeseeable newness. The two lovers who suffered and loved so much now have no relation whatsoever—save for their shared bionics.

In her hospital bed, Jaime tests out her bionics by bending one of the bed's metal bars. She no longer confronts the reality of her bionic enhancements with the emotional pain she exhibited on first learning of them. Instead, her attitude bespeaks a detached uncertainty. She asks Steve after bending the bar, "What does that make me?" He responds, "Like me." What initially began as a lifesaving operation emerges as the foundation of an entirely new relation between the two—one that is no longer a romance.

I have been positing that the series—intertextually engaging with the woman's film—thematizes Jaime's ambivalence over heterosexual romance and allegorizes this ambivalence as biomedical breakdown. Jaime's amnesia functions similarly, an allegory for becoming a new being, someone not defined by Steve Austin, his love for her, or their romance, but a person whose life looms before her as uncharted territory, mysterious, frightening, thrilling. The gender and sexual politics of this plot and character development are acute. Jaime Sommers is a female character who has left compulsory heterosexuality, certainly compulsory marriage, behind or at least at a remove.

Admittedly, Jaime's tentative romance with Dr. Michael Marchetti—which comes to a clear halt in "Welcome Home, Jaime, Part 1"—reintroduces a heterosexual romantic possibility into the narrative. But that Jaime and Steve no longer pursue marriage is one of the most daring decisions that Kenneth Johnson made in devising this narrative. Even in the newly feminist, women's-liberation 1970s, a woman without the social legitimatization of marriage was, in some eyes, a femininity gone rogue.

Similarly provocative, Jaime is allergic to her hometown. While she returns to Ojai in "Welcome Home, Jaime, Part 1" after regaining partial memory, in "Return of the Bionic Woman, Part 2" Jaime becomes ill—distraught—with prolonged exposure to her childhood home, where Steve has brought her to jog her memories. As we have noted, new generations of women since the late nineteenth-century were leaving their familiar surroundings in search of excitement and possibility in larger urban centers. Symbolically, Jaime's aversion to Ojai allegorizes a resistance to being redomesticated and normalized, which marriage to Steve, given the circumstances and his feverish protectiveness towards her, also threatens to do. Fascinatingly, deftly, and persuasively, *Bionic* will make Jaime's return to Ojai at the start of the series seem like an authentically positive choice—one choice that Jaime herself makes.

As a young child, I was greatly compelled by Steve Austin as he battled Bigfoot, the Death Probe, and other foes. As I got older, I found his stoic and at times expressionless masculinity harder and harder to take. Revisiting these episodes as a grown man, I find much to admire in Steve and appreciate Majors' performance—which I once found wooden—as perfectly suited to the role. Especially in these four episodes involving Jaime, Steve becomes a far more nuanced and complex character. His burden in "Return of the Bionic Woman" is an acute one. He cannot tell the woman he would "sell his soul for" that he loves her; he must watch as Jaime appears to be falling in love with someone else crucial to her care, and he with her. Throughout, Steve maintains his integrity and sensitivity, never pushing Jaime one way or the other, silently enduring private torment.

The Bionic Woman and Feminist Ethics

In some ways this behavior reflects traditional modes of taciturn, silently-suffering masculinity. But given the equally typical tendency for males to act out violently when confronted by female sexual indifference, infidelity, or self-determination that has become increasingly public in our moment, Steve's demeanor strikes an admirable note. He patiently and selflessly offers himself as a resource to Jaime as she finds her human and bionic way. It is very moving when Jim Elgin says to Steve, "I've never been prouder of you, son"—one good and tender and loving man recognizing these qualities in another. Another way of putting this is that in "Return," Steve treats Jaime like an autonomous person, not the fanatically monitored object of his masculine oversight. What is much less admirable is Dr. Marchetti's violation of medical ethics, the doctor wooing his patient while claiming all the while that Jaime is merely demonstrating typical feelings of gratitude and infatuation with the medical authority who saved her life.

Jaime chooses to work as a spy, and in this episode her decision makes sense—unsure of who she is and at a loose end, she wants to do something of value. While Steve protests, still feeling protective of her, he listens to her requests and agrees to go on a mission with her. While this mission is a disaster, a rare unsuccessful one for the bionic heroes, it is a necessary catharsis. Steve realizes something significant. As he says to Oscar and Marchetti, "I'm no good for Jaime." He decides that it would be best if he and Jaime did not spend any more time together for the time being and recommends that Jaime be sent to Rudy Wells's Colorado medical base to continue her recovery.

In a standout sequence at the oil refinery of the villainous tycoon Carlton Harris (Dennis Patrick), Steve and Jaime attempt to coordinate their efforts to knock out the refinery's power and impede Harris' nefarious deeds. Jaime, posing as a reporter (a ruse she devises on the spot, a plan uneasily accepted by Steve), walks around with the "ladykiller" Harris, charming him as he aggressively flirts with her. Just when Jaime is supposed to hold up her end of the plan, pressing a lever down in one location so that Steve can do the same where he is, she begins having a breakdown, overcome by flashbacks to her traumatic run through the storm on the night she died, but now believing it is Steve who is in trouble, calling out to *her* for help. Jaime breaks free of Harris, bionically knocking him down as she does so. In an amazing shot, the director holds Jaime's/Wagner's face in agonized yet also supremely controlled close-up as she wrenches a locked metal door loose. These early episodes are full of found art like this shot, which seems an artistic meditation on Jaime's struggles, courage, and unknowable possibilities.

1. Mrs. Steve Austin

Putting Down Roots

"Welcome Home, Jaime: Part 1." Directed by Alan Crosland.
Written by Kenneth Johnson. Original airdate: January 14, 1976.

"Welcome Home, Jaime: Part 2." Directed by Alan Crosland.
Written by Kenneth Johnson. Original airdate: January 21, 1976.

Evoking classical Hollywood woman's films such as the beautiful *The Stranger's Return* (King Vidor, 1933) starring Miriam Hopkins, the first episode of this two-parter depicts Jaime Sommers' return to her hometown of Ojai, where she will pursue life as a schoolteacher by day, OSI agent by night. "Welcome Home, Part 1" begins with Jaime waking up in the OSI hospital after undergoing yet another round of surgeries to restore her memory. Rudy Wells and Michael Marchetti ask her a series of questions that demonstrate that Jaime has regained memories of her childhood, her parents' death in a car accident when she was sixteen, being adopted by the Elgins, who became her legal guardians at that point, going to Carnegie Tech to get a degree in education with the intention of teaching, and her career as a tennis star. She remembers Steve as a childhood friend but does not remember their romance or impending nuptials.

Diane Negra, in her discussion of postfeminism and movies of the 2000s, has discussed the resurgence of "retreatist cinema," in which urban, cosmopolitan women return to their hometowns. The return of women to the idealized hometown reflects the ways that women are "exhorted to re-secure local, communal, regional, and in some cases even national meanings through their rejection of global cosmopolitanism. They must do this not only to enrich family life, but to play a (gendered) part in staving off class and economic others."[9] The 1970s New Hollywood cinema showcased women who left their literal and symbolic hometowns to light out, Huck Finn–like, for the territories—such as the heroine of Martin Scorsese's 1974 *Alice Doesn't Live Here Anymore* (not to mention its television spinoff *Alice* [1976–85]) does—so the retreatist return to the hometown was certainly not inevitable. And, to be sure, Jaime's embrace of Ojai—which when we last saw her made her ill—and of her role as schoolteacher can be read as a rejection of global cosmopolitanism.

All of this granted, "Welcome Home, Jaime, Part 1" is a remarkable episode, certainly one of the standout moments in female representation of the 1970s. It acutely charts Jaime's return to Ojai as a self-determining and autonomous journey. While her return to Ojai can be read as "retreatist," in execution the episode resonates with themes of female transformation exemplified by indelible woman's films such as *Now, Voyager*.

The Bionic Woman and Feminist Ethics

As I argue in *Representations of Femininity in American Genre Cinema* (2011), the heroines of the woman's film frequently undergo a profound change. Often, this change first occurs on the level of physical appearance, a bodily transformation that serves to signify a later and more resonant emotional or material change. In *Now, Voyager*, the once overweight, lonely, deeply insecure, unhappy Charlotte Vale (the incomparable Bette Davis), freed from her controlling patrician mother's grasp, blossoms into a self-reliant, independent person. The change that marks the woman's film heroine's maturation can also occur on economic and class levels; in passing narratives, they much more ambiguously and problematically occur on the level of race. (I return to these themes in the chapter "Bionic *Vertigo*.")

Another extremely important theme of "Welcome Home, Jaime, Part 1" that will recur throughout the series, and that has profound queer implications, is the non-biological and/or chosen family. *Bionic* emphasizes the bond—adumbrated in the *Six Million* episodes introducing both Jaime Sommers and Steve's parents Helen and Jim Elgin—between Jaime and Helen and Jim. Given that they are Steve's parents and that Jim Elgin is also Steve's stepfather, the series goes to great lengths to deroutinize the idea of family ties, demonstrating that non-biological relations can be just as powerful—more powerful, even—than biological ones.

Moreover, the love that Helen and Jim feel for Jaime transcends, or dovetails with, the love they have for Steve, transcending any conflict of loyalties. In one of the most moving moments of the series, Helen takes Jaime on a tour of the new property that the Elgins have bought (There is a sweetly humorous moment when the memory-deprived Jaime admits that she does not recognize the property, and Helen says that makes sense since they just bought it.) Helen offers Jaime a loft apartment over the barn, but she protests, saying that she does not feel she has the right to accept help from these kind people. Helen firmly and lovingly insists, "We're family." "It's so good to be home," Jaime responds, to which Helen answers, "It's good to have you home again." As a gay viewer, I have always found this exchange between extraordinary women deeply resonant, a tribute to the bonds that develop on emotional lines and through mutual and loving tenderness and respect, ties not determined by biological familial necessity but reflective of alternative lines of kinship and affinity.

Reinforcing this scene, a later exchange between Jaime and Helen emphasizes the bond between them. Helen and Jim having very sensitively revealed her marriage plans to Steve, Jaime sits in her loft apartment alone. Lindsay Wagner, as always, makes Jaime's emotional state palpable. Jaime

1. Mrs. Steve Austin

seems outwardly cheerful; when Helen walks in, asking if anyone's home, Jaime responds, "Just us schoolteachers" in anticipation of her new position at the Air Force Base. Helen invites Jaime over for dinner, but Jaime says she's just going to whip up a tuna salad and prep for class. The infamous bit with Jaime opening the can of tuna with her bionic fingernail follows. "You wouldn't happen to have an extra set of those fingernails, would you?" Helen playfully asks. Equally playfully, Jaime responds, "I'll have Rudy check the parts department."

There are no explanatory words to prepare us for the shift in conversation, but Helen suddenly says, "It isn't easy, is it?" "No, it's not," Jaime immediately responds. The women are emotionally linked. Jaime discusses her difficulties with missing memories, especially when it comes to her relationship with Steve. There are so many ways that this scene could have been written, but Kenneth Johnson emphasizes the bond between Jaime and Helen, and Wagner and Martha Scott achieve a wholly authentic equilibrium in their performances. Helen explains to Jaime that even before her parents died, Helen always considered Jaime her daughter. "So, you see," Helen says, "I win either way." There is no conventional mother-in-law manipulation, no "Why don't you give my wonderful son Steve another chance?" Instead, Helen sensitively hears what Jaime shares with her and gives Jaime back her love without any qualifications or conditions. Though the episode shows the women in conflict, "Jaime's Mother" will overwhelmingly affirm the importance of Jaime and Helen's bond.[10]

Jaime's bewilderment when she learns that she and Steve were to be married, and especially the scene between Jaime and Steve in this episode, are crucial to a feminist reading. Jaime does not identify primarily as the female half of a heterosexual relationship. Nor does she immediately want to reenter the marriage plot. Instead, she foregrounds her ambivalence about the prospect.

When she and Steve talk as they walk around Ojai together—in so markedly distinct a mood from their promenades in "The Bionic Woman, Part 1"—Steve tells her that they met as children. She dared him to eat one of everything in the cafeteria. He got sick as a result but got revenge on her by putting a lizard down her back. At this point, Steve is sitting on a swing. Jaime, in a playful mode, bionically pushes him into the air, and as he goes flying upwards, she suddenly stares, transfixed, at his image, which has transformed into that of Steve's boyhood self. The freezeframe of the boy on the swing suspended in the air is a visual expression of Jaime's flash of memory. But it's more than that. Suddenly, Steve is rendered a child again. For one thing, this effect completely desexualizes him

The Bionic Woman and Feminist Ethics

as a romantic prospect. It also makes him like one of the children Jaime might be teaching. Most importantly, the shot stands in for an entire relationship that Jaime can no longer access. The boy on the swing sits with his back to Jaime and to us—he could be anyone; he is random, anonymous, any boy in the world. At the same time, the weird aural effect of a plane roaring into the sky—perhaps a bionic sound effect discarded after this episode—as Jaime pushes him into the air almost subliminally reminds us of Steve's fateful plane crash that resulted in his being made bionic.

As they did in "The Bionic Woman" and "The Return of the Bionic Woman," Steve and Jaime go to the spot in the park where the tree with the heart-carving that says "Jaime + Steve" is planted. Steve once again tries to avoid it. "Why did you hide this from me?" Jaime asks. Steve explains that he did not want, once again, to trigger her painful memories; he asks her if he has, now. "No, not anymore," Jaime responds.

What follows is an extraordinarily direct speech from Jaime to Steve in which she says, "I can't remember what's it's like to be in love with you." This speech is significant. First, Jaime unequivocally rejects a renewal of their romantic bond, thereby absenting herself from compulsory heterosexuality. She does leave open the possibility that they may develop a new relationship, but she says that at the end of the scene and makes it clear that this would be a "new beginning" for them. Second, the subtle suggestion is that Jaime is not attracted to Steve. For a leading man like Majors, playing the hero of an action series, such an assessment is deflating. I do not think the intention is to deflate Steve or diminish his magnetism. Rather, it is to establish that Jaime has—the alternative to what Mary Ann Doan calls the desire to desire—the right *not* to desire. Romantic feelings and heterosexual coupling will not be her chief goals; instead, she will pursue her own ambitions and dreams. It is to his character's credit that Steve Austin responds, "I understand."

"Welcome Home, Jaime, Part 2," is exciting, though much more conventional. Jaime is surveilled and terrorized by Carlton Harris, the ladykiller tycoon of "Return of the Bionic Woman." He stages scenes that force Jaime to use her bionics. Eventually, Jaime devises a ruse, at which Oscar initially balks: she will appear to join forces with Harris, using her bionics to help him steal top-secret plans from the government, in order to expose his criminality.

There is, however, a truly remarkable sequence early in this episode when—putting her ruse into action—Jaime agrees to meet Carlton Harris in an empty alley behind the Bank of Ojai. After Jaime hangs up the phone, she contemplates what she is about to do. One of the most characteristic

1. Mrs. Steve Austin

and fascinating aspects of Wagner's performance is her ability to convey Jaime's private thought process. Sometimes she appears in a realm of her own thoughts, looking inwardly. The effect is enigmatic and beguiling. Here, Jaime appears to be considering her own plan, weighing it carefully. Does she really want to enter such a dark realm even though in doing so she will expose it?

When Jaime meets Harris in the alley, he has a surprise waiting for her. Not only does his limousine speeds towards her, but an enormous truck on the other side does so as well. Harris's son Donald, newly graduated from college and still naïve about his father's nefarious practices, cries out, "She can't get out! Stop!" Suddenly, Jaime looks upwards. She bionically leaps up to a fire escape high above. This sequence conveys a great deal about Jaime's quick-witted and instinctual skills as not only a survivor but also a strategist. The fan side of my scholar-fan sensibility succumbs utterly to this moment, the thrill of the bionic action as Jaime saves herself so dramatically from the hurtling vehicles. As always with *Bionic*, the score—this one written by Jerry Fielding, who also wrote the wonderful opening credits music—adds immeasurably to the dramatic effect.

In the next chapter, I discuss the first season's immersion in feminist ethics, indicated by Jaime's loving bonds with animals and her strong relationships with girls and other women. Another important theme, the double, is significant to two of this season's signature episodes.

Chapter 2

Feminist Ethics

With Jaime Sommers established as a schoolteacher who undertakes the occasional covert mission for the OSI, *The Bionic Woman* was on a clear-cut path to emulate the action-adventure format of *The Six Million Dollar Man*, albeit with a softer, domestic, hometown feel given its consistent setting in Ojai, California. Lindsay Wagner complained of the ABC network executives that they wanted her to be "Steve Austin with cleavage." She fought to make *Bionic* more meaningful. In creating *Bionic* and the character of Jaime Sommers, the producer, writer, and director Kenneth Johnson, a supporter of feminism, strove to write a positive and inspiring female character. Johnson's auteurist vision and, especially, Wagner's commitment, integrity, and luminous lead performance gave *Bionic* an unusually personal momentum, an urgency and a depth that was largely lacking in *Six Million* and other TV SF series of the day. (Johnson would invest his next series, *The Incredible Hulk*, starring Bill Bixby and airing on the CBS network from 1978 to 1982, with similar qualities.)

Bionic self-consciously broke new ground: it seemed *aware* of itself, in pointed contrast with its parent series. The achievement of *Bionic* is that it did not simply emulate the series it spun off from, dispatching Jaime to various exotic locales where she outwits and outmatches foreign foes with makeshift accents. This is not to say that *Bionic* did not do precisely that at times; some plots, such as the S1 "Fly Jaime," were directly lifted from *Six Million* episodes; some episodes, such as "Winning is Everything" (S1), were transparent knockoffs. Though it was unkind of him to say, Lee Majors' angry description "The *Bionic* Rip-Off" aptly described such episodes, though not the series as a whole.[1]

Bionic oscillated between rote, predictable derring-do and a critical, self-aware mode that allowed the series to explore the psychology of its protagonist and the specific gendered and technological challenges she faced. Within the conventional action drama, an audaciously personal, emotional, introspective, and at times disturbing account of woman's experience in the gendered spheres of work, family, and covert affairs thrillingly emerged.

The frustration for any loving fan who also wants the series to be a feminist critique—to be this consistently—is that some moribund thinking about gender roles and also about the point of an hour-long action drama, some of it imported from *Six Million*, much of it inherent in the ABC network's constitutional love of genre cheese, dragged the series down from its own ambitions. While *Bionic* was almost always wildly entertaining, it was at times only that. Acknowledging its inconsistent level of quality in the first season, I want to explore, with seriousness, the episodes that defied expectations and achieved something meaningful and memorable, transcending the inherent limitations, format, and guidelines of commercial television.

At its best, and it was often at its best, *Bionic* foregrounded feminist ethics and explored Jaime's relationships with girls, other women, and nonhuman animals in a manner that exemplified feminist ethics' goals. This chapter expands on the concept of feminist ethics, discussing *Bionic*'s evocations of Greek mythology, first-wave feminism and nineteenth-century American women's fiction, and the woman's film.

Classical Mythology and the Woman's Film

In many ways, this study is a sequel to my book *Representations of Femininity in American Genre Cinema*, where I focused on the woman's film, one of classical Hollywood's most important genres, and its afterlife in other forms, primarily modern horror. I call female-centered horror movies such as *Carrie* (Brian De Palma, 1976) and *Alien* (Ridley Scott, 1979) "concealed woman's films."[2]

The myth of Demeter and Persephone, one of the mainstays of classical mythology, is central to my argument. In the myth, Demeter, the goddess associated with the earth, agriculture, and the seasons, plunges into mourning when she learns that her daughter, the young maiden Persephone, has been abducted by Hades, the king of the underworld, and forced to be his bride. In her grief, Demeter wanders the earth and casts the world into endless winter. Finally, a bargain is reached—Persephone, queen of the underworld, will spend half the year with her mother, the other half (the wintry months, when her mother mourns her again) with her husband in Hades.

The woman's film and female-centered horror evoke the Demeter-Persephone myth by thematizing mother-daughter conflicts. The heroines of these genres both want to maintain ties to their mothers and forge independent lives, to be faithful daughters and autonomous agents. Marriage and heterosexual relationships loom as life-changing events, exciting new possibilities that also threaten to sever women's maternal ties. Moreover, the singular, distinctive personality of the heroine hangs in the balance: should she stay with her mother and in her familiar surroundings, or should she leave her family and enter the world of adult sexuality? The stakes are high: she may gain much but lose herself in the process. Or, if she has forged a new life for herself but remains single, is becoming a man's wife and mother to his children a path she personally wants to follow? Marriage, men, and motherhood threaten to take away the woman's autonomy and conform her to conventional roles. Exemplary films in this regard are *Alice Adams*, with the singularly distinctive young Katharine Hepburn in the title role, falling in love with a well-born young man who gradually realizes that Alice's class status makes her an unsuitable romantic match (the movie adds a happy ending that doesn't take away the narrative's sting or the plangency of Hepburn's performance); *Now, Voyager*, in which the heroine undergoes profound changes but moves farther and farther away from the marriage plot, defying her mother's wishes and declaring that she may "Get a cat and a parrot and live alone in single blessedness."

One of the most important dimensions of the woman's film genre is its tie to melodrama. The inherently melodramatic nature of the genre achieves acute articulation and comes under scrutiny in the 1950s films of Douglas Sirk, a German émigré to Hollywood, such as *Imitation of Life* and *All That Heaven Allows*. I discuss the Sirkian and Hitchcockian elements of S2's "Deadly Ringer" in the chapter "Bionic *Vertigo*." *Bionic* upholds the tradition of female-centered melodrama, thereby revising its own categorization as an SF series.[3]

First-Wave Feminism and Nineteenth-Century American Literature

An important precedent for these dynamics in the woman's film exists in female-centered late nineteenth century fiction, the literary era asso-

2. Feminist Ethics

ciated with realism. Works by American authors such as Sarah Orne Jewett, Edith Wharton, Kate Chopin, Frances Harper, Charlotte Perkins Gilman, and others tracked the emergence of a newly independent femininity (the figure of the New Woman), struggling over maternal and home ties and the desire to break out into the social world.

An important reworking of the Demeter-Persephone myth, Jewett's novel *The Country of the Pointed Firs* and its follow-up short stories take place in the coastal village of Dunnet Landing, Maine.[4] A model of first-wave feminism, Jewett's work makes for a fascinating parallel with the second-wave feminist *Bionic*. The unnamed protagonist of *Firs*, a schoolteacher, enjoys a deep and fulfilling bond with Almira Todd, a maternal, loving older woman to whom she is not biologically related. Associated with nature, Almira is a gifted creator of natural remedies, always concocting healing balms from her garden.

Like Jewett's protagonist, Jaime Sommers is a schoolteacher who maintains an extremely close relationship with an older woman to whom she is not biologically related, Helen Elgin (Martha Scott), Steve Austin's mother. Helen and her husband Jim Elgin (Ford Rainey)—Steve's stepdad—became her adoptive parents after Jaime's parents died in a car accident. Jewett's work provides a template for several key issues in *Bionic*—intergenerational and non-biological ties and love between women and the importance of women's bonds with nonhuman animals. The first *Bionic* episode I discuss in this chapter, "Claws," focuses on the latter, thereby providing a foundation for a recurring theme of the series.

"Claws." Directed by Phil Bondeli. Written by Sue Milburn.
Airdate: February 25, 1976.

One of *Bionic*'s significant achievements is its consistent depiction of female friendship and intergenerational female relationships: bonds between younger and older women and between women and girls. *Bionic*'s female-centered themes figure prominently in "Claws." The episode evokes something of Jewett's world in *The Country of the Pointed Firs* and related stories, in which bonds among women are multivalent, collaborative, and empathetic. At the same time, the episode suggests the deep limits of social community especially when independent women and vulnerable girls must face off against brutal and myopic male power.

"Claws" was written by Sue Milburn, who would write television films with female protagonists such as *The Child Stealer* (1979), starring Blair Brown and Beau Bridges, about a young woman whose ex-husband kidnaps their children after she is granted sole custody after their divorce,

The Bionic Woman and Feminist Ethics

but is given no help whatsoever by the authorities, and *This Is Kate Bennett...* (1982), about a determined female reporter who risks her life to report on a sniper who targets nurses.

"Claws" focuses on the struggles of Susan Victor (Tippi Hedren), an animal trainer for television and the movies who lives with the several different animals she trains—an elephant, a monkey, a parrot, and her prize possession, the noble lion Neal—on a sprawling ranch in Ojai, California. A girl in Jaime's class, Katie (Alicia Fleer), works for Susan as her assistant, sharing her fierce love of the animals. The shy, awkward Katie stuns her classmates one day when she brings in Neal for show and tell. Presumably, Jaime has met Susan through Katie; Jaime visits the older woman and her young assistant the next day (images of Jaime riding the elephant Tusker and beaming all the while evoke a peaceable kingdom, the title of a short-lived television series Wagner later starred in). Susan reveals that money troubles have made caring for the animals and the property difficult; moreover, a series of mysterious attacks on livestock in the area have sparked local farmers' anger and suspicion. Many blame Susan and specifically Neal for these attacks.

Susan gets a phone call. She has been invited to interview for a TV series that could be her, and the animals', big break. Encouraging Susan to chase this opportunity, Jaime commits to looking after the farm with Katie's help while Susan meets with the producers.

More attacks occur, however, and a particularly gruff, unpleasant, blowhard farmer, Charles Keys (Jack Kelly) and his easily-led compatriots invade the Victor property, determined to kill Neal. The episode largely involves Keys' attempt to kill Neal and Jaime's determined quest to exonerate and protect the animal. Accompanied by her uncle, of sorts, Bill Elgin (William Schallert)—he is Jim Elgin's brother—Jaime discovers the true culprit, a cougar, but not before Keys wounds and maddens Neal. To prevent the Sherriff and Keys from killing the crazed lion, Jaime faces off against Neal in a barn. While she suffers some injuries, Jaime is ultimately able to calm Neal down. When the irate men open the barn door, she beams at them, Neal's prodigious mane in her hands.

The men in this episode come across as brutal, unreasonable, relentless in their persecutory zeal, and pathetic and cowardly. The exception is Uncle Bill, who initially, if uncomfortably, sides with Keys but ultimately aligns himself with Jaime and Katie. Clearly, Keys' resentment against Susan insinuates his larger disapproval of her independent lifestyle, one that is not marked by heterosexual marriage or biological offspring (which may suggest something about her sexuality as well). The episode engages in a discourse about women and animals that intersects with the concerns of feminist theory while evoking Greek mythology and nineteenth century American women's literature. The theme of bonds between women and animals as resistance against patriarchal oppression re-emerges in Season Three with the introduction of Max, the titular "Bionic Dog."

Women and Nonhuman Animals

The connection between women and nonhuman animals informs Greek myth, which echoes in *The Country of the Pointed Firs*. Several critics have discussed Jewett's references to the Demeter and Persephone myth. One of Jewett's most memorable personae is Esther Hight, who could be a prototype for the character of the animal-trainer Susan Oliver in "Claws."[5] A former schoolteacher turned shepherdess, Esther resists expectations. She is elderly but physically strong. Caring for her fierce old mother, Mrs. Thankful Hight, Esther has not been able to fulfill her own desires. But just as most Maine homesteaders are giving up giving up sheep-raising, Esther decides to pursue it. Though eventually marrying a man about her age, Esther is initially introduced as a solitary shepherdess. Her social company largely consists of animals, an interspecies community that rejects the commonly held beliefs that only humans provide community and contentment, presaging the theories of Donna Haraway.[6]

As Paula Blanchard writes of nature in Jewett's work, it plays a role that "remains essentially transcendentalist, wild creatures and plants being both embodiments and messengers of a universal anima."[7] To put it another way, there is an organic unity in this world in which humans and animals and plants share equal billing and stature. As Marian Scholtmeijer puts it in an essay about the ways that women writers depict animals in fiction, "In view of the radical, ontological separation of humans and animals in contemporary life, the mere thought of a community of animals and humans demands full-scale revisioning of the ways of the world."[8] *Bionic* envisions just such a world in "Claws" and "The Bionic Dog."

Scholtmeijer continues:

> In their work on animals ... women writers perform that most anti-androcentric of acts: thinking themselves into the being of the wholly "other," the animal.... Women writers use fiction to concretize, affirm, and empower the state of being "other," which dominant ideology objectifies as a site of weakness, but which finds living expression in nonhuman animals.[9]

The Bionic Woman and Feminist Ethics

Sue Milburn wrote an episode that evokes these possibilities. Much like Jewett's Esther Hight, Susan Victor in "Claws" creates an alternative community that includes her animals, numerous and peacefully co-habiting species that embody diversity, apprentices like Katie, and friends like Jaime.[10]

Esther's adventurousness of spirit and animal associations allow Jewett to inscribe her with ancient female heroism. Jewett likens Esther to the Greek female hero Atalanta, a rebel who defied conventionality, remaining solitary and unmarried for most of her life.[11] If Esther inherits a Hellenic tradition of animal women, she also inherits this tradition's complexities. As Ellen Reeder puts it, "In Greek thought a woman's bestial side was viewed as the heart of her sexuality and fertility."[12]

Jewett also likens Esther to Joan of Arc, who battled against patriarchal power, willing to die for her convictions.[13] Joan of Arc, a young shepherdess before she became a woman warrior, has consistently been associated with animals and the bucolic tradition. These references contextualize *The Bionic Woman* within a dynamic, evolving feminine discourse about women's roles in society. If it is inaccurate to call *Bionic* a feminist series, it is a series with several important feminist elements, and in that regard one with a great deal of relevance for queer spectatorship as well.[14]

To return to "Claws," the episode establishes Susan Victor as an older woman who, like Helen Elgin, cares for Jaime and strives to protect her. At one point, Susan is aghast to discover that the elephant Tusker has placed his immense, imponderably weighty foot on Jaime's own (her bionics protect her from injury). And when Susan returns from her meeting with the prospective series' producers (happily announcing that she has secured the job), she expresses concern to see Jaime's bandaged left hand (which Neal mauled in the barn before Jaime calmed him down).

The casting of Tippi Hedren in the role of Susan Victor is significant. Hedren famously starred in Alfred Hitchcock's 1963 masterpiece about nature gone awry, *The Birds*. The casting of Hedren, Martha Scott, and Barbara Rush (in the episode "Jaime's Mother") in the first season signaled the series' connections to classical Hollywood (a period that I define as commencing with the emergence of the sound film in the late 1920s and roughly ending with the decline of the traditional studio system in the 1960s). Wagner's tall, cool, blonde beauty evokes Hedren's in *The Birds* (a mainstay on television when *Bionic* aired), a connection that will be nearly explicitly referenced in the S2 two-parter "Deadly Ringer," a meditation on the Hitchcock blonde.

Moreover, Hedren became a notable animal-rights activist. She and her husband Noel Marshall co-produced and he directed the infamous 1981s nature-gone-awry movie *Roar*, where wild lions prey on the visiting family of a man who lives in Africa with the lions; Hedren's soon-to-be-famous daughter Melanie Griffith also stars. (The film was out of circulation for many years has been recently restored and made available on DVD and Blu-ray.) Admittedly, "Claws" removes Susan Victor from much of the action so that Jaime can occupy center stage. Still, Jaime does not work alone. She allies herself with the young Katie and with her notably solitary, non-conventionally masculine Uncle Bill. Continuing the series' investment in the non-biological family, Jaime's "Uncle" Bill is the brother of Jim Elgin, Steve's stepfather—and Uncle Bill regards Jaime with no less love and protectiveness than a blood relative would. Uncle Bill also has an inkling of Jaime's bionic powers, which he discreetly references as "something special about" Jaime.

The several, stunning images of Jaime running through the vast, rocky landscape in search of Neal archetypally figure her as a benevolent force of Nature. Jaime's nurturing of the shy and withdrawn Katie, who truly comes alive in the company of the animals and with Jaime and Susan, recalls the poignant narrative of the woman's film *Now, Voyager*, in which the once-repressed spinster Charlotte Vale (Bette Davis), helped not only by her psychiatrist but also by her loving sister-in-law, in turn helps the painfully shy, awkward girl Tina. Just as Jaime has been nurtured by others—Drs. Wells and Marchetti, Steve Austin in "The Return of the Bionic Woman" on *Six Million*, Helen and Jim Elgin, and Oscar Goldman—she in turn nurtures.

Her climactic battle with Neal in the barn shows Jaime eluding his rampage rather than inflicting harm on him. She manages to connect to him in his frenzy and fear, just as Steve Austin does with her in the several episodes of *Six Million* before *Bionic* begins. Jaime reaches out to an adversary here, as she does at the climax of "Deadly Ringer, Part 2" when she attempts to help her once evil, now mentally unstable doppelgänger.

"Claws" ends largely as it began, with the image of an intergenerational group of women—the triumphantly returned Susan Victor, the victorious Jaime, and the exultantly fulfilled Katie—surrounded by the animals, who cry out in joyful and humorous unison at Susan's return—a non-normative, non-heterosexist, collaborative community of women and nonhuman animals.

"Jaime's Mother." Directed by Leo Penn. Story by Worley Thorne. Written by Arthur Rowe. Airdate: March 24, 1976.

The Bionic Woman and Feminist Ethics

"Welcome Home, Jaime, Part 1" lay the groundwork for several key themes and preoccupations of *The Bionic Woman* series, especially the theme of the non-biological family, connections forged through emotions, not blood; women's emotional and psychological life, resistant to and inaccessible by male authoritarian forms of control and analysis. "Jaime's Mother" brilliantly expands on these ideas while foregrounding a figure that will be fundamental to *Bionic*: the doppelgänger, foil to the seeming normalcy and desirability of the original. The series invests the figure of the doppelgänger with feminist and queer possibilities.

A mysterious woman in a drab, dark business suit tensely drives on the open road in the teaser. The traditionally male-identified symbol of the open road now becomes a female domain. She anxiously stares at her rear-view mirror, bites her lip, and massages her right arm, obviously in pain. We cut to a terse dialogue scene between two drab-looking men, paid assassins hunting her down, one of whom shot and nicked her in the arm. They have discovered that she's headed for Ojai, California. The other man, identified as Vic, surmises, "She's going to tell Jaime Sommers that she's her mother." In the backstory established for Jaime Sommers on *The Six Million Dollar Man* and in "Welcome Home, Jaime, Part 1," Jaime's parents were killed when she was a child, and Helen and Jim Elgin adopted Jaime. This strange woman's identity is this episode's central mystery: could she really be Jaime's mother? Is she a ghost? Or is she a figment of Jaime's troubled imagination, the theory that Helen Elgin and Oscar Goldman develop till proven otherwise?

After the main credits, a scene time-stamped 6:14 a.m. begins in Jaime's sunlit bedroom; clearly agitated, she twitches as she dreams. In hazy, Vaseline-lens-covered dream images, or flashbacks, we see shots of Jaime as a young girl, and an elegantly dressed woman with a charming voice. This woman is Ann Sommers, Jaime's mother. These dream images of young Jaime depict her as beaming, fulfilled, energetic, and curious about the world around her. In these shots of the physically active young girl, her mother is a key element, supporting her with verbal praise and warmly encouraging laughter. Her approbation accompanies Jaime as she rides on horseback, plays tennis, and other activities. Indeed, her mother plays tennis *with* her, cheering her on and clearly a crucial influence for Jaime's budding tennis career.

Later, Jaime visits the family's old home and notices yellow roses in the garden. The yellow roses play an important role. The sight of them triggers another memory. We flash back to the child Jaime happily digging up a messy garden. Offscreen, her father indicates that he disapproves of

2. Feminist Ethics

Jaime's botanical romping. Also offscreen, her mother chides him for being sexist: "Now, a girl has just as much right to play in the dirt as boys do. It's part of her development." Her father complains that he wouldn't like his son to be digging up his roses, either. Jaime's father speaks in voiceover but is never seen in the flashbacks; only a framed photograph by Jaime's bedside—showing the child Jaime, flanked by her parents and holding the family dog, Puzzles—contains the paternal image. The father's importance cedes entirely to the mother's.

The early morning flashbacks include an image that is mythic, a feminine variation of the Excalibur myth: Ann holds up and bestows a golden necklace on Jaime ("I brought you a present, Jaime. Do you like it?").[15] Jaime will go on wearing this necklace, a material link to her mother that, like the roses, signifies their connection. Ann symbolically anoints Jaime, sending her on a journey and honoring her as a person of strength and courage. (Shades of *Wonder Woman*, the magnificent comic book heroine who had her own 1970s television series at the same time. Diana Prince's mother also gives her gifts, talismans of power, before Diana leaves Themiscyra for the human world.)

In these flashbacks, Ann Sommers is a vital presence, supportive of Jaime in every way; in contrast to her father, Jaime's mother nurtures her ambitions, talents, athletic training, and scientific curiosity. Both of Jaime's parents were university professors, but Ann was a Cold War–era spy, "top echelon" as Oscar tells Jaime, for the United States government. That Jaime's mother was the spy, not her father, concretizes the suggestion in the flashbacks that she was by far the more interesting person.

A strange woman—the one we saw driving and nursing her injured arm—begins making mysterious appearances. Jaime begins to imagine that this woman is her mother returned from the dead. Jaime receives a call—from the strange woman—telling her, falsely, that her parents' graves have been vandalized. Examining the gravesite of both deceased parents, Jaime can see that the site remains intact. Suddenly, a dog runs up to her, and when she pets him she notices his nametag reading "Puzzles." From a distance, a woman in a car impatiently calls out, "Puzzles!" and the dog runs back to her. As the car speeds away, Jaime softly inquires, "Mother?"

The mysterious woman is Chris Stewart (Barbara Rush), an actress hired by the U.S. government and augmented with plastic surgery to look like Ann Sommers and be her spy double. For the bulk of the narrative, Chris pretends to be Jaime's mother. Jaime, after initial resistance, accepts that she really is her mother. The viewer is kept in suspense about this mysterious woman's identity until the end. The early portions of the episode focus on Jaime's conflict over whether to trust her own impressions given the mental anguish she endured after being made bionic, including her loss of memories.

Much of Wagner's portrayal of Jaime Sommers in her pre–*Bionic* episodes focused on the character's physical and, increasingly, emotional agony. In *Bionic*'s first season, Jaime, restored to life but suffering from memory loss, determinedly wins her spurs as a government agent in her own right, capable and confident. The idea that Jaime may still be suffering from emotional as well as memory loss-related difficulties is carryover from *Six Million*, since even in "Welcome Home, Jaime, Part 1," much less fear over a potential mental breakdown permeates.

Back at the Coach House, Jaime, visibly confused and upset, has a tense conversation with Helen, who gently offers, "Maybe it was the power of suggestion." Jaime becomes incensed despite Helen's nurturing and mild tone. Given that Ann died several years ago—"I was at the funeral, and so were you," Helen says—it is hard to believe that Jaime could have actually seen her mother again. Helen has good reason to doubt the truth of Ann's reappearance; nevertheless, her worried insistence that Jaime is besieged by recurring memory and emotional problems—"funny little troubles" she says, quoting Jaime back to herself—agitates Jaime. Still, the extent to which Jaime blows up at Helen is surprising. Defending herself in response to one of Jaime's challenges, Helen says, "We all care for you!" Jaime provocatively responds in turn, "Well, I'll make that unanimous!" The series' general emphasis on Jaime's generosity and selflessness (a generally admirable stance while also endemic to the series' idealization of her as a good American) notwithstanding, Jaime threatens to lose both Helen's and the audience's sympathy here.

Against Jaime's explicit wishes, Helen contacts Oscar Goldman, who pays his secret agent a concerned visit. In an offscreen consultation with Rudy Wells, Oscar explores the possibility that Jaime's encounter with the returned Ann is a hallucination deriving from Jaime's unconscious memories and/or knowledge of Ann's having been a spy. He shows her the redacted government document that identifies Ann as such. But Jaime has no memory of her mother's secret identity. If this plot device is somewhat heavy-handed a piece of retrocontinuity, it nevertheless has fascinating possibilities.

First, Jaime and her mother share double lives spying for the United States government, a staggering coincidence given that Jaime's spy career has no connection to Ann's involvement with covert affairs. Second, this plot allows *Bionic* to explore women's social possibilities in a comparative

2. Feminist Ethics

manner, holding up the second-wave-feminist 1970s to the Cold War 1950s and its postwar redomestication of women, ennobled and imprisoned at once as maternal guardians. This female redomestication inspired commentators like Betty Friedan, Helen Gurley Brown, and Gloria Steinem to revolt against American sexism. Third, the notion of a female spy with a double life alerts us to the instabilities that make the 1950s such an enduringly complex period, along gender as well as racial lines. Inevitably, one thinks of Eve Kendall (Eva Marie Saint), the blonde siren revealed to be a U.S. spy in Alfred Hitchcock's great comic thriller *North by Northwest* (1959). Eve is both a *femme fatale* and a woman nobly assisting the U.S. government's effort to combat Cold War villainy.

The casting of Barbara Rush as Chris Stuart, like the casting of Tippi Hedren and Martha Scott, signifies *Bionic*'s links to classical Hollywood femininities. Rush acted in several important films of the 1950s such as *Bigger Than Life* (Nicholas Ray, 1956) and *The Young Lions* (Edward Dmytryk, 1958). (Rush was also no stranger to the science-fiction genre, a star of movies like *When Worlds Collide* [1951] and *It Came from Outer Space* [1953].) Her big-screen career faded after that initial high point. On the IMDb website, Barbara Rush is quoted as saying, "I can safely say that every movie role I was ever offered that had any real quality went to someone else." A meta-fictional touch, her casting as Chris (and Ann in the flashbacks) works beautifully because it draws on Rush's own status as a quasi-star. As Chris explains to Jaime in the extremely moving coda, playing Ann, and having Jaime believe her, has been her "big moment. I finally got to be your real mother." A minor actress's hunger to play a great role and a discarded woman's final chance to be of importance to someone dovetail in Chris's perilous performance as Ann.

At one point, Ann/Chris, responding unflinchingly to Jaime's challenging questions about her identity, coolly responds: "You like Helen, and you trust her. Let's go and see her." Helen will be a particularly discerning audience, and if Chris can carry off her role in front of *her*, Chris's performance will be a triumph indeed. Jaime brings Ann/Chris to see Helen. There is a peculiar thrill in seeing Rush, Martha Scott, and Wagner in the same scene, gifted performers with distinct yet complementary acting styles; it is also interesting to see Scott and Rush, veterans of the classical Hollywood cinema, together on the small screen.

Helen has steadfastly maintained that Jaime has been imagining seeing the dead Ann again. In the meantime, however, Oscar has learned about Chris's role as Ann's double, and raises the possibility that this resurfaced woman is indeed Ann, and Chris the woman buried in her stead.

The Bionic Woman and Feminist Ethics

Informed by Oscar about this, Helen wonders if this really is the returned Ann, not just Jaime's mother but also Helen's old friend. "So, Ann, then it really is you?" Helen asks. "The shattered remains," Ann (Chris) responds, with the dark humor that Rush's performance and Arthur Rowe's teleplay bring to the role.

This scene in which two women try to determine a mysterious woman's identity allegorizes *Bionic's* evocation of classical Hollywood styles, preoccupations, and especially the woman's film genre: first, in its use of two women stars of the older period as a contrast to Wagner's contemporary stardom as well as acting style; second, in its depiction of female suffering. Rush employs a melodramatic acting style that recalls the German expatriate Hollywood auteur Douglas Sirk's passionate and ironic woman's films, such as the 1956 *Magnificent Obsession* with Jane Wyman and Rock Hudson, which featured Rush in an emotive supporting role. Martha Scott's acting cites melodramatic style at times. In the later scene between Helen and Oscar Goldman when he informs her that the returned woman is Chris, *not* Ann, Helen wrings her hands in a self-consciously motherly manner over Jaime's troubles, lamenting, "Oh, I should have known better!"

But in this scene among the three women, Scott gives a notably taut, detached performance. She more than holds her own against Rush and Wagner's intense emotionalism. When Jaime asks Ann/Chris for proof that she really is her mother, Chris draws on her knowledge of Ann's private life. She looks at Jaime's necklace and identifies it as the one Ann gave her daughter on the day that Jaime's parents died, leading both women to display a fierce outpouring of feeling. The free flow of tears as Jaime and Chris embrace—Jaime believing that Chris really is her mother, Chris, perhaps, seizing the emotional fulfillment of making Jaime believe this, while Helen looks on—evokes the woman's film genre, its inducement of sympathetic and shared tears and its central theme of mother-daughter relationships.[16]

The woman's film genre, as we have noted, emphasized mother-daughter relationships and female anxieties over marriage. The definitive woman's films—*Imitation of Life* (both its 1930s and '50s versions), *Stella Dallas, Alice Adams, Now, Voyager, Mildred Pierce*—paralleled the heroine's simultaneous rebellions against maternal control and the prospect of marriage, the latter desirable but also threatening to the heroine's identity, singularity, specialness. *Bionic* reflects the transformation, after its popular period ebbed in the 1960s, of the woman's film genre, associated with melodrama and emotional floridity, into other genres. As I have argued, horror films took up many of the themes of this once central genre; horror classics such as *Carrie* and *The Silence of the Lambs* (Jonathan Demme, 1991) can be described as "concealed women's films."[17] Given its parallels with the horror genre, science-fiction narratives could also be read as concealed women's films. *The Bionic Woman* emerges as a crucial example of such a genre-blending possibility.

What's most interesting about "Jaime's Mother," however, is that it preserves the centrality of the mother-daughter relationship while eschewing the question of heterosexual desire and romance and marriage. The real romance here is between women, between mothers and daughters, and between mothers and daughters whose ties are not biological. The science-fiction elements of *Bionic* allow it to explore the emotional dynamics of female characters' interrelationships while conceding to the mainstream audience's presumably insatiable need for action and adventure. (This is not to patronize the bionic aspects of the show, or its adventure series-elements. It would be hypocritical of me to do so, since I enjoy them so.) Several key bionic suspense sequences in which Jaime battles against the petty thugs hunting down Chris ensue, allowing the other, quieter, emotionally intense moments to occur unfettered.

At the climax, Jaime rescues Chris, whose identity she has learned by bionically overhearing a conversation between Chris and her would-be assassins. (In a spellbinding moment, Jaime hears the imposter's name echo: "*Hello, Chris... Chris... Chris...*" She adds to the incantatory chain by also saying, in recognition, "Oh, Chris.") Chris knows about Jaime's bionics, knowledge that would provide the desperate woman with a get-out-of-jail-free gambit.

But Chris has no intention of hurting Jaime. Instead, she saves Jaime's life, twice, first by deflecting the hit men's intentions to kill her for being a witness and second when Chris takes the bullet meant for Jaime when she intervenes to save Chris life. When Jaime comforts the older woman in the car as she bleeds out from the gunshot, Chris finally confesses. "I'm not your mother." As Jaime holds her, she says, "I know, Chris." This moment—this gesture—is characteristic of *Bionic*'s sensibility. In comforting Chris and holding her close while Jaime says her name, Jaime affirms Chris's humanity, conveying the message that she deserves love and care *because* she is Chris, not Ann.

The yellow roses associated with Ann and the child Jaime and the family home emerge as an important symbol for Chris and the adult Jaime. Chris brought a bouquet of yellow roses to her mother's graveside when Jaime first discovered her. In the penultimate scene, Jaime brings Chris,

The Bionic Woman and Feminist Ethics

recovering from the gunshot wound, a bouquet of yellow roses when she visits her in the hospital. If one Googles "yellow roses" today, the information that comes up associates them with friendship. But in the Victorian language of flowers, yellow roses signify "Infidelity and Jealousy. Bad Luck Gift to a Woman."[18] The yellow roses link Jaime to her mother and her love for her daughter. But they also symbolize Chris's love for Ann. As she tells Jaime in the hospital, "I loved Ann. I admired her. I wanted to be like her." In many ways, Chris's love for Jaime is an extension of, perhaps, her deeper love for Ann. Her competitive moment, which she herself stages, with Helen comes to seem a power play, a battle with a living rival for a dead woman's love and friendship.

In the scene between the three women Chris, as Ann, surveys the old furniture that Helen has brought to her new house. (Helen explained to Jaime in the first episode of the series that she and Jim have just bought this property.) Ann/Chris says, "The old furniture looks good in the new house. Twenty years ago, I was telling you to sell it." "And I was telling you—" Helen begins to say, but the other woman cuts her off: "To mind my own business, that you were comfortable with it." This densely loaded dialogue is suggestive, hinting at the possibly less than perfect character of Ann, who chided Helen over her drab furniture, and the feisty strength of Helen beneath her maternal warmth.

Back to the yellow roses: Chris's bouquet signifies the jealousy of the rival but also that of the double, the copy who has been made to feel inferior to the original. Ann has it all, being clearly the head of her family and a university professor in an era in which women's employment prospects were routinely diminished if not foreclosed altogether. The theme of the double's simultaneous love for and rivalry with the original will animate the greatest of *Bionic* episodes, S2's two-parter "Deadly Ringer."

Unmistakably, a note of same-sex desire hovers over the depiction of Chris's love for Ann, one made especially palpable by the themes of doubling and the covert nature of espionage and the suspect air of treason. Chris, on some level, represents the closeted 1950s, or, more historically, the masks that gays and lesbians had to don to pass as straight in homophobic society, the enclaves of the United States government as well as the halls of the university and the garden-lined rows of suburbia.

The final scene between Jaime and Chris is deeply moving, concluding with Jaime wiping a tear from Chris's face. ("It was my big moment. I finally got to be your real mother.") The last scene of the episode takes place between Jaime and Helen, who is, not insignificantly, working in her own garden. In this scene, through laughter and warm jokes, the women reaffirm their bond. "I wasn't very happy when I thought she was Ann," Helen explains, sheepishly admitting that she was jealous, to which Jaime responds, "Oh, Mom, mothers aren't like used cars, you don't change a model on a whim." As the women walk off together, arm in arm, they tell one another that they love each other. What makes this finale so moving, tender, and fulfilling is, in part, the sense that this bond between nonbiologically-linked women has a power and an integrity all its own, not being inferior to the love Jaime shared with Ann but instead its complement. Nevertheless, the episode leaves you with a lasting sting. One cannot forget the discarded woman alone in her hospital room, facing a future whose only certainty is incarceration and isolation.

"Mirror Image." Directed by Alan J. Levi.
Written by James D. Parriott. Airdate: May 19, 1976.

Though not played for the wrenching emotional depths of its sequel in S2, "Mirror Image" is a significant *Bionic* episode, especially given its themes, so central to the series, of the double and the copy's relationship to the original. If *Bionic* always understands itself in relation to *Six Million*, the series allegorized its own status as copy in several episodes, such as "Jaime's Mother" and this one.

The villainous Dr. Courtney (Don Porter) is a plastic surgeon who runs a clinic in Bethesda, MD. Through his surgical arts, he has transformed his secretary Lisa Galloway into an exact lookalike for Jaime Sommers. Lisa will be a crucial component of Courtney's effort to steal government secrets from the OSI, a plan that involves killing Jaime when she's on a vacation in the Bahamas while Lisa infiltrates the OSI. Lindsay Wagner plays Lisa as well.

Lisa/Jaime's first interaction with Oscar Goldman is a telling one. Oscar expresses incredulity that Jaime would want to leave the Bahamas for drudgery at his office. "Oscar, I do a lot of work for you—and I love it." But, Lisa/Jaime explains, she still does not know very much about the agency she secretly works for, hence her decision to cancel her trip and come to the OSI instead. Oscar, cheerful but perplexed, arranges to get Jaime a "security building permit," shrugging incredulously at her as he leaves the office. Lisa swings into action, talking photographs on her nifty bracelet-camera device of a top-secret document called the Howlett Report. Meanwhile, Jaime, wooed by a handsome seeming native of the island, enjoys drinks with him on his boat. This man, played by Herbert Jefferson, Jr., is really an American, working for Dr. Courtney. He drugs Jaime and with the help of his assistant places her in a chest, which they

The Bionic Woman and Feminist Ethics

lock and dump into the water with the line, "Nothing is more moving than a burial at sea." Cut to a commercial; when we come back, Jaime bionically bursts through the chest and swims back to shore.

An extremely suspenseful scene follows in which Jaime, desperate and frightened, calls Oscar in his office as Lisa looks on. Rather casually, he asks his secretary—dumbfounded that a woman on the other end of the line claims to be Jaime Sommers—"Where is she calling him?" When his secretary responds, "Nassau, in the Bahamas," Oscar takes the phone, and as the real Jaime begins speaking, Lisa makes use of another of her devices, a small weapon that shoots poisoned darts. She just misses Oscar, who ducks under his desk right after pressing the panic button; security guards rush into his office.

In certainly one of the most chilling moments in the series, Oscar, asking "What is this? Who are you?," grabs Lisa/Jaime's face, twisting it in his hand. Though the doppelgänger, having just tried to kill Oscar, is clearly dangerous, seeing a woman being manhandled in this manner on the series gives one considerable pause. The gesture and its effect prefigure the shocking and controversial moment in *Star Trek VI: The Undiscovered Country* (Nicholas Meyer, 1991) in which the Vulcan Spock (Leonard Nimoy) forcibly mind-melds with Lt. Valeris, a female Vulcan (played by Kim Cattrall) exposed as a double agent.[19]

The subversive function of the doppelgänger is her ability to draw out, tap into, the unspoken, less obvious, and dark energies of the protagonist and her narrative. Lisa brings out a hidden potential for violence lurking in the warm, collaborative, supportive rapport between Oscar and Jaime. Oscar's body language and banked rage here reveal his investments in power and the wielding of it, the ruthlessness of his covert operations. To be clear, this is only one dimension of his persona on the series, which consistently depicts his behavior as conscientious and his treatment of Jaime as both respectful and caring. But it *is* a dimension, one *Bionic* usually leaves out.

Lisa also brings out—more positively and provocatively—a more resistant potentiality in Jaime. By questioning Oscar about the inner workings of the OSI, Lisa demands accountability in a way that Jaime, at this point, does not. Jaime does not yet question the structures of power within the government institution she quite willingly serves. By the last episode of the series, however, Jaime will not only be questioning but also actively defying this government.

Dimitris Vardoulakis, in his study of the doppelgänger, theorizes that the figure "puts the notions of the beginning and end into question. If

2. Feminist Ethics

there is an endlessness proper to the doppelgänger, it is the infinite possibility of interruption between an absolute beginning and an absolute end." The doppelgänger is a "liminal subject," exposing the limitations of notions of subjectivity and exemplifying the "relation between being creative and been created."[20] The idea that the doppelgänger disrupts questions of beginnings and endings has suggestive possibilities for a queer reading of the double, which I will expand on in the chapter "Bionic *Vertigo*."

We never see Lisa Galloway before she transforms into Jaime. First introduced in the teaser, she is a faceless stranger swathed in surgical bandages, reminiscent of film noir works such as *Dark Passage* (Delmer Daves, 1947), in which Humphrey Bogart's face is surgically altered. When one of Courtney's henchmen unravels her bandage-mask and shows her an image of herself in the mirror, Lisa is *already* Jaime, whose image stares back at her. But the smile, in its knowingness and pleasure with a slightly amoral air, conveys a different affect, and it is this difference in affect that signifies Lisa-ness.

The destabilization of temporal priority—the end of beginnings and endings and therefore of a hierarchy of originals and copies—figured in the doppelgänger makes Lisa's presence unsettling and disturbing. If Lisa takes Jaime's place, the entire backstory so carefully woven into the series disappears. So, no heartbreaking romance with Steve, no loving non-biological parents in Helen and Jim, no tennis pro past and schoolteacher present, no passionate desire to work on behalf of the government that brought her back to life, only a void where that heroine was.

But Lisa is also far from a void. With her Southern twang and zestful appetite glutted with cigarettes and alcohol, and with an impatient, amoral determination to get what she wants, Lisa is a singular entity. Singular, certainly, is her lack of any sense of obligation to Oscar, the OSI, and the integrity of the United States.

The original and the copy confront one another in two eerily effective moments. First, Jaime, back from her near-death experience in the Bahamas, is shown into a room at the OSI's DC office where a woman with long blond hair sits in a chair, her back turned. She turns around in her chair to face Jaime, and Jaime beholds a woman who looks exactly like her. Jaime's stunned expression is countered by Lisa's slightly amused, even prideful one. The double's pleasure in being a copy is a delicious and subversive touch.

Second, at the climax set in the basement of Courtney's hospital facility, Lisa confronts Jaime as she tries to break into a vault containing

The Bionic Woman and Feminist Ethics

criminal evidence. "Jaime," Lisa hails her foe. Jaime swings around, and Lisa, again with a surprising level of self-contented humor, says, "I believe it's time for you and me to have it out, sugar pie. There's only gonna be *one* Jaime Sommers now." Wagner's delivery of these lines, with Southern twang adding to the effect and a certain witty fire in her eyes, makes Lisa a lively character—one wants to learn more about her, see how her mind works.

The shot of Lisa sitting in Oscar's chair, her feet up on his desk, leading to his great surprise when he returns to his office to find "Jaime" in that position reading his files, encapsulates Lisa's subversive appeal. Lisa's inevitable defeat at Jaime's hands fulfills the demands of the hero's narrative—the villain must be defeated, and the hero must prevail. But traditionally the double carries knowledge of the subject's death, of which the double is a harbinger. The double's power to unsettle the subject will be extensively developed in S2.

Much more pronounced in this episode than in "Deadly Ringer," Lisa Galloway's associations with fashion, beauty culture, and what Joan Riviere would call the female masquerade distinguish her from Jaime, always presented as a lovely physical being but never emphasized as shallowly fashionable nor presented in a sexually objectifying manner. In the S1 "Bionic Beauty," Oscar corrals Jaime, who adamantly balks at his request, into going undercover as a beauty pageant contestant. Helen expresses shock that Jaime is participating in the Miss United States beauty contest. When she learns that Jaime's participation is only a covert ruse, she says, "You always hated beauty pageants." Jaime is never shown putting on make-up or even choosing her clothes with discretion (there are no scenes in which she equivocates over which ensemble to don). Her style, even when elegantly toned, is always warm and inviting—earth tones, comfortable fabrics, yarn, floral patterns all connote an accessible, commonsensical sensibility. Lisa, however, is associated with the stereotypical feminine arts of masquerade and fashion—in other words, the hallmarks of the narcissistic woman.

The narcissistic woman has long been a figure of opprobrium throughout the Western tradition. The frequent subject of paintings, a woman stares in self-mesmerized abandon at her reflection in a mirror. This image of female vanity expresses the idea that pride is inherent in femininity and offers a cautionary message: the woman who succumbs to pride is damned.

Yet the narcissistic woman can also be read as a resistant figure. In "On Narcissism," Freud theorizes that women, "especially if they grow up with good looks, develop a certain self-contentment which compensates them for the social restrictions that are imposed upon them in their choice of object." Narcissism compensates the woman for the constrictions of sexist society; at the same time, it tantalizes men, seduced by the "great charm" of the woman's narcissism.[21]

Feminist psychoanalytic theorists have recuperated Freud's theorization of female narcissism as potentially politically useful. For Kaja Silverman, Freud's theory is valuable in that it differentiates "the female subject ... from her male counterpart" in terms of desire. "She must embody," Silverman makes clear, "both lack and its opposite; lack, so that the male subject's phallic attributes can be oppositionally articulated; plenitude, so that she can become adequate to his desire." The woman's identification with beauty culture is a phallic maneuver that "protests," in Silverman's words, against "her forced identification with lack."[22]

In "Mirror Image," Lisa Galloway is associated with surfaces—her outward appearance, especially, but also her clothing. When Jaime offers to infiltrate the criminals' lair by reversing their strategy and impersonating Lisa impersonating her, Oscar responds, without missing a beat, "How are you going to match her dress?" Jaime responds, "Oscar, if she can match my face, I can match her dress!"

Lisa, being interrogated in Oscar's office after attempting to kill him, refuses to answer anyone's questions. Oscar, disgusted by her silence, is about to walk out when Lisa finally does utter something. "Mr. Goldman?" she asks. "Well, she can speak after all," Oscar marvels. Tear-tracked mascara running down her face and Southern accent unfettered, Lisa asks for an item in her purse: "Mr. Goldman, I fear that I look a fright. Do you mind if I put some lipstick on?" Oscar, however disgusted, agrees to her request before exiting the room; his personnel hand Lisa her bag. In a bravura moment, Lisa takes the lipstick—actually a weapon given her by Courtney—and throws it to the ground, where it becomes a cloud of gas that knocks her captors out, allowing her to flee.

Associated with the shallow vanity of the siren, Lisa seems interested only in her appearance, even when being faced with criminal charges and held in a government office, surrounded by tough male agents interrogating her. Seemingly interested only in superficialities even when her fate hangs in the balance, Lisa cunningly exploits the sexism inherent in the male enclave surrounding her. Oscar makes the foolish mistake of handing Lisa's bag back to her because he believes that she *would* be shallow enough to apply make-up at such a decisive moment. Lisa weaponizes the accessories of female beauty, turning her very performance of femininity into a weapon.

The Bionic Woman and Feminist Ethics

"The Ghosthunter." Directed by Kenneth Johnson.
Written by Kenneth Johnson and Justin Edgerton.
Airdate: May 26, 1976

With box-office hits such as *The Exorcist*, *The Omen*, and *Carrie*, the 1970s were awash in supernatural horror. This episode of *Bionic* capitalizes on the '70s prevalence of such works, especially those focusing on mother-daughter relationships (though Brian De Palma's movie *Carrie* was released on November 3, 1976, a few months after "The Ghosthunter" aired, its source material, Stephen King's novel, was published in 1974).

The exceptionally talented young Kristy McNichol plays a girl named Amanda Cory, whose scientist father, Alan Cory (Paul Shenar), is working on the top-secret Alpha Sensor project for the OSI. Cory's now dead wife Elizabeth Putnam Cory, Amanda's mother, was a descendant of Rebecca Putnam, who was executed during the Salem witch trials. Elizabeth was also said to be a witch. The unexplainable events happening in the Cory home located—predictably—near Salem, Massachusetts are upsetting the local townspeople, convinced that Amanda's mother has come back from the dead to wreak havoc. Oscar Goldman is worried that this unexplainable force is interfering with the Alpha Sensor unit. Enter Jaime, undercover as a new governess for young Amanda.

Jaime arrives and introduces herself as the governess, a scene with shades of Robert Wise's 1965 movie musical *The Sound of Music* (incidentally, Wise directed the 1973 film *Two People*, co-starring Wagner and Peter Fonda) and of *Jane Eyre*, the famous gothic novel by Charlotte Brontë published in 1847. Cory, in a brusque manner that recalls Captain von Trapp (Christopher Plummer) summarily disciplining the newbie Maria (Julie Andrews), complains that he has little time for the social niceties and will assign Jaime her duties in the morning. But suddenly he spies a thick old volume titled PUTNAM in the bookcase (supernaturally overturned when Jaime first arrived, now bionically restored to its usual position along with its big heavy books). Distressed, Cory picks up the tome and places it in the next room, where a portrait of his wife Elizabeth hangs on the wall.

After her father has left, Amanda, in hushed, conspiratorial tones, informs Jaime, "It's a witch book." It contains the account of her "great-great" Rebecca Putnam's trial for witchcraft during the Puritan era. Intrigued, Jaime takes the book with her and the next scene occurs in her room as she reads through it.

Directed in a clean, graceful manner by Johnson, the episode does a remarkable job of conveying supernatural dread. The I-camera perspective

2. Feminist Ethics

allows us to see through the eyes of the seeming ghostly presence invading Cory's house and the town. With it, we careen through spooky, somber leaf-strewn graveyards, scuttle across a long bridge lit by kerosene lamps and twinkling with a supernatural sheen in the nighttime air.

The episode contains two extraordinary sequences. The first contains the following action: Jaime, reading through the historical account of the Salem witch trial of Rebecca Putnam, imagines that she hears the voices of those involved: the accused woman pleading her innocence, the stern judge denouncing her as a witch and sentencing her to death. Jaime then hears strange noises beneath her and, investigating, looks out of her window. She watches the forward-moving progress of what appears to be a ghostly entity, an invisible force knocking over things and brushing leaves aside as it travels ahead. Jaime bionically leaps down and follows this invisible force to the graveyard housing both Elizabeth Cory and her witch ancestress. There, she meets the titular ghosthunter.

Johnson begins this sequence with a superbly suggestive image: Jaime stares into the painting behind a glass frame that hangs on a wall in her room. The painting depicts Rebecca Putnam's hectic trial scene. Jaime's own image as she stands peering at the painting is captured in the glass, held at its center, creating the uncanny effect that *Jaime* is encased within the action. And in her elegant white suit, Jaime looks rather ghostly herself—like a contemporary version of one of Rebecca's inquisitors or jurors.

The horrific nature of the Salem witch trials overwhelms a visibly affected Jaime as she reads the Putnam history while seated on a bed. She reads the first line of the trial aloud, the judge's stern question to the accused woman, once again oddly aligning Jaime with the prosecution. In many ways, that makes sense—Jaime is here to investigate, to judge, a female entity accused of witchcraft.

But as Jaime becomes absorbed by the trial history, the soundtrack blares with the voices of the judge and Rebecca Putnam herself, his hectoring and unrelenting, hers desperate and adamant. Clearly, from her troubled expression, Jaime identifies with Rebecca and her plight. Jaime becomes affected by a real-world historical event and offense against women (predominantly, those killed during the trials were women). Her empathy with the unjustly accused and murdered woman gives the episode a feminist perspective on the longstanding persecution of women, especially women marked off as alien and threatening. Such a designation would include the bionic woman herself.

The episode's reworking of the feminist literary classic *Jane Eyre* deserves scrutiny. The novel centers on the plight of the young orphan

The Bionic Woman and Feminist Ethics

Jane who becomes, when older, a governess for Adèle, the ward of the brooding, enigmatic Edward Rochester, who presides over Thornfield Hall. Once there, Jane falls in love with Rochester. She also discovers that something terrible is afoot. Mysterious assaults and unexplainable sounds eventually reveal their source: the abandoned Mrs. Bertha Rochester, the infamous "madwoman in the attic" as described by Sandra Gilbert and Susan Gubar in their 1979 book by that name. (In *Jane Eyre*, racial themes play a crucial if muted role. Bertha Rochester is from the West Indies. Jean Rhys' novel *Wide Sargasso Sea* focuses on Bertha Rochester, providing an expanded backstory and an analysis of the buried politics of race in the source text.) "The Ghosthunter" very much seems to be following the *Jane Eyre* route of having the wife wreaking havoc. A vengeful apparition appears to substitute for Rochester's wife in the *Bionic* episode; in the novel, Rochester's servants believe a ghost is to blame for Bertha Rochester's malevolent antics.

But as Jaime eventually deduces, it is not the dead Elizabeth but instead *Amanda*, gifted with matrilineal telekinetic abilities, who unleashes destructive energies. Feeling abandoned by her workaholic father, the bereft and motherless Amanda feels jealousy and rage over her father's inattentiveness and burgeoning romance with Jaime, especially when the doctor drops his work and beholds anew the governess's entrancing beauty.

William Friedkin's film *The Exorcist* (1973) is another intertext for this episode. While Friedkin's film has some inescapably misogynistic elements, it is ultimately a progressive horror film, in my view, given its central relationship between Chris MacNeil (Ellen Burstyn) and her daughter Regan (Linda Blair), who becomes possessed by the ancient demon Pazuzu. So much of the drama of this film lies in Chris' desperate attempt to heal her horrifically afflicted daughter (and, to be sure, in the spiritual and emotional crisis of Father Karras, played so powerfully by Jason Miller, who must be convinced that Regan is indeed possessed but then sacrifices his own life to save her).

Cory reveals that he performed experiments on his wife to determine the scientific basis of her paranormal activities (shades of John Boorman's much-maligned but fascinating 1977 sequel *Exorcist II: The Heretic*, which takes the possession-gothic narrative of the first film into the realm of scientific analysis of supernatural events). That the series affirms this kind of research as one a scientist would plausibly undertake speaks volumes about the 1970s' comfort level with the paranormal. (Later, the series will delve into another obsession of the decade, extraterrestrials and UFOs.)

2. Feminist Ethics

Cory's experiments on his wife evoke the nineteenth century and its focus on the female hysteric, a late Victorian phenomenon popularized by Freud's case studies. The episode foregrounds what Michel Foucault has called the "hysterization of woman."[23] As Foucault argued, the earlier views of female sexuality as hysterical in nature permeate twentieth-century pathologizations of women's mental states and sexuality. (Though not sexualized, Jaime's mad scenes in her early appearances on *The Six Million Dollar Man* evoke the hysteric.)

Corey's experiments on his wife similarly recall the nineteenth century's fascination with mesmerism and the spirit world. Most disturbingly, they evince a patriarchal exploitation of women in a biomedical context that includes Michael Marchetti's romantic manipulation of the mentally fragile Jaime Sommers in "The Return of the Bionic Woman" on *Six Million*.

The flip side of Cory's exploitation of his wife is his aloof distance from Amanda. "She seems so melancholy," Jaime tries to alert him. Given his indifference to his troubled daughter, is it possible that Cory mistreated Elizabeth? (One is reminded of Nathaniel Hawthorne's great tales on this theme, "The Birth-Mark" and "Rappaccini's Daughter." In "The Birth-Mark," a science-fiction cautionary tale, the foolish and sadistic scientist Aylmer relentlessly attempts to remove the titular mark from his beautiful wife Georgiana's cheek, resulting in her death.)

As Jaime deduces, however, neither Elizabeth nor Rebecca Putnam is wreaking havoc on scientific rationalism and suburban peace. It is the troubled, sad, lonely, bereft Amanda, unconsciously expressing her grief through seemingly supernatural acts of revenge. When Cory leaves Amanda behind so that he can take Jaime out on a canoe trip while the three enjoy a lakeside picnic, Amanda looks visibly rejected, and then falls asleep. Her father and the new governess taking him away from her then endure a series of supernatural assaults. Long, menacing, phallic logs uncannily move with relentless purpose through the water, puncturing the canoe. (This sequence oddly suggests a symbolic rape: Amanda may want to punish these incipient lovers and especially Jaime for her sexuality.)

Jaime returns to shore with Cory, knocked unconscious during the lake assault. Jaime narrowly saves her own life with a bionic jump as a monstrous log hurtles toward her. As she lands on the ground, she bionically hears Amanda crying out, "Mother!" Jaime and a revived Cory return to the sleeping Amanda. Now awake, Amanda informs them, eerily, "Mother was here." Jaime's fierce expression as she stares at the solemn,

The Bionic Woman and Feminist Ethics

haunted girl insinuates a growing suspicion of her complicity in these intensifying attacks.

Corey announces his plan to visit MIT. Given the circumstances, he brusquely abandons his paternal duties in leaving his daughter behind at this time. Adding to her injury, Amanda witnesses her father giving Jaime an amorous farewell kiss. The girl grows more openly moody; she sharply informs Jaime, wearing a pair of slippers she found in the lab, "Those were *mother's* shoes."

The rather stereotypical German ghosthunter Emil Lazlo appears at the house, investigating the case. Lazlo recalls the Universal horror movie tradition of the 1930s and '40s. He also evokes the titular figure in *The Exorcist*, Father Merrin (Max Von Sydow). The ghosthunter nearly divulges the cause of the supernatural pestilence, but the bookcase falls again, an attack meant for Jaime. Lazlo pushes her out of the way, taking the blow himself. Before he drifts into unconsciousness, he cries out, "Poltergeist!" Jaime takes him to the hospital, leaving Amanda, at her behest, home alone. ("I can't go to that hospital, Jaime. Mother died there.")

While at the hospital, Jaime, armed with Lazlo's knowledge and speaking on the phone with Cory, begins to theorize that, if the poltergeist-energy attaches itself to a troubled young person, it is very likely that Amanda, rather than a maternal ghost, is responsible for these attacks. Cory initially scoffs at the idea, saying Amanda has never exhibited telekinetic ability or been consciously aware of having it. Jaime muses, "But what about her subconscious mind?" Unfortunately, Jaime commits the layperson's typical error of talking of the subconscious when she means the unconscious. But the main point is that, through her intelligence and imaginative empathy, Jaime can interpret the situation correctly, especially notable given the obtuseness of the apparently brilliant scientific male mind at the other end of the line. (Indeed, male scientists often come across quite poorly on this series in terms of devising solutions to scientific dilemmas. See, for example, Michael Marchetti's utter incompetence regarding extraterrestrial intelligence and mind control in S2's "The Vega Influence.")

In the second extraordinary sequence of the episode, Jaime, driving back to the Corey estate, must get out of her car and traverse a collapsing bridge to get to Amanda. She then faces a series of telekinetic assaults in the Corey house. Once she gets through this gauntlet, she must then convince a nightmare-maddened Amanda that she, not her mother, is unleashing telekinetic wrath.

Kenneth Johnson, director of this episode, brilliantly seizes on the collapsing bridge as a metaphor for the thematic action. Jaime is a technologically enhanced woman and also completely alone as she traverses the collapsing bridge. This image encapsulates the gender politics of her struggle and the rich cultural resonances of the bridge, one of the major symbols of modernity. We noted that "Jaime's Mother" evokes the usually male-identified symbol of the open road, imagining the lonely and desperate woman's navigation of its uncertain possibilities. (Shades of Hitchcock's *Psycho* and Janet Leigh's desperate trip in the rain-pounded night.)

Here, the bridge, associated with masculinity and technology, modernity and progress, acts as a nearly insurmountable obstacle to a connection between an intergenerational female pair. The bridge not only collapses, in stages, but hurls parts of itself—an enormous beam that Jaime bionically deflects and jumps over—at the heroine. That it does so gives the structure a strange agency of its own, as if it were sentient and attacking the defiant woman.

Jurgen Hasse notes,

> [M]any peoples have attributed mystical qualities to bridges. In Christian mythology the bridge was the "loci of the souls' probation on the way to the hearafter" and was therefore associated with the iniquitous; the earthly world of the sinful was on this side, while hellfire and brimstone threatened the other.[24]

While the narratives of modernity no longer foreground "dark, allegorical tales of gloomy, mystical worlds," these myths endure well into the present. They endure within the structures of modernity and "atmospherically colour our experience of the seemingly mundane," functional objects such as bridges, "in an imperceptible way."[25]

Given an eerie kaleidoscopic glow as it shimmers in the supernatural dark, the bridge looms as portal to a hellish world of night, recalling ancient beliefs, while also being a hyper-modern image of the subject's relationship to the material world and technology. Jaime embodies this techno-material world but more importantly symbolizes the human struggle to adapt to and make use of it.

The episode's Gothic themes, however, imbue the narrative with a sense of timelessness and the archetypal. Jaime endures a high-tech modern version of a Salem witch trial, battling the forces of elemental female nature—symbolized by Amanda's unconscious mind running amok and taking flight in the natural world—and masculinized techno-modernity. Amanda's furious unconscious struggles are another kind of ancient power battling against the techno-modernity embodied in Jaime.

Johnson uses a superb overhead shot of Amanda, asleep but writhing

The Bionic Woman and Feminist Ethics

on an enormous bed as the blankets toss around her. This complex image signals the creative mind at work while recalling the famous, frightening painting *The Nightmare* (Henry Fuseli, 1781). Fuseli's painting, the signature image of the Gothic, allegorizes the mind's vulnerability to the unconscious life, which takes the form of dreams. The subject is most vulnerable at night, during sleep, when the body is most helpless, the mind prey to indecipherable torments. In Fuseli's painting, the torment is embodied in a demonic creature atop an unconscious (or dead woman), from which position the demon leers at the spectator; the vulnerable body by the woman who lies in disarray on the bed beneath the demon.

In *The Exorcist*, two male priests heroically battle an ancient demon possessing the body and mind of Regan, an adolescent girl in a nightmarishly cold, dark bedroom. Her mother, Chris, terrified and helpless, waits outside. At one point, Regan's violently thumping bed lifts from the ground. In "The Ghosthunter," Jaime performs a secular exorcism, reaching out to the half-asleep Amanda as her bed. In a clear citation of *The Exorcist*, her bed moves up and down violently, like a boat on a stormy sea. As Jaime persists in reaching the troubled girl, she first applies a tough-love logic, informing Amanda that she nearly killed her father on the lake (the tempest-tossed bed echoes the lake attack). Hearing this, Amanda whimpers, "No!" The bed stops shaking and sinks, with her realization, to the ground. Then Jaime embraces the girl as she achingly weeps.

As we have noted, the genre of melodrama, which was at its height in the classical Hollywood era, informs *Bionic*. Many horror films from the 1960s forward can be read as concealed woman's films, *The Exorcist* very much included. "The Ghosthunter" brilliantly fuses these two modes. Jaime's hard-won, emotionally cathartic connection with Amanda recalls such intergenerational female relationships as that between Bette Davis's Charlotte Vale and the shy, socially withdrawn young girl Tina in *Now, Voyager* and the initially rocky and eventually mutually supportive one between Audrey Hepburn's Susy Hendrix, the blind heroine of *Wait Until Dark* (Terence Young, 1967), and Gloria (Julie Herrod), the shy, socially withdrawn girl who initially torments her and then becomes her chief ally.

"The Ghosthunter" revises *The Exorcist* to focus centrally on a maternal bond between a woman and a girl, an idea present, very much so, in the film but much more clearly articulated in this *Bionic* episode. This female bond transcends the horrors of the Gothic plot, restores the mind and heals the spirit of a young woman besieged by demons, chiefly those of loss and abandonment.

2. Feminist Ethics

The episode ends with a poignant image of father and daughter reunited, with Corey announcing that he will apply his investigative skills, along with the neuropsychiatrists in his service, to the study of Amanda's telekinetic abilities. While one hopes for the best, the episode ends uneasily. Without Jaime's tough but loving intervention, will Amanda thrive? Will her father develop a selflessness necessary to support and love her through her trials? Will she fall victim to the hysterization of women that most likely afflicted her mother? These questions remain unresolved, but that the episode raises them and lets them linger bespeaks its complexity. In Nathaniel Hawthorne's story "Rappaccini's Daughter," a morally corrupt scientist performs experiments on his daughter that turn her into a superbeing whose very touch is poisonous; "The Ghosthunter" could be the backstory for Hawthorne's tale.

Onlyness

Jaime traverses the haunted bridge alone. Johnson's indelible image encapsulates not only this episode's thematic action but many of the first season's themes. I surmise that one of the crucial points of intersection for both female and gay fans of the series is Jaime's aloneness—which, to avoid any pejorative tone, I am going to theorize as her *onlyness*. As the only bionic woman in the world, Jaime has a unique status.

From the time I was a child—a closeted one, living very much within the realms of my own imagination, where I throve—Jaime's isolation resonated for me. In "Welcome Home, Jaime, Part 1," she enters the loft that will become her home, in a state of disarray that she rights with bionic finesse. What's amazing about this sequence of her homecoming, as it were, is that she does it by herself: no man carries her over the threshold, no female friend pitches in. (*The Mary Tyler Moore Show*, which ran from 1970 to 1977, led the way in presenting independent women forging a new life and identity.) While Helen Elgin beams approvingly from below—we see her from Jaime's POV high up in the loft—the chief impression is that of Jaime's onlyness.

In "Welcome Home, Jaime, Part 2," she prowls an alleyway alone, summoned by the villain who wants more proof of her superpowers. In the excellent S1 episode "The Jailing of Jaime," which intersects provocatively with the paranoid thrillers of the decade such as *The Parallax View* (Alan J. Pakula, 1974), Jaime must clear her name after being falsely accused of a crime. To do so, she exposes the treason of those who have framed her, but does so with no help from anyone, save for a largely hamstrung but ever-loyal Oscar Goldman. "The Ghosthunter"'s climactic passage narrows the entire world down to Jaime, confronting an unloved girl who unleashes her grief-stricken wrath on the physical world. No other cars on the road, no other people in the street: Jaime makes her way to the scientist's cold and menacing realm as if the only person left in the world.

Overview of Season One

The radicalism within the depiction of Jaime's onlyness lies in its connection to her refusal of heterosexual identity in "Welcome Home, Jaime, Part 1." This is not to argue that Jaime is queer, but that her declaration of independence from romance and marriage, in its break with the normalizing demands of heterosexual and marital ties, has queer potentialities. One could argue that Jaime's refusal was merely an expedient maneuver on part of the series, a way to keep its heroine and her lover, on a linked but rival series, discrete, and therefore more commercially viable, entities. I think that would be a mistake. The series brings Jaime's feelings of ambivalence in the face of this normative relationship into articulation: *she* articulates her feelings, telling Steve "I can't remember what it was like to be in love with you." Kenneth Johnson deserves credit for writing dialogue that gave an autonomous woman a voice and an opportunity to articulate this autonomy, and Lindsay Wagner deserves inestimable credit for making Jaime so palpably real.

To be sure, the series backtracked from its initial radicalism in this first season. There are numerous, if brief, moments of Jaime and Steve bantering flirtatiously. Perhaps the oddest, and most uncomfortable, moment occurs during "Bionic Beauty," in which Jaime goes undercover in the "Miss United States" beauty pageant. Talking, during her sleuthing, to Oscar on the phone about Steve, Jaime sounds positively fragile as she asks her boss about her ex-fiancé. (The most interesting aspect of her phone call is the evidence it gives that Jaime sees Oscar as a confidante, a decidedly non-manly role for the staunchly masculine head of a government agency.) Such moments seem designed to keep the flames of Jaime and Steve's romance alive.

For the most part, however, the series keeps its focus on Jaime's efforts to establish herself not only as an independent person (we might say she reestablishes herself as such, given that in her pre-bionic days she

2. Feminist Ethics

was already quite independent as a tennis star) but also as a competent, skilled, successful spy. In many ways, S1 is the most realistic and grounded of all *Bionic*'s seasons. The series strove to depict Jaime as an independent single woman juggling two jobs and forging a fulfilling life.

Chapter 3

In the Shadow of Sasquatch

In S2, Jaime Sommers battles dark doppelgängers: the infamous Fembots—robot women who successfully masquerade as human ones—and her own super-powered double Lisa Galloway, who takes a drug to simulate Jaime's bionic strength. Before tackling Fembots and super-powered doubles, however, we must discover the secret of Bigfoot.

The crossover *Six Million Dollar Man* and *Bionic Woman* two-parter "The Return of Bigfoot," written by Kenneth Johnson, commenced the fourth and second seasons of these series, respectively. Given that this storyline is a sequel to a third-season *Six Million* two-parter, it makes sense to turn our attention to *Six Million* first. That Bigfoot, or Sasquatch as he is more often called, enters the Bionic mythology as a foe, then friend, to Steve, but becomes an important character in Jaime Sommers's narrative as well, evinces the overlaps but more importantly the distinctions between each series. Jaime's encounter with Sasquatch focuses on the creature's emotional life, which seems nonexistent when Steve first tangles with him. Giving Sasquatch a subjectivity, *Bionic* continues its feminist ethical exploration of the life and value of nonhuman animals, a theme that reaches its culmination in season three with "The Bionic Dog."

"The Secret of Bigfoot: Part 1." Written by Kenneth Johnson. Directed by Alan Crosland. Airdate: February 1, 1976

"The Secret of Bigfoot: Part 2." Written and produced by Kenneth Johnson. Directed by Alan Crosland. Airdate: February 4, 1976

As the cultural studies book *Paranormal America* notes, "By many accounts, a mysterious ape-man known variously as Bigfoot or Sasquatch has long inhabited the United States. Native American myths and legends

3. In the Shadow of Sasquatch

include a rich body of tales of hairy, man-like beasts that roam the forests. Depending on the tribe, such creatures are known as *Wendigo, Tornit, Strendu, Chenoo, Oh-mah, Snookum*.... The popular media often depicts Bigfoot/Sasquatch as a solitary creature roaming the Pacific Northwest. Most believers think of Bigfoot as a separate *species*."[1]

Introduced in third season of *Six Million*, the character of Bigfoot is a most unexpected hybrid. Kenneth Johnson gave the traditional creature of American legend—the immensely tall and shaggy ape-man in the wilderness—an SF twist. This Bigfoot is a gigantic beastly creature with—surprise—bionic limbs. He is the creation of Shalon (Stephanie Powers), a scientist who specializes in bionics. Shalon lives with her fellow deep-space travelers in a volcanic vent-powered complex beneath the San Andreas (called San Angelo here, however), California fault-line. The immense bionic creature Bigfoot, or Sasquatch (the aliens adopt the name given the creature in Native American lore), is an outer-space Golem. He protects the colony of aliens and does their bidding, which includes testing Steve Austin's strength in battle. When Steve grabs Bigfoot's right arm during a forest brawl, it shears off, the dismembered limb smoking in Steve's hand.

This episode is legendary for its Steve/Sasquatch showdown, but it boasts several stunning visuals. The passageway to the underground complex is a dreamlike wonder, a long, spooky corridor encased within a revolving, cylindrical wall that emits an eerie hum. Inside the complex, Steve meets Shalon, the scientist who created the Bigfoot creature from one of the aliens' lower species. It's an appealing touch that Johnson imagines this creator of futuristic cybernetics as female, a counterbalance to bionics creator Rudy Wells. Played by Stephanie Powers, Shalon is conventionally feminine, tender, funny, and womanly, but also a sharp, exacting scientist who thoroughly scans Steve's body, inventorying his bionic capacities (her cyborg technology greatly exceeds it).

One of the most interesting aspects of the two-parter is the depiction of Steve as both rescuing prince and the princess cast under a spell. Unconventionally for a male action hero, Steve spends a substantial portion of the episodes in a drug-induced slumber as Shalon and her team examine his exposed, vulnerable body.

In an extraordinary shot at the denouement of the second episode, the immense, towering Bigfoot carries Steve's unconscious body out of the complex, Steve's memories of his time with the aliens having been erased. This mythic image synthesizes the fairy tale aspects of the Bionic shows. Only it's a gender reversal, with Steve in the feminized role of being carried—swept away—by a powerful masculine force. These themes will be revisited in the crossover sequel episodes.

> "The Return of Bigfoot: Part 1." *The Six Million Dollar Man.*
> Directed by Barry Crane. Written by Kenneth Johnson.
> Airdate: September 19, 1976.
>
> "The Return of Bigfoot: Part 2." *The Bionic Woman.*
> Directed by Barry Crane. Written by Kenneth Johnson.
> Airdate: September 22, 1976.

Jaime's battle and eventual alliance with Bigfoot reprises that between the male hero and the cybernetic creature in the *Six Million* episodes but subjects this relationship to a critical analysis. Whereas Steve and the Sasquatch eventually form an alliance to save the underground alien colony from extinction during an earthquake, Jaime appeals directly to the creature, attempting to deprogram him from the duplicitous ideology of the villain, Nedlik (John Saxon).

Nedlik leads a faction of the aliens who have defected from the colony, the Sasquatch in tow. They seek dominion over the Earth and use the Sasquatch to steal precious minerals. Nedlik controls the creature by convincing it that Shalon will suffer if it refuses to comply. To reinforce his control, Nedlik uses a wristband control-unit—a torture device—to inflict pain on the creature. Jaime eventually overcomes Nedlik, wresting the control unit from him. Urgently trying to stop him from killing Steve, Jaime, speaking into the device, convinces Sasquatch that the villain cannot hurt Shalon.

In staging a confrontation between Jaime and Bigfoot, *Bionic* revises the *Six Million* template, giving the woman the chance to win her spurs in battle while developing her own relationships with the Sasquatch and the alien colony. Most significantly, Jaime develops relationships with two of the colony's prominent female members, Shalon and a newly introduced character, Gillian (Sandy Duncan), who tries to stop the rebel aliens with the bionic duo's help.

If the Fembots and Lisa Galloway represent the double, Bigfoot adds something both similar and wildly dissimilar, a concept I call the *like unlike*. On the one hand, Bigfoot is a fellow bionic being ("nano-synthetic," as Shalon puts it). On the other hand, the Sasquatch recalls not only the wild man archetype but also the Male Medusa. This historical icon, the male image of Nature, usually depicts a male face flowing with flora, typically vines and leaves. Fusing man, animal, and machine, Sasquatch combines the raw, unleashed potentialities of our disavowed animal nature

3. In the Shadow of Sasquatch

and cyborgian strength taken to the *nth* power. The oppressed and intimidating monster darkly doubles the bionic otherness of Jaime and Steve, the potential for destruction and wrath in those reserves of meta-human might.

Jaime's relationship with Sasquatch evinces feminist ethics, especially women's alliance with nonhuman animals. Nedlik boasts that while he cannot harm Shalon, he is able to control Sasquatch because "the stupid animal doesn't know that." This harsh description denies the creature his dignity, replacing Shalon's love with hate. Jaime's recognition of Sasquatch restores his dignity and extends Shalon's love. The special bond Jaime develops with the creature allows her to liberate him from Nedlik's mind control and, symbolically, from male oppression.

The Sasquatch can be read as the racial other. If so, his and Jaime's relationship signals a union between oppressed groups, women and people of color and others whose rights are trampled by the masculinist status quo.[2] When Jaime and Sasquatch engage in battle, Nedlik stands to the side, controlling and creating the mayhem. "Hey, you with him?" Jaime shouts at the villain. Nedlik isn't *with* anyone; despite being the leader of a faction, he works for himself alone, pitting the powerless—or the seemingly powerless—against one another. The poignancy of the Sasquatch is that for all of his heft and might he is essentially a passive, vulnerable creature forced to do evil against his will.[3]

The first episode of the two-parter, a *Six Million* episode, commences with some indelible images. Nedlik's faction plot to take over the earth by building a "phase-lock magneton," an invincible shield that will protect them from any human counterattack as they colonize the planet. To build this device, they need certain minerals, using the Sasquatch to steal them.

The pre-credits teaser opens at night outside of a bank vault. Rather than seeing the Sasquatch, we see his shadow cast against the institutional building, an image that suggests ancient, primal energies staining the edifice of capitalist modernity. An interesting discourse flows throughout these episodes about the ancient, the modern, and the futuristic, all qualities combined within Bigfoot, a creature with highly advanced bionics but made from a "lower life form."[4] The creature poses a paradoxical challenge, being at once the product of a far more technologically advanced culture and a throwback to prehuman life.

Steve's affect throughout Part One is notably unconventional for a male hero. From the moment he sees the evidence of a bionic theft—strewn rubble, stretched-open vault bars, broken-apart walls—he seems pensive, troubled, distracted. And then with his infrared eye Steve scans

The Bionic Woman and Feminist Ethics

the Bigfoot footprint, a seething gray blotch in a red field. Because Steve's memories have been wiped, he cannot remember the significance of the footprint—and yet he verges on remembering.

After the credits, the episode proper begins with a sequence of Steve doing a bionic run on the grounds of the OSI facility in Los Angeles, California as Rudy Wells monitors him and examines his readouts. Rudy asks him if he notices a sluggishness in his performance, and Steve says, curtly, "No," and walks off. As he does so, Rudy, obviously concerned, stares at him. The Bionic shows were always graced with excellent scores, and J.J. Johnson's brooding music creates an atmosphere of anxiety as Rudy and Steve walk toward his lab.[5]

The building used for this OSI facility has a terrifically appropriate look for a structure associated with scientific advancements—tall, horizontal, with a balcony on its top level. This building, with its chilly, distancing appearance and ambience, connotes the modernity of the OSI's scientific research.

In one of the most brilliant shots in a Bionic show, Steve and Rudy, seen in long shot, walk back to the lab, and the camera zooms in on Jaime Sommers pensively watching, from her vantage point high up on the facility's balcony, the two men below. This shot amply conveys Jaime's apprehensiveness—as we learn, she is concerned because Steve has been acting strangely, as she tells Oscar. The shot metaphorically conveys a sense of Jaime's position in this world of men, a homosocial enclave that she has, as a woman, surprisingly and singularly joined. The shot conveys her apartness, but also her thoughtful, questioning, considering, alertly attentive personality. These are the qualities that distinguish *Bionic* from *Six Million*, Jaime from Steve, and her interactions with Oscar and Rudy from those between them and Steve. Jaime's pensive gaze connotes an awareness, a critical intelligence: she does not just live within the action and events of the series but submits them to analysis. These qualities distinguish Jaime's presence from that of the other personae, including Steve Austin.

What is especially fascinating in "The Return of Bigfoot, Part 1," however, is that Steve experiences mental distress that links him to Jaime, specifically her character's psychological turmoil in the early episodes. When Jaime asks Steve if something's wrong, he says, "Let me show you something." He shows Oscar, Rudy, and Jaime the gray cast of the enormous Bigfoot footprint. As he stares at it, subliminal but indecipherable images of Bigfoot flash in his mind (his repressed memories are being weakly reactivated by Gillian, though she lacks the power to restore them fully).

3. In the Shadow of Sasquatch

Jaime immediately senses Steve's pain, asking him what's wrong. "It's like I'm on the verge of remembering … it's frustrating." Jaime responds, "Hey, I'm the one who wrote the book on partial memory, remember?" Jaime now attempts to help Steve cope with memory loss, a reversal of their dynamic in "The Return of the Bionic Woman, Parts 1 and 2." When Gillian finally makes her presence known to Steve and attempts to jog his memory more directly, Steve truly seems vulnerable and apprehensive: he flinches as Gillian applies the alien memory device to his temple. This *Six Million* episode expands Steve's emotional range.

Through the presence of strong female characters such as Jaime, Gillian, and Shalon, the two-parter can be said to be a female-centered narrative. To my mind, "The Return of Bigfoot, Part 2" makes a feminist statement. No scene better exemplifies this claim than the extraordinary one in which Shalon, Gillian, and Jaime work together to find a way to defeat the rebel aliens and restore the dying Steve to life.

Steve lies dying, having been nearly fatally injured by his climactic encounter with Sasquatch in Part One. Determined to save him, Jaime has defied the odds and the limits of credibility by going on a search for the mysterious San Angelo aliens. As she searches for the aliens in the forest near their complex, Nedlik's people detect her presence on their video monitor, and Nedlik, taking Sasquatch with him, teleports there to vanquish the bionic woman. As Jaime battles the Sasquatch, Gillian, now the rebels' prisoner, manages to wrest a time-teleporter from her captor and rescues Jaime from the villain's clutches. Gillian teleports Jaime to the aliens' complex deep within the mountains and brings her to meet Shalon. (This sequence, like the episode, is considerably enhanced by Joe Harnell's spellbinding score for the episode, which is available on CD.) Once in Shalon's presence, Jaime explains that Steve is dying, and she needs the aliens' help to save him.

Given that it is initially all about Steve, Jaime's discussion with her newfound female allies about her rescue mission fails the Bechdel test (which, to be passed, must be a discussion between two or more female characters about concerns other than the men in their lives). Yet this only characterizes the discussion in its initial stages. After agreeing to help Steve, Shalon in turn asks Jaime for *her* help in defeating the evil rebels. Shalon's appeal to Jaime recognizes Jaime as an autonomous being whose worth and abilities exceed her ties to Steve.

Shalon asks Jaime to save not only the alien colony but humanity and the Earth itself. And working together, Shalon and Gillian in turn save

The Bionic Woman and Feminist Ethics

Steve. It's wonderful to watch this scene in which three women—a scientist, an ambassador from another world and in her own right a woman warrior, and the loving, formidable Bionic Woman—all collaborate and devise a two-fold plan of salvation.

It's especially appealing that Shalon and Gillian save Steve not through some alien magic or witchy hocus-pocus (which is not to denigrate witchcraft, only the pop deployment of it as a conventionally feminine, enigmatic art) but instead through carefully developed and applied, if futuristic, science. Gillian transports into his hospital room and, with Shalon's monitoring guidance, administers Neotraxin, a wonder drug devised by the aliens. Nedlik and his faction have stolen most of the drug for themselves, leaving most of the aliens to die of incurable radiation poisoning. Shalon, though dying from the radiation poisoning, gives Gillian the last vial of the drug left in the colony; the afflicted scientist sacrifices herself to save Steve.

If anything, the presence of Rudy Wells and Oscar Goldman in Steve's hospital room are hindrances to his recovery, which can only occur when the women take over. And it has been, after all, Jaime's determination to help Steve—her willingness to believe his outlandish story about the aliens, her faith in his goodness and credibility and sympathy for his vulnerability—that allows the entire rescue mission of Steve, the alien colony, and humanity to occur in the first place. These truly are wonder women. And that description includes Stephanie Powers and Sandy Duncan as well as the great Wagner, all performers who undertake these roles with the utmost conviction and integrity.[6]

Jaime's plan to infiltrate the rebel base in Mexico by being taken prisoner proves successful. Locked in a seemingly inescapable prison cell, Jaime attempts to communicate with the brainwashed Sasquatch: "I just came from Shalon ... she's very upset that you've turned against her. But I don't think you have. They're making you do this, fighting Steve and me." Sasquatch listens with interest. But when Nedlik summons him away, the creature complies. Seemingly in a hopeless, disappointed position, unable to break through the titanium-alloy prison door, Jaime remains undeterred, refusing to submit to her jailers. She fights back, bionically barreling her way out of her stony prison cell, smashing the rock wall holding her in (recalling the great S1 episode "The Jailing of Jaime," in which she similarly breaks out of a jail cell).

This act of resistance is a crucial one, allowing Jaime to fulfill her first goal—saving Steve—so that she can, with his help, fulfill her second one, saving the world itself. She manages to escape the cell just as Ned-

3. In the Shadow of Sasquatch

lik issues the command that Sasquatch kill Steve. Gillian and Steve attempt to join Jaime in her effort to stop the rebels. They soon see the Sasquatch raging toward them; he and Steve do battle, the hero trying to communicate with the creature all the while. Knocked down during their fight, Steve, restored to health but still weak, lies on the ground as Sasquatch holds an enormous boulder in his hands, about to smash it on Steve.

Grabbing the control unit and bionically knocking out Nedlik, Jaime speaks to Sasquatch as she did from her prison cell, appealing to his better nature and his love. "Sasquatch, Nedlik cannot hurt Shalon. He can't hurt you, either—I have the control unit. Sasquatch trust me, please—*please*." And, as he could not do earlier, Sasquatch decides to trust her, hurling the huge rock into the forest and helping Steve to his feet, Gillian now joining them. *Bionic* pursues feminist ethics: the woman appeals to the oppressed other by restoring his dignity.

The sheer ambitiousness of Kenneth Johnson's vision in this two-parter merits recognition. The rebel aliens' plans go horribly awry, and their efforts to use a volcano to create their world-domination device leads the volcano to erupt beyond control. In order to save the world, Jaime and Steve essentially do battle with a volcano. In a thrilling moment, the pair run out of the rebel compound in bionic unison to confront the volcano, their plan being to hurl one of the futuristic alien devices—a TLC, a "time-line converter"—into the lava and freeze it in its tracks.

I will admit to being disappointed that Jaime is the first member of the pair to give up the attempt to stop the lava flow. Verging on collapse from exhaustion, heat, fumes, Jaime gasps, "I can't make it." Given Steve's weakened condition and that it was Wagner's own series, I think that it would have been appropriate to allow Jaime to keep going. The decision to have Jaime falter first accommodates the heterosexist and sexist standards of viewing tastes, making it clear that the man's stamina will outlast the woman's.

That having been said, Steve falters, too—while he does begin to throw the device into the lava, his efforts will also fail. "Even he can't throw it that far," observes a deeply anxious Gillian, watching the bionic pair's progress on the viewscreen.

Startlingly, Sasquatch comes to the rescue, wresting the device from Steve's hand and climbing—staggering—to a perch high enough for him to hurl it into the ferocious lava tide. That Sasquatch himself nearly dies in the process confirms just how impossible a task the whole endeavor was for either Steve or Jaime. The climactic action concludes with a lovely

The Bionic Woman and Feminist Ethics

shot of Jaime and Steve converging around the fallen Sasquatch, comforting him with warm smiles and affection.

The fairy tale elements of the Bionic shows inform the image of the near-death Shalon, frozen in time and awaiting the arrival of the alien mother ship. Serenely encased in a glass tube, she recalls Sleeping Beauty. "The Return of Bigfoot" is genre-blending. One could call it science fantasy, but science fairy tale seems even more apt. In this regard, it anticipates the tonal textures of Guillermo Del Toro's lovely (and often poignant) 2017 film *The Shape of Water*, set in the 1950s, in which a mute, kindhearted janitress falls in love with a South American anomaly, a fish-man being used by nefarious government forces in a Cold War–era plot. In contrast, though, the Jaime/Sasquatch relationship is entirely chaste.

The aliens offer Jaime and Steve the chance to slumber like Shalon and wake up one hundred years into the future, an offer they appreciate but decline. As the bionic pair make their way out of the complex, walking across that long, humming, eerie sci-fi corridor, they thank the aliens for allowing them to keep their memories of having met them. Saying their goodbyes, Jaime turns to Sasquatch and says, "And you! You get a big bionic hug!" The trademark bionic sound effect hums as she hugs the creature. Bionics signify kinship; bionic *sound* expresses a shared, species-crossing, transgressive, healing language, a code and a communication between and beyond the like unlike.

CHAPTER 4

Bionic *Vertigo*

In his extraordinary documentary *Tarnation* (2003), Jonathan Caouette chronicles his childhood, focusing on his relationship with his schizophrenic mother. This film is a hallucinatory amalgam of found art from the young director's own life, an archive of snapshots, Super-8 film, answering machine messages, video diaries, early short films, and the like. At one point, Caouette includes a drag performance he did as a female neighbor revealing her years of abuse at the hands of her husband. In an interview with the online magazine *Bomb*, Caouette described the inspirations for his performance:

> Basically, I had watched this episode of *The Bionic Woman* where Lindsay Wagner gets cloned. It was called "Deadly Ringer." Sort of a Stepford Wives episode where she gets replaced by this other person, and they locked the real Jamie Summers in an asylum. My mother reminded me of Lindsay Wagner somehow, because Lindsay Wagner was this very emotional, over-the-top actress, really underrated for prime-time TV. And she just did this kick-ass performance. I watched that during the day, it was on in syndication. Then that evening, on PBS, I saw Ntozake Shange's *For Colored Girls Who Considered Suicide When the Rainbow Is Enuf*, an American playhouse production with Alfre Woodard. Alfre Woodard is staring into the camera, and I don't remember it verbatim, but she says something like, "I'll kill that bitch!" So, I took both of those elements and I fused them into this fictitious character in which, as I said, I'm essentially imitating my mom. What you see in the film is a result of that.[1]

Having been profoundly affected myself by this two-parter when I was a child, I empathize with Caouette's identification with Jaime Sommers and with the dual characters she plays. Caouette's film is a personal odyssey about both his relationship with his mother and his queer sexuality. In a remarkable fashion, "Deadly Ringer" thematizes queer desire and estrangement as well as the longing for a healing maternal embrace in much the same way that *Tarnation* does. That black women's experience and Ntozake Shange's representation of it in her famous play also affected the director in his childhood speaks to the overlaps between these female-centered works. As I will discuss, while issues of race are not explicitly discussed in "Deadly Ringer," an implicit racial discourse, the narrative of passing, is suggested here. And a related theme of class longing and passing, which is explicitly represented here, resonates and dovetails with the racial passing one. Caouette in his superbly realized film articulates what I aim to do in this chapter and book, evoke and pay homage to the transgressive achievement of *The Bionic Woman* at its most daring.

Theorizing the Double

Given the centrality of the doppelgänger in *Bionic*'s second season, it behooves us to consider the theoretical and symbolic implications of the figure. We discussed the double in Chapter 2, which analyzed the season one episodes "Jaime's Mother" and "Mirror Image," both of which thematize the double, in depth. In addition, we discussed the bionic woman's solitary nature, which one could view as her loneliness, or, as I call it, her *onlyness*.

The doppelgänger allegorizes the isolation and loneliness of the subject. But the relationship between the subject and the doppelgänger, while typically described as disturbing and menacing, can also transform isolation into community. As Dimitris Vardoulakis writes, "The loneliness of the doppelgänger exposes a lack in the autonomous subject, but this does not mean that the subject as such is rejected. ... The transfiguration of loneliness from what leads to isolation to that which makes it possible for the subject to return from isolation is essentially an attempt to give a place back to the subject."[2] If we follow doppelgänger theory, the double's purpose is to expose a lack in the subject, but this lack can lead the subject to a process of self-critique. The results of this self-critique are open-ended and ambiguous. If the self-critique is rigorous and produces a change of attitude, it can lead to insightful renewal. Such is the case with *Bionic*'s thematization of the double in the second season's two-part episode "Deadly Ringer."

The "doppelgänger's expression of loneliness can no longer be taken at face value as a lamentation. ... [The] final utterance of loneliness is transfigured into an expression of mirth. Here is the doppelgänger's laughter at the logic of identity that had sought to pin it down."[3] Lisa Galloway

4. *Bionic* Vertigo

in "Mirror Image" certainly transfigures the double's loneliness into an expression of mirth. As we have noted, she takes great pleasure in confronting Jaime with Lisa's perfect physical imitation of her. Lisa smiles at Jaime in their first encounter. Walking into an office where Lisa is being held after attempting to kill Oscar Goldman, Jaime beholds her double. Sitting with her back to us, Lisa dramatically swivels around to look at Jaime, a sight that causes the heroine visible shock. Instead of conveying evil, twisted anger, Lisa simply, mildly, somewhat mischievously smiles, a far eerier effect. At the episode's climax, informing her rival that "There's only gonna be one Jaime Sommers now," Lisa smiles when Jaime turns around to behold her double, who challenges her: "I believe it's time for you and me to have it out, sugar pie." Lisa doesn't just want her criminal plans to succeed; she also wants to annihilate Jaime and her claim on her own identity.

An important intertext for *Bionic*'s use of the double, specifically the female double, is a superb first season-episode of Rod Serling's legendary television series *The Twilight Zone*. "Mirror Image" (the same title as the first Lisa Galloway episode on *Bionic*) originally aired on February 26, 1960. Vera Miles (who plays Janet Leigh's sleuthing sister in Alfred Hitchcock's 1960 horror classic *Psycho*) stars as a solitary young woman at a nighttime bus station who sees her own double. Throughout the course of the episode, the double periodically appears. Despite the alarm she increasingly feels at the double's appearances, Miles's protagonist, Millicent Barnes, cannot convince anyone that the double exists.

In an indelibly chilling moment, Millicent, believing that she can finally escape her menacing doppelgänger by boarding a long-overdue bus, sees her double already sitting in the bus, staring back at Millicent from a window seat, a subdued but triumphant smile on her face. Millicent is defeated by the implacably persistent presence of her double, a harrowing conclusion that *Bionic* thankfully avoids.

Confirming at once the significance of the double and its treatment in this episode, the notable director and screenwriter Jordan Peele has cited *The Twilight Zone*'s "Mirror Image" as an influence on his brilliant (if messy) film *Us* (2019), in which a family on vacation find themselves confronted by their own doppelgängers, hell-bent on terrorizing the family. The female-focus of "Mirror Image" finds its parallel here in the dual roles that Peele wrote for Lupita Nyong'o, who plays the wife and mother Adelaide Wilson and her frightening, vengeful double Red.

Peele makes incisive use of the double motif to critique America's treatment of its underclass and its ongoing agonies over racial difference and racism. Red at one point emits a laugh as she lays out her menacing intentions to Adelaide that is more sinister than most effects in horror films. As she explains, Red and her family of doubles are the "Tethered," who live in a metallic warren under the sewer system that looks like abandoned luxury malls from the 1960s. Discarded and forgotten, the Tethered are left to perform mindless mock-reenactments of their human counterparts' actions and eat nothing but "cold, raw rabbit" (the opening credits show rabbits scampering about unsupervised in the Tethereds' lair). Now, the Tethered infiltrate the human world determined to wreak havoc and enact retribution for having been abandoned.

Works such as *The Twilight Zone*'s "Mirror Image" and *Us* signify a tradition of negative images of the double as menacing, threatening, and ultimately harbingers of death. They synthesize longstanding negative readings of the double in psychoanalytic theory. As Slavoj Žižek writes, "'seeing oneself looking' ... unmistakably stands for death ... in the uncanny encounter of a double ... what eludes our gaze are always his eyes: the double strangely seems always to look askew, never to return our gaze by looking straight into our eyes—the moment he were to do it, our life would be over...."[4] Millicent Barnes's confrontation with her double terrifyingly embodies this paradigm.

Otto Rank influentially theorized the role of the double in psychology, folklore, and literature. The double, he argued, is a transformation of one's narcissistic self-love into a horrifying mirror image, "the feared and loathed other of one's own desires."[5] Certainly, Red, Adelaide's villainous double, conforms to Rank's model. Revisiting Rank through the lens of the famous queer theorist Eve Kosofsky Sedgwick's work, Steven Bruhm notes that Rank associated the narcissistic double with paranoia and homosexuality.[6] As we will discuss, the double, whether in the form of Lisa Galloway or Fembots, has queer implications on *Bionic*. As another critic parses Rank, the classic doppelgänger plot is resolved by "the slaying of the double, through which the hero seeks to protect himself permanently from the pursuits of his self." The slaying, however, "is really a suicidal act."[7]

Lisa Galloway's deadly smile, like that of Millicent Barnes in the *Twilight Zone* episode, signifies the triumph of the double when the double is associated with murderous intention, nullity, and death. In Lisa Galloway's second appearance, in "Deadly Ringer" (S2), her smiles and laughter come at greater cost, transmitted sparingly. This two-parter presents Lisa as the double who unravels, her initial mirth dissolving into unexpected, bewildered, and finally abject tears. It also depicts Jaime's mental

4. *Bionic* Vertigo

breakdown once her identity is called into question. The genius of *Bionic*'s "Deadly Ringer" is its decision to depict the psychological dissolution of both the villainess and the heroine, a dissolution that results from their mutual experience, even if on opposite sides, of the double. Their shared mental unraveling, not only a plot-driven but also a thematic and narrative doubling, has potent implications for feminist and queer readings.

> "Angel of Mercy." Directed by Alan J. Levi.
> Teleplay by James D. Parriott. Airdate: January 28, 1976
>
> "Deadly Ringer: Part 1." Directed by Alan J. Levi.
> Teleplay by James D. Parriott. Airdate: February 2, 1977.
>
> "Deadly Ringer: Part 2." Directed by Alan J. Levi.
> Teleplay by James D. Parriott. Airdate: February 9, 1977.

James D. Parriott wrote many excellent *Bionic* episodes, beginning with the wonderful "Angel of Mercy" (S1). In this episode, Jaime and the grizzled, cantankerous pilot Jack Starkey (Andy Griffith) fly to the fictional South American country Costa Brava in hopes of rescuing the American ambassador George Morehouse (James Karen) and his wife Judith (Jean Allison), trapped beneath rubble during a war. In one extraordinary moment, Jaime reveals her powers to Starkey, who constantly snipes at her about their ill-fated mission and her inadequacy. (Truth be told, Jaime is pretending to be a nurse but doesn't have the requisite skills, leading to his comic suspicion when she has difficulty bandaging his wounds after their chopper crashes.) After enduring his negativity for hours on end, Jaime has had enough. Starkey hollers at her when she attempts to restart an abandoned plane, "Sommers, when I tell you we can't do it, we can't do it! This bird won't fly." Jaime responds, "And I am sick and tired of you telling me what *I* can't do." As she bionically adjusts one of the bent-out-of-shape landing struts, Starkey, astonished, says to her, "What kind of woman are you?" She responds, "A very frightened one. Now what's next?"

In another notable moment, Jaime bionically hears Judith Morehouse's desperate tapping. Mrs. Morehouse is not only trapped beneath rubble with her husband but also incapacitated by a large stone slab that has fallen on her legs. When Jaime breaks through the rubble to discover the endangered pair in a dark pit below, George Morehouse immediately climbs up and walks out into safety and freedom, telling Jaime that his wife remains trapped below. Jaime ventures down into the dusty darkness, and helps the woman break free of the slab. Subtly and movingly, a "sisterhood is powerful" bond develops between the women. The ambassador all too readily leaves the scene and his wife to Jaime's care. Jaime works

The Bionic Woman and Feminist Ethics

with Judith Morehouse to free her from her predicament, bionically lifting the slab but telling the trapped woman that she must pull herself out from beneath, which, with palpable difficulty but successful resolve, she does. Jean Allison's brief but intensely believable performance as Mrs. Morehouse immeasurably deepens the impact of this moment, one that has always stayed with me. The heroism of both women undergirds the scene, especially given the desperate but unceasing effort, throughout the episode, on the part of the trapped and injured Mrs. Morehouse to keep tapping, despite her husband telling her it's no use, so that a rescuer might be alerted to their predicament. Mrs. Morehouse's refusal to give up hope even as her husband tells her all hope is lost parallels Jaime's defiance of Starkey's sexist naysaying. Parriott also wrote the superb season three two-parter "The Bionic Dog," which we will discuss in a later chapter. But nothing matches his brilliant teleplay for "Deadly Ringer," which is in my view one of the most sophisticated narrative treatments of the oft-tread theme of the double.

At the end of "Mirror Image," Oscar informs Jaime that Lisa Galloway will be sent to prison but also that she'll be wearing Jaime's face for another year, the amount of time necessary for it to be safe to perform plastic surgery on Lisa again. "You'll have a jailbird for a twin," Oscar cavalierly remarks, adding, "That won't be bad," so long as Lisa stays put. "Deadly Ringer" continues this storyline, depicting the ongoing machinations of the evil plastic surgeon James Courtney (Don Porter) and Lisa Galloway to infiltrate the OSI using Lisa as a double for Jaime. Courtney's henchmen go to Jaime's carriage house at night, drug and abduct her, bring her to the prison where Lisa is serving time, put Jaime in Lisa's prison cell, and bring Lisa to a plane where Courtney is waiting for her. As he lays out the plan, Lisa will once again masquerade as Jaime, this time to steal a top-secret drug designed by Rudy Wells, the creator of bionics.

This drug, called Adrenalizine, was developed by Rudy to help paraplegics. As Rudy later explains to Lisa, whom he believes to be Jaime, "It's a plastic compound; it works about the same as our own adrenaline." Courtney, also in prison and doing medical research while serving time, encounters the drug when he tests it out on a prisoner who has been paralyzed by a fall. The prisoner miraculously regains use of his limbs. As Courtney explains, he then tested out the drug on himself, curious about what effect the drug might have on a "normal body." The effect is fantastical; the drug "generalizes" its impact on Courtney's entire body, giving him powers remarkably like Jaime's bionics. The only problem is that eventually Adrenalizine powers wear off. Courtney, unaware of Jaime's bionics,

4. *Bionic* Vertigo

assumes that the drug must be the reason why she is so powerful. He has broken Lisa out of prison to impersonate Jaime once again and steal the Adrenalizine from Rudy's medical lab.

The scene between Courtney and Lisa on his private jet where he explains the plan to steal the Andrenalizine merits consideration. Though a hateful person, smug and diabolical, Courtney nevertheless conveys something like human warmth to Lisa as he describes the effects of Adrenalizine and his admiration for Rudy Wells's "reputation for breakthroughs." Lindsay Wagner, in her brilliant dual performance here (she won an Emmy for "Deadly Ringer, Part 2"), primarily depicts Lisa, apart from a theatrical Southern twang, as childlike. That quality comes through in her first appearance, smoking feverishly in her prison cell. In response to the guard's efforts to make the switch between her and Jaime as hastily as possible, Lisa petulantly demands, "Just get me out of here!" In her interaction with Courtney as he recounts his tale of brief superheroism, Lisa/Wagner reacts with a child's sense of wonder and incredulity, as if she were being read a fairy tale, which isn't too far off. Courtney describes his Adrenalizine-fueled escape from prison; at the fact that the guards didn't notice till too late, Lisa responds with a wide-eye unabashed manner: "And by then you were long gone!" With an almost endearing wistfulness, Courtney explains what it was like to feel such power when he escaped and how disappointing it was to "become human again" when the drug's effects wear off. Assuring her that she can pull off her end of the scam, Courtney tells Lisa something that will continue to haunt her, his words repeated in hypnotic voiceover: "Remember, you *are* Jaime Sommers."

The significance of Wagner's decision to play Lisa as a child lies in its intuitive rightness given the two-parter's themes overall, chief among them the child's longing for connection and desire to be loved. As Lisa tells Jaime at the end of Part 2, she *must* be Jaime and she *cannot* be Lisa "because no one ever loved Lisa, not her parents, not her teachers…" As Jaime, Lisa can finally experience love and nurturing. Jaime's adoptive parents Helen (Martha Scott) and Jim (Ford Rainey) clearly love her, which Lisa disguised as Jaime gets the chance to experience. In a poignant and audacious narrative turn, Lisa Galloway, once she believes that Jaime has been killed, actually returns to Jaime's home in Ojai, California, her schoolteacher's world and especially the demonstrably loving world of Helen and Jim.

Lisa attempts to explain this to Courtney, who sees through the absurdity of her plan: "You'd be discovered before long." He then tries to

The Bionic Woman and Feminist Ethics

placate her with satanic offers of glamor and luxury: "I'll change your face, make you the most beautiful woman in the world." At this point, Lisa, wearing Jaime's face, looks at her reflection in a glass wall, ponders for a moment, and says, "I like the way I look." Wagner plays the moment with an utter simplicity that makes everything seem plausible despite the outlandishness of the premise; she makes Lisa's desire and hopes palpable.

"Deadly Ringer" evokes the dead-end world of film noir, movies such as *Dark Passage* (Delmer Daves, 1947), where Humphrey Bogart, a prison escapee falsely accused of murdering his wife, uses a plastic surgeon to give himself a new appearance and identity. Along these lines, Lisa Galloway emerges as a new-style *femme fatale*. Pauline Kael described Debra Winger's character Angela Crispini in the neo-noir thriller *Everybody Wins* (Karel Reisz, 1990) as "something new in thrillers: a schizophrenic *femme fatale*."[8] Lisa Galloway anticipates Winger's character. Julie Grossman, noting the misogynistic tradition behind the *femme fatale*, writes, "The persistent projection onto women of mutually exclusive categories of being in the world often has tragic implications for women who stray from their roles or want to break down the oppositions that bind them."[9] "Deadly Ringer" makes the difficulty of transition from one kind of role to another, and in this case one kind of class status to another, agonizingly evident. In making us sympathetic to Lisa's desire for change and longing for someone else's life, "Deadly Ringer" breaks astonishing new ground for the kind of genre television that *Bionic Woman* was thought to typify. It's hard to imagine an episode of *The Six Million Dollar Man*, *Wonder Woman*, or *Charlie's Angels* reaching for the ambitious thematic goals of *Bionic*. "Deadly Ringer" comes close to making us root for the imposter rather than the heroine, the copy over the original, the "bad" woman over the good, the criminal over the enforcer of the law.

Our fierce identification with Jaime Sommers as *Bionic* fans encounters a radical disruption in our sudden allegiance with and sympathy for Lisa Galloway, producing a split in the spectator. We root, as we always do, for Jaime as she manages to outwit, elude, and simply endure the sadistic stratagems of Courtney and his associates, in particular the malevolent prison doctor Harkens (played, unexpectedly, by the comic actress Katherine Helmond, best known for the ABC sitcoms *Soap* and *Who's the Boss?*). Yet, once she has escaped and rejoins Oscar and Rudy in the hunt for Lisa Galloway, Jaime becomes, momentarily, an oppressive force threatening to sever Lisa from the fulfilling and satisfying and love-filled life she has finally discovered as Jaime and in Ojai.

4. Bionic **Vertigo**

Imitation of Life

As I have argued, the woman's film, after its classical Hollywood heyday, thrives in concealed form in the horror film (works such as Brian De Palma's *Sisters* [1972] and *Carrie* [1976] and the *Alien* films).[10] While the horror film is arguably the most significant site of overlap with melodrama, the dialogue with the classical Hollywood woman's film in the New Hollywood cinema of the 1970s and also in genre television series such as *The Bionic Woman* is notable. In terms of film, works such as Martin Scorsese's 1974 *Alice Doesn't Live Here Anymore* (not to mention its television spinoff *Alice* [1976–85]) and *The Way We Were* (Sydney Pollack, 1973) evoked woman's film narratives: *Alice Doesn't Live Here Anymore*, with its scenes of Ellen Burstyn as a single mother desperately looking for work and eventually becoming a waitress, is a virtual pastiche of *Mildred Pierce* (Michael Curtiz, 1945), whereas overlaps abound between *The Way We Were* and *Alice Adams*, a 1935 film starring Katharine Hepburn and directed by George Stevens, two films about nonnormative, unclassifiable women's romantic travails.

As we have discussed, *Bionic* frequently engages with classical Hollywood. The season one episode "Jaime's Mother," uniting the classical Hollywood films stars Martha Scott and Barbara Rush in a female-centered narrative about mothers and daughters, is the most explicit citation of the woman's film. Several key woman's films explore relationships between mothers and daughters, most prominently *Now, Voyager* (Irving Rapper, 1942), *Mildred Pierce*, and the two versions of *Imitation of Life* (John M. Stahl, 1934; Douglas Sirk, 1959). I argue that "Deadly Ringer" engages with classical Hollywood melodrama through its intertextual relationship with Sirk's *Imitation of Life* and Alfred Hitchcock's *Vertigo* (1958).

Based on Fannie Hurst's novel, both versions of *Imitation of Life* explore the bonds between a white single mother and a black single mother, both of whom have daughters; these mothers and their daughters; and to a certain extent the white woman and the black woman's daughter. In the 1935 version, the white woman uses the black woman's pancake recipe to catapult into wealth; in the 1959 version, the white woman becomes a famous Broadway musical star, bringing her black maid and daughter along when she achieves stardom and plusher living.[11]

In Sirk's *Imitation of Life*, the widowed and white Lora Meredith (Lana Turner) and the black single mother Annie Johnson (Juanita Moore), both have young daughters. An important theme this version shares with the 1934 one is the longing on the part of Annie's light-skinned daughter,

The Bionic Woman and Feminist Ethics

Sarah Jane (Fredi Washington in Stahl's film, Susan Kohner in Sirk's) to pass as white. Sirk's distanciated treatment of white femininity as a prolonged and shifting masquerade, a series of facades, informs his ironic treatment of Lora's rise to musical theater fame. As I will discuss, Hitchcock's treatment of white femininity in *Vertigo* has similar ironic aspects.

The most acute overlap between Sirk's film and *Vertigo* is the theme of maternal loss. Sirk's film includes a devastating scene where Annie visits her now grown-up daughter Sarah Jane, a performer, in a disreputable nightclub. Sarah Jane refuses to acknowledge her mother's identity, and a heartbroken Annie tells her daughter that she will not bother her anymore. Shortly thereafter, Annie dies, and at the funeral, Sarah Jane, utterly distraught, clings to Annie's longtime employer Lora/Lana Turner, the implication being that Lora may be not only consolation for the devastating loss of her own mother but also the symbolic white mother Sarah Jane has long sought.

I dwell at length on Sirk's film because its theme of passing within a female melodramatic narrative has important implications for *Bionic*. Though primarily associated with racial passing, the theme of passing has expanded greatly in recent critical treatments. In their collection *Passing: Identity and Interpretation in Sexuality, Race, and Religion*, the editors Maria C. Sanchez and Linda Schlossberg gather a wide-ranging series of essays of the forms of passing ranging from Jack Halberstam's study of the transgender male Brandon Teena (the basis for the film *Boys Don't Cry*) to Jewish chameleonism to a study of femme queens and butch queens to a particular form of class passing known as slumming.

Class passing is the underlying theme of "Deadly Ringer." Lisa Galloway's desire for Jaime's life entails a desire to live as Jaime does. At the end of Part 2, Jaime tries to help Lisa, being poisoned by the Andrenalizine and mentally unraveling. In response, Lisa tries to kill Jaime ("I'm gonna kill you... I have to kill you!"), once again fulfilling the double's role as the inflictor of death on the original subject. Jaime uses psychology-speak to try to reach Lisa ("We love you, Lisa"); Lisa counterattacks Jaime's therapeutic language with a blisteringly defiant line: "You just don't want me to live like you!" Jaime responds, "No. I want you to live like *you*." Her pointed response is well-taken, but it doesn't dispel the stinging accusation her double levels at her.

In her book *Women Without Class: Girls, Race, and Identity*, Julie Bettie writes,

> Little attention has been paid to thinking about class as a performance or as performative.... The normalization of class inequality and its institutionalization reg-

ulates class performances. For example, class-specific styles of speech, such as the use of standard and non-standard grammar, accents, mannerisms, and dress (all of which are also racially/ethnically and regionally specific), are learned sets of expressive cultural practices that express class membership.[12]

Bettie explains that she uses the term "performance" to signify "agency and a conscious attempt at passing" and the term "performativity" to signify "the fact that class subjects are the effects of the social structure of class inequality." Of crucial importance, performativity signals nothing about essence but only that "institutionalized class inequality creates class subjects who display differences in cultural capital."[13]

Lisa Galloway's class performativity comes across in both the season one episode "Mirror Image" and in season two's "Deadly Ringer" whenever she is speaking to Dr. Courtney, who makes her over to be Jaime's lookalike, her boyfriend Perkins (John Fink), called "Perc," her various handlers among Courtney's henchmen, her encounters with Jaime, and also in her private moments, to which we are privy. In "Mirror Image," we assume that Lisa's desire for financial gain motivates her involvement in Courtney's espionage plot. In "Deadly Ringer," however, Lisa eschews the material rewards and Courtney's offer to "change your face ... make you one of the most beautiful women in the world" in favor clinging to the identity of the woman she has impersonated.

Jaime Sommers' middle-class status and privilege, never a focus of the series, is suddenly thrown into relief by Lisa's ardent yearning to inhabit and possess it. When Lisa enters Jaime's carriage house for the first time, Jaime having been transferred to Lisa's prison cell, Lisa experiences ecstatic joy, exclaiming "Oh, boy!" when she surveys the kitchen, four-poster bed, and other indications of Jaime's apparently enviable lifestyle, which her abode embodies. Lisa yields to an overwhelming ardor for "capitalist kitsch," in the words of Tom Kulka.[14] Beholding these surface emblems of middle-class comfort and stability, completely banal in themselves, with a sense of abandon and wonder, she lends them a kitsch radiance.

"Deadly Ringer" closely corresponds to *3 Women*, also released in 1977, directed by Robert Altman and in my view his masterpiece. The film, starring Shelley Duvall, Sissy Spacek and Janice Rule, explores similar themes of the blurring of women's identities, transformations of personality, and descents into madness. Duvall's poignant Millie Lammoreaux behaves in a manner that echoes Lisa in "Deadly Ringer," as Millie obsesses over banal consumer goods and invests them with meanings well beyond their value. Sissy Spacek's character Pinky Rose, initially submissive and wan, emerges from a comatose state as a fully transformed character, raucous and heartless, recalling the Lisa of "Mirror Image" who acted so remorselessly and avidly on her desires. One might even see "Deadly Ringer," in its self-awareness as a portrait of woman's confrontation with the surface world of consumer capitalism and subsequent loss of identity, control, and agency, as an anticipation of Todd Haynes' extraordinary portraits of female despair in capitalism: *Safe* (1995), featuring a superb performance by Julianne Moore as a housewife whose mental breakdown is inextricable from her belief that she is being poisoned by household products, and his legendary banned short film, *Superstar: The Karen Carpenter Story* (1988), in which he links the real-life music star Karen Carpenter's struggles with anorexia to the crushing socialization of femininity in American capitalism. Haynes is best-known for revisiting the Sirkian melodrama, as he does in *Far from Heaven* (2002), making his work especially relevant for our discussion.

Starting up the fireplace so that she can light up a cigarette, Lisa says—to herself, to the viewer—"Mama always said I had a little Indian in me," a line that in its offhand racism Jaime would never utter.[15] But the suggestion that Lisa is of mixed racial heritage extends her class passing to a racial one as well. Indeed, Jaime's privileged class status becomes a visible aspect of her persona once Lisa desires it, and by extension that also applies to Helen and Jim Elgin and Steve Austin (Helen being Steve's biological mother and Jim his stepfather, both Helen and Jim being Jaime's adoptive parents and potentially Jaime's mother- and father-in-law had she married Steve).

Lisa renounces her criminal past and alerts the authorities—the D.C. police and the OSI—about Courtney's whereabouts, aligning herself with Oscar Goldman, Rudy Wells, Jaime, the OSI, and the United States government and against her father in crime. For Courtney comes across as a fatherly figure albeit a sinister one: Oscar's double, he gives Lisa assignments and appears attentive to her well-being. Courtney conveys a fatherly demeanor when he extols Lisa for her ever-more successful attempts at masquerade—"You're losing your Southern accent even when you're talking to me!" he praises her over the telephone—and when he chastises her for losing focus ("Forget about Ojai, we have work to do.").

Lisa renounces the obscene father, whose enjoyment of his own evil he invites Lisa to share, and embraces the superego father, the giver and enforcer of the law. This shift in allegiances signals Lisa's moral shift from the criminal to the ethical. It also signals a shift in class status. In exposing Courtney to the authorities, Lisa ratifies her now upstanding nature, her

4. Bionic Vertigo

status as a good citizen with the proper education, background, and sense of social responsibility to help law enforcement catch criminals who betray their nation.

Lisa's boyfriend Perc does not appear in "Deadly Ringer," save for the moment when, interestingly, Jaime picks up his framed photograph in Lisa's jail cell. The suggestion is that Lisa has left Perc and perhaps heterosexual desire aside in favor of pursuing her narcissistic identification and obsession with the ideal ego, to put it in psychoanalytic terms, that Jaime represents. In giving up Courtney, then, Lisa forfeits her one close personal tie to embrace the unsteady, unlikely, but hopelessly alluring prospect of Jaime's class status and its overflowing familial and affectional rewards.

Sarah Jane's efforts to pass as white amounts to a form of what Lauren Berlant calls "cruel optimism," a desire for something that, instead of facilitating fulfillment, prevents one from attaining it. Sarah Jane destroys her relationship with her mother and experiences retaliation from her abusive white boyfriend as a result of her passing. Similarly, Lisa loses her freedom, being jailed as a result, by passing as Jaime. But "Deadly Ringer" also suggests that passing is Lisa's best hope for fulfillment. Passing ultimately leads her to self-knowledge and an embrace of her circumstances—dire ones, given that she will return to jail for however many years—as well as a desire to make amends.

"Deadly Ringer" submits Lisa's seemingly uplifting arc to the kind of ironization we have come to call "Sirkian," given his self-conscious ironization of melodrama, intended to distance the viewer from what she is watching, to inspire her to watch herself watching—and crying—from a critical remove. "In the 1970s," writes Kimberly Chabot Davis, "Marxist-influenced critics began to celebrate Douglas Sirk's 1950s family melodramas for their use of irony and a parodic form of excessive *mise-en-scène*; these 'distanciation' techniques were said to undermine the bourgeois ideology of the surface narrative."[16] At the same time, Sirk movies always deliver the emotional goods: few could watch a movie like *Imitation of Life* without the accompaniment of tears (for me, it's that scene where Annie tells Sarah Jane goodbye and that she won't bother her anymore).

Sirk's masterpiece *All That Heaven Allows* (1955), more or less remade by Todd Haynes as *Far from Heaven*, has relevance to our analysis. A New England widow, Cary Scott (Jane Wyman), attempts an ill-fated affair with her gardener, Ron Kirby (Rock Hudson). At one point, Cary meets some of Rob's friends, a married couple, and Cary has a discussion with the wife about the saying "To Thine Own Self Be True," Rob's rugged,

The Bionic Woman and Feminist Ethics

self-made mantra. Though long since passed down, denatured, and recirculated, the phrase originally appears in *Hamlet*, Polonius's lines to his son Laertes before he embarks on a trip: "This above all—to thine own self be true,/ And it must follow, as the night the day,/ Thou canst not then be false to any man./Farewell" (1.3.564–7). (Given that Polonius, Ophelia's father, is a comic figure whom Hamlet brusquely murders, and that Laertes is hardly the hero of the tragedy, these lines must be taken with the proverbial grain of salt.) Cary and Rob's relationship is destroyed by their class differences, viciously mocked by those in Cary's more elite circle. Class and social and familial pressures force Cary to give up Rob, meaning she cannot be true to herself. (There is a vague suggestion that they may reunite at film's end after Rob suffers some serious injuries.)

At the start of "Deadly Ringer," Jaime is doing an embroidery, and stitching the words "To Thine Own Self Be True." The saying is, therefore, initially associated with Jaime as she stitches in the letters. Jaime will have to be true to herself, especially as she endures a debilitating mental collapse in the hospital due to the psychotropic drugs pumped into her by the evil Dr. Harkens. That the saying is first associated with Jaime suggests that she is always and already true to herself but may darkly hint at some instability in her own character, especially given that she so dramatically questions her own identity during her mental breakdown (recalling Jaime's first appearances on *The Six Million Dollar Man*). In solitary confinement, Jaime believes that she sees dozens of photos of Lisa on the wall, taunting her with the possibility that *she* will soon become Lisa. Dr. Harkens threatens her with just this prospect, telling Jaime before she is placed in solitary, "It's time for you to get your own face back." Holding up a black and white picture of Lisa before Jaime's disoriented face, she adds, "You're going to look like yourself again: Lisa," and her articulation of the word "Lisa" ominously reverberates.

For Lisa Galloway, the lines from *Hamlet* have an obviously ironic meaning, since she is unable to be true to herself, if by "herself" we mean her own identity as Lisa. Yet the episodes also call into question what that self could possibly be. The chief indications of Lisa's own identity are a Southern twang and some black and white photos of the real Lisa, who, of course, looks nothing like Jaime/Wagner. (The first time we are introduced to Lisa in season one, she is wearing post-plastic surgery bandages, and when they are dramatically removed before the opening credits begin, she is wearing Jaime's face and smiling contentedly at her own image in the mirror.)

Moreover, "Deadly Ringer" strongly suggests that in becoming Jaime,

4. *Bionic* Vertigo

Lisa comes closer to creating a personal identity than she could before. That having been said, one remembers the lively, amoral, tough, determined, impatient, sly Lisa of "Mirror Image." The Lisa of "Deadly Ringer" belongs to the world of film noir (movies like *Possessed* and *Whirlwind*) and melodrama, the woman of uncertain identity and mind contending with her overwhelming emotions, what Stanley Cavell calls the "melodrama of the unknown woman."[17] More on this topic in the next section.

"Deadly Ringer" employs a Sirkian distancation technique at a key moment. Lisa successfully convinces Oscar and Rudy at the OSI headquarters in D.C. that she is Jaime. The small dose of the drug that Courtney gave her allows Lisa to duplicate Jaime's strength during Rudy's bionic tests. He then asks Lisa/Jaime if she will deliver the remaining Adrenalizine to another lab.

Having now successfully stolen a large dose of the drug, Lisa strolls contentedly through the cosmopolitan avenues of a posh D.C. neighborhood. Lisa, at her most resplendently Jaime-like, wears an exquisite white and beige ensemble. Her fashionability mirrors her newfound confidence and joy in her identity, however borrowed. (I return to the issue of fashion below.) All the while, an eminently inauthentic, hollow, sentimental song, "Time Changes," sung by Sally Stevens, plays non-diegetically. The song was written by Joe Harnell, who also composed yet another brilliant score for these episodes.

Harnell ingeniously incorporates the song's insipid but beguiling notes into his score, so that the song emerges as Lisa's theme song, one that rivals the familiar heroic strains of Harnell's musical motifs for Jaime. The "Time Changes" motif, including the cooing, insinuating, hummed version of the song, plays like a seduction into madness, infiltrating the soundtrack the way madness does Lisa's mind.

As Mike Joffe writes in the liner notes for a CD of Harnell scores for *Bionic*, he "was able to display his skill at quickly writing music in different styles, switching gears between the bright, optimistic music for Lisa as she finds herself settling into Jaime's life of family and friends and then darker atonal music augmented by electronics as Lisa slowly loses grip on reality because of her addiction."[18] Moreover, the song, with its lulling, repetitive, maddening qualities, suggestively conveys Lisa's spiral into madness as she lulls herself into the fantasy of inhabiting Jaime's life—indeed becoming Jaime. The glamorous white outfit that Lisa wears here recalls Madeleine Elster's wardrobe in *Vertigo*, which leads us to the next section.

The Bionic Woman and Feminist Ethics

Bionic Vertigo

Alfred Hitchcock's masterpiece *Vertigo* haunts many cinematic works, ranging from Chris Marker's *La Jetée* (1962) to Brian De Palma's *Obsession* (1976) to Christian Petzold's *Phoenix* (2014). I claim *Vertigo* as a woman's film, despite its longs years of being considered the signature example of the male gaze, as established by Laura Mulvey's classic 1975 *Screen* essay "Visual Pleasure and Narrative Cinema."[19] "Deadly Ringer" intertextually engages with Hitchcock's film.

Qualifying my argument to a certain extent, *Vertigo* was one of five Hitchcock films that had been pulled from circulation since their original release due to legal conflicts. Therefore, unlike other well-known Hitchcock films, it was not consistently televised at this point. My use of the term "intertextual" is meant to suggest that one text interacts with and sparks off another, not necessarily a direct form of influence of one text on another, though of course it's entirely possible. *Vertigo* was well-known to film scholars, buffs, and the film industry before its re-release in theaters in the 1980s, as De Palma's *Vertigo*-like *Obsession* demonstrates. It should be noted that Hitchcock had a longstanding relationship with Universal Studios and even appears in a promotional video for the Universal Studios amusement park—performing a bionic jump when shilling for the two *Bionic* shows! Lindsay Wagner starred in an episode of the updated, 1980s version of the series *Alfred Hitchcock Presents*, made well after Hitchcock's death. In the episode, "Prism," which aired on February 20, 1988, Wagner plays a woman with several different personalities, a fascinating parallel with "Deadly Ringer."

As I have been arguing, though a science-fiction action drama, *The Bionic Woman* continues the tradition of the woman's film given its concerns with a woman's experience, the "emotional, social, and psychological problems that are specifically connected to the fact that she is a woman," as Jeannine Basinger put it.[20] (In the series finale "On the Run," Jaime becomes a fugitive from a government that believes it owns her along with her bionic limbs. One of the government agents hunting her down warns, "We know you're a bionic woman." Jaime defiantly responds, "No, sir. I'm just a woman." Jaime's adverbial qualification of her status as woman—"just"—belies her hard-won triumph in reclaiming her status as woman rather than government commodity, signifying that she has made peace with her bionics.)

Hitchcock is rarely placed within the company of the great directors of the woman's film of the sound film era: Josef Von Sternberg, Edmund

4. *Bionic* Vertigo

Goulding, Dorothy Arzner, George Cukor, Michael Curtiz, Irving Rapper, William Wyler, Max Ophuls, King Vidor, and Douglas Sirk. Yet many of the major Hitchcock films correspond to the defining themes of the woman's film genre even as they reimagine it radically. The major woman's films—such as *Alice Adams* (1935), *Now, Voyager* (1942), *Letter from an Unknown Woman* (Max Ophuls, 1948), *The Heiress* (William Wyler, 1949), *Beyond the Forest* (King Vidor, 1949), *Autumn Leaves* (Robert Aldrich, 1956), and, I would argue, many Hitchcock films—place a woman's desire at the center of their plots and themes, as Robert Lang argues.[21] Several of Hitchcock's most significant works follow suit: *Rebecca*, *Suspicion* (1941), *Shadow of a Doubt* (1943), *Spellbound* (1945), *Notorious* (1946), *Under Capricorn* (1949), *Vertigo*, *Psycho* (1960), *The Birds* (1963), and *Marnie* (1964)—and aspects and sections of other films as well—belong to the genre of the woman's film.

Bionic's casting of Tippi Hedren in the season one episode "Claws" explicitly nods to Hedren's breakthrough first appearance in a Hitchcock film, the dystopian thriller *The Birds*, especially given that "Claws" focuses on animals, albeit in a positive, affirming fashion. Hedren's status as Hitchcock blonde has a relevance for Wagner's star persona in *Bionic*. And Hedren's titular unstable heroine in Hitchcock's masterpiece *Marnie*, with her constantly shifting masquerades and clothing styles and mental illness, provides a foundation for Wagner's performances as Jaime Sommers and her double Lisa Galloway in "Deadly Ringer."

Vertigo is the Hitchcock film that most deeply intersects with "Deadly Ringer." It will be helpful to remind the reader of *Vertigo*'s plot. John "Scottie" Ferguson (James Stewart) is a San Francisco detective who discovers that he suffers from acrophobia when he hangs suspended from the ledge of a building during the nighttime pursuit of a criminal across rooftops. As Scottie explains to his friend Midge (Barbara Bel Geddes), an old acquaintance from their college days, Gavin Elster (Tom Helmore), has contacted him. When Scottie meets with Elster, he tells the now-retired detective that he wants him to follow his wife. Suspicions of adultery are not the motivation; instead, Elster has come to fear that his wife, Madeleine (Kim Novak), has become possessed by the spirit of a nineteenth century female ancestor named Carlotta Valdes, who took her own life when her married lover abandoned her and kept their illegitimate child for himself and his wife (who have no children of their own). Initially reluctant, Scottie decides to take the job after beholding the beautiful Madeleine. Believing that Madeleine is going insane because she believes herself possessed by the spirit of Carlotta, Scottie, utterly caught up in

The Bionic Woman and Feminist Ethics

her plight, gathers evidence to prove to her that she is merely remembering events from her own childhood. At one point, beneath a church tower, he tells her that he loves her; Madeleine, obviously in distress, tells him that she loves him as well. But she runs into the church, and though Scottie races up the tower steps after her, his vertigo prevents him from making it all the way to the top of the tower, and Madeleine plummets to her death. Grief-stricken and in a near-catatonic state, Scottie is institutionalized; upon his release, he sees a woman, Judy Barton (also played by Novak), who looks remarkably like Madeleine, although she is a brunette and obviously, in contrast to the regal blonde woman Scottie still pines for, working-class in looks and manner. He follows her back to her apartment and speaks with her. Initially, she rejects him, but gradually softens and agrees to go out to dinner with him that night. In one of the most famous moments of the film, we shift our identification from Scottie to Judy as he closes her front door behind him and she looks directly into the camera. A flashback sequence begins that reveals that Judy had impersonated Elster's wife, the real Madeleine. It was all part of Elster's plan to kill his wife; knowing of Scottie's malady, Elster ingeniously plotted to use Scottie as a patsy who would corroborate that Mrs. Elster had gone mad. Scottie then, as Elster had done, transforms Judy—back into Madeleine! Despite her protestations, dark-haired Judy eventually morphs back into Madeleine's physical identity—same coiled blonde hair and gray suit. Eventually, Scottie discovers the truth, and drags Judy back to the scene of the crime, the bell tower at the church. While it seems that, after a horrible confrontation, the lovers may find a way to connect at last, Judy is startled by the sudden appearance of a dark figure, actually a nun, but to the guilt-ridden Judy the return of the murdered woman. Now, Judy falls to her death from the tower, and Scottie is left alone.

What we discover immediately upon comparing *Vertigo* to "Deadly Ringer" is that the latter eschews the heterosexual romance at the center of the former. Instead of a narrative about a man in pursuit of and then in love with a mysterious blonde woman, "Deadly Ringer" focuses on one woman's obsession with another. The theme of obsession unites both texts, but the fact that in the television narrative one woman obsessively pursues another in hopes of becoming the other is significant.

What makes *Vertigo* so significant as a woman's film is that it becomes one half way through its narrative, through one of the most controversial decisions that Hitchcock made as a filmmaker. At the time of *Vertigo*'s release, many critics complained that Hitchcock spoiled his suspense film by placing its big reveal—that Judy really is Madeleine and that she par-

4. *Bionic* Vertigo

ticipated in the murder of the real Mrs. Elster—at the mid-point of its narrative. But this radical gesture gives Hitchcock's heroine (as I feel we must call the flawed but deeply sympathetic Judy) an agency and subjectivity that do not depend on the male protagonist. From this point, we experience the remainder of the narrative from her point of view as well as Scottie's.

The parallels with "Deadly Ringer" now deepen. Unlike "Mirror Image," where we are never asked to identify with Lisa Galloway even though she commands much of the action, "Deadly Ringer" forces us to identify with Lisa and therefore to identify *against* Jaime. Or, at the very least, it asks us to hold two opposing thoughts in our minds and give each one equal weight: to identify with both Lisa and Jaime at once, even though both are entirely at cross-purposes.[22] We are asked to identify with both Judy and Scottie, and moreover to call Scottie's actions into question because we identify with Judy as well, experiencing her disappointment, pain, and finally terror as he transforms her back into Madeleine, a prospect that Judy abhors and dreads even as she submits to it. So, too, do we identify with both Jaime and Lisa and begin to see Jaime more critically because we identify with Lisa as well.

Film theory focusing on spectatorship, such as Laura Mulvey's essay "Visual Pleasure and Narrative Cinema," argues that we in the audience identify with the male protagonist of the film, whether biologically male or not, because he is the film's narcissistic center of attention and dominance. The spectator, gendered male, joins the protagonist in a narcissistic merger of shared power. His gaze objectifies woman and the nonnormative figures subjected to his dominance. This theory has been much debated, especially in feminist and queer film theory.[23]

Freud argued that, in the Oedipus complex through which the child becomes socialized, an initial homosexual desire for the same-sex parent must be renounced in favor of a normative identification with the same-sex parent. Identification with the same-sex parent is the goal of this process of socialization; desire for either the same-sex or the opposite sex parent, however, must be renounced, redirected to a properly heterosexual object outside of the family (exogamy). As decades of feminist and queer film theory have shown, the seamless split between identification with and desire for a figure, whether the Oedipal parent or the screen protagonist, is rarely achievable (or desirable).

Judith Butler, in an essay entitled "Melancholy Gender/Refused Identification," has brilliantly analyzed the implications of this Freudian theory of a split between desire and identification.[24] As she discusses, if the successful resolution of the Oedipus complex frees the subject from incestuous desire, that achievement depends on a prior prohibition on homosexual desire.[25] An open question about "Deadly Ringer" is whether Lisa's identification with Jaime is also desire for her, and whether this desire should be considered sexual in nature.

Another film text helps us to work through the theoretical problem posed by identification, desire, and class envy, Anthony Minghella's 1999 film adaptation of Patricia Highsmith's 1955 novel *The Talented Mr. Ripley*. In Minghella's film, class longings intersect with sexual longings. Sent to Italy by the powerful tycoon Herbert Greenleaf (James Rebhorn) to persuade his errant son Dickie Greenleaf (Jude Law) to return to the United States, Tom Ripley (Matt Damon) "discovers" Dickie in Mongibello, lying on the beach with his girlfriend, a writer named Marge Sherwood (Gwyneth Paltrow). Tom insinuates himself into the couple's life and also uses a series of tricks to ingratiate himself with the strong-willed, passionate Dickie, such as faking a shared history of being students at Princeton and an interest in jazz. A gifted mimic, Tom does great impressions of Dickie, and also learns how to forge his signature. Eventually, Tom murders Dickie and begins living his life as the rich expatriate. Minghella's film emphasizes the sexual component of Tom's class-based envy of and desire for Dickie's life, which he seizes as his own.

Lisa certainly shares Tom Ripley's class envy and ruthless determination to acquire someone else's class status and the life that comes with it. It is less clear that "Deadly Ringer" thematizes, as Minghella's film does, a gay/queer dimension to this class envy. While I believe that a lesbian/queer dynamic potentially informs "Deadly Ringer," there is no particularly salient imagery to support such a reading, which therefore remains implicit in a narrative about one woman desiring another's life. In contrast, the episodes "Fembots in Las Vegas, Parts 1 and 2" do contain imagery that supports a lesbian/queer reading, and I therefore discuss lesbian sexuality in the chapter "Fembot Theory."

This having been said, there is a profound level of allegorical queer material in "Deadly Ringer." As we have noted, the gay filmmaker Jonathan Caouette cites Wagner's performance in "Deadly Ringer" as a queer touchstone. "Deadly Ringer" thematizes what Mab Segrest has described as the "deep loneliness of being queer."[26]

As I have argued, Hitchcock's films lend themselves resonantly to both feminist and queer readings.[27] *Vertigo*'s allegorical resonance for both critical perspectives is richly complex. For a film that has been read as exemplary of the reactionary workings of the male gaze, it is an astonish-

4. *Bionic* Vertigo

ingly desperate and agonized portrayal of male inadequacy in the face of desire. James Stewart's Scottie is both victim and perpetrator—that is his tragedy. Most powerfully of all, subsequent viewings of the film reveal *Vertigo* as not only Scottie's but also Judy's film, not only when her character is introduced but from Madeleine's first appearance onscreen.

Madeleine is an ideal of feminine beauty, with her sculpted blonde hair, courtly manners, immaculately tailored clothing, and poised and vaguely English-sounding voice. Novak's vocal performance as Madeleine denotes the polished speaking style often used by classical Hollywood actors to convey well-educated and posh society. Her remarkable performance extends to Judy's comparatively rougher, not at all polished tones. But there are slippages. Remote and inaccessible, Madeleine verges on passionate outcry, and with knowledge of the entire plot we realize that it is Judy's wracked emotionalism beneath the studied façade that lends Madeleine such a poignant emotional complexity.

Throughout *Bionic*, Jaime is an accessible, lovable, humorous, deeply human heroine. Yet from the Judy-like Lisa Galloway's perspective Jaime emerges as Madeleine-like, a poised, controlled, and socially approved ideal of femininity, someone that the working-class, brash, socially irresponsible, rejected Lisa not only longs to be but self-consciously models herself after, in ways that far exceed the espionage plot that Courtney engineers. When Courtney asks the Southern-twangy Lisa about her level of preparation to play Jaime—"Have you studied Jaime's biography? You're going to have to fool her family now."—Lisa suddenly code-shifts into Jaime's properly accented mid-range voice, saying "I know Jaime Sommers inside and out." That Lisa believes she possesses such knowledge of Jaime suggests that she understands her as a conventional personality type, her printed-out bio a descriptive label on a product. But as the narrative develops, Lisa becomes more and more enraptured by Jaime and the life she has built for herself, or least Lisa's fantasy of both. She becomes entranced with Jaime's personhood, a commodity denied Lisa. Overwhelmed with palpable personal loss when she peruses Jaime's scrapbook, Lisa gets a catch in her throat (and so do we) when she pauses and looks at a picture of the young Jaime, surrounded by loved ones, and remarks, "Aww, ain't she cute?" Clearly, seeing Jaime's life in pictorial nostalgic form awakens and provokes feelings of deep loneliness in Lisa.

Now, I wish to turn to a rather remarkable confluence of thematic and aesthetic choices between *Vertigo* and "Deadly Ringer" that center on wardrobe. So much of *Vertigo*'s thematic power revolves around the power of surfaces and appearances. Scottie falls in love with an apparition,

The Bionic Woman and Feminist Ethics

someone who does not exist, the masquerade that Gavin Elster devises and Judy performs according to his plan. (In a devastating turn later in the film, Scottie discovers Judy's crime by noticing that she has kept one of the pieces of jewelry worn by Carlotta Valdes and as an heirloom by Madeleine. Judy has also kept the clothes she wore, including the famous gray suit. Scottie buys her expensive clothes she already owns, a subtle account of frustrated and futile desire.) Nearly everything that Judy says or does as Madeleine has been scripted by Elster. As Scottie bitterly accuses Judy at the climax, Elster "made you over just like I did, only better.... Not only the clothes and the hair, the looks, the manner and the words, and those beautiful phony trances." Along with his henchman, we see Courtney training Lisa in "Mirror Image" to speak and act as Jaime does. Courtney, if anything, has done one better than Scottie and even Elster, imposing a new female identity on Lisa Galloway's very flesh, changing her body itself.

The famous costume designer Edith Head did the costumes for *Vertigo*. Regarding the effect that Hitchcock creates (given his careful instructions to Edith Head about costumes, such as his insistence that Madeleine/Novak wear a gray suit), Tania Modleski observes that the ghostly figure of woman in *Vertigo* is as an effect created through camera work and costumes. Madeleine/Novak is "photographed through diffusion filters, shot in soft light, dressed in a white coat, and accompanied by haunting music on the soundtrack."[28] Bernard Herrmann wrote arguably the greatest of all film scores for *Vertigo*; it is high praise indeed to say that Joe Harnell wrote a television score that honors Herrmann (who never disdained the television medium, having written scores for numerous television programs, especially *The Alfred Hitchcock Hour* and the original Rod Serling *Twilight Zone*). Harnell's score for the episodes emphasize the lulling, siren-like call of obsessive envy as Lisa descends into madness.

According to the wonderful website thebionicwomanfiles.com, Charles Waldo designed the costumes for "Deadly Ringer" as well as numerous other *Bionic* episodes. In a key intertextual overlap, Madeleine Elster wears a long white trench coat at one point, and Lisa Galloway wears an all-white ensemble. The commentator at the website wwwbionicblonde.com, who dissects every *Bionic* episode and includes an astute discussion of fashion with each analysis, enthusiastically describes Lisa's white outfit this way: "I really loved this white wool suit and skirt combination Lisa wore with a white ribbed turtleneck, and the matching white dress hat with beige trim."[29]

4. *Bionic* Vertigo

Lisa wears this outfit when she heads to the OSI headquarters in D.C. with the intention of stealing the Adrenalizine. We have already discussed this sequence, but it demands further attention. Once there, greeted warmly as Jaime by Oscar and Rudy, Lisa must use the one dose of Adrenalizine that Courtney gave her to pass Rudy's bionic tests. (While this is happening, poor Jaime is finally escaping the prison where Harkens and her assistant Webber have drugged her. The episode intercuts scenes of Jaime bionically escaping with those of Lisa using her Adrenalizine powers to pass Rudy's tests.) After triumphantly passing/faking her bionic exam, Lisa, asked by Rudy to deliver the remaining Adrenalizine to a lab, sets off.

So begins an extraordinary sequence in which Lisa, in her Madeleine Elster–like high fashion white ensemble, delivers the drug to the lab (secretly retaining the larger portion for herself), drives for a time, then walks through the streets of a cosmopolitan D.C. neighborhood (Georgetown, perhaps), has a phone conversation with Courtney, and then boards a plane headed, of all places, back to Ojai. (These scenes are intercut with those of Jaime's escape through the forest beyond the prison, being hunted by police officers and bloodhounds.)

As in *Vertigo*, the costume here carries symbolic weight and makes implicit statements about character and narrative. Lisa's outfit—did Courtney pick and choose it for her? Was it one of Jaime's outfits? Its typical qualities as a white suit suggest calm, tranquility, and, problematically, racial purity and cleanliness. The iconography of the Western is relevant here, white typically symbolizing heroism, dark symbolizing villainy. The effect of Lisa/Wagner's blonde hair and white outfit is particularly Madeleine Elster–like, recalling Hitchcock's legendary cool blondes. But Lisa, brooding and tormented and yearning and hopeful at once, is anything but cool. Madeleine, once she becomes intimate with Scottie, reveals her fears of impending madness and imminent death ("Oh, Scottie, Scottie, I'm not mad, I'm not mad. I don't want to die. But there's someone inside telling me that I must die."). Lisa truly is going mad, and thanks to the poison she is ingesting, risking imminent death.

In the lab, a medical technician greets Lisa and takes the Adrenalizine from her. He then proceeds to hit on Lisa, who rebuffs him deftly. But as she drives away, his questions and her response reverberate in her mind: "Well, where do you live?" "That's a very good question." Adding emotional heft, Courtney's directive also echoes in a dreamlike register: "You *are* Jaime Sommers." Imagine if *throughout Vertigo* we'd been privy to Judy's thoughts and feelings and desires, and we might have something like these scenes. Later, the "Time Changes" song non-diegetically playing, Lisa walks through the well-appointed D.C. streets, and feels—Lindsay Wagner peerlessly makes her feelings palpable—a sense of joy and possibility. She's a Judy Barton who finds pleasure, fulfillment, and agency as Madeleine Elster. (Though she bitterly resents Scottie's forcing her back into that role later, who is to say that Judy did not feel some sense of these positive emotions during her training and at least the initial stages of her performance as Madeleine?)

Courtney's plan has been to kill Jaime in the prison. The coldly evil Dr. Harkens, looking down on what appears to be an unconscious Jaime, remarks to her co-conspirator the prison guard Webber, "Pretty face. I almost hate to touch it." But, she pitilessly intones, "Jaime Sommers will be buried with Lisa Galloway's face." Triumphantly, Jaime, not unconscious after all, later removes the drugged sandwich she sequestered within her shirt and makes a break for it. Lisa speaks with Courtney on the phone, facing a glass wall. She believes that Jaime has been murdered. Lisa asks, "Can I go on being Jaime Sommers, now that she's dead and all?" Lest we idealize Lisa, her affectless tone when she matter-of-factly mentions "now that she's dead and all" powerfully conveys Lisa's sociopathological nature. At the same time, Lisa rejects Courtney's horrifyingly glib offer to give her ten million dollars and especially to "change your face, make you the most beautiful woman in the world." At these words, she looks at her reflection in the glass and says "I like the way I look." Wagner's superb simplicity conveys the emotional authenticity of Lisa's self-regard. Lisa's new identity proceeds from the basis of external confirmation, her borrowed appearance giving her assurance and tranquility.

The poignancy of Lisa's costuming and appearance generally lies in the disjunct between her outward show of glamor and her inner turmoil. One recalls Bette Davis's immortal heroine Charlotte Vale in *Now, Voyager*. Once miserably unhappy, overweight, and lonely, Charlotte Vale emerges from a long period of therapy having been physically made over. Her psychiatrist and loving sister-in-law book Charlotte on a cruise to take her first independent voyage, freed from her tyrannical patrician mother's tight grip. When Charlotte emerges from her cabin for the first time, the object of a collective gaze, she looks stunningly attractive, but her outward show of strength, confidence, and glamor is at odds with her inner struggles, lack of self-confidence, and history of emotional pain. Something similar is conveyed in "Deadly Ringer," which draws out the ongoing relevance of the woman's film and its resonances in the Hitchcock film.

Charles Waldo's incisive costuming choices here also affect how we

4. *Bionic* Vertigo

view Jaime. Accused of being Lisa by the prison warden and Oscar himself, Jaime is finally rescued and just as importantly *believed* by Oscar when she forces him to ask her a question from a great distance and without a bullhorn so that Jaime can bionically hear and answer it. ("Who are you? What's your name?" "I'm Jaime—I'm Jaime Sommers!" She and Oscar run to each other and embrace.)

Back in D.C., the freshly recovered Jaime discusses the case with Oscar and Rudy at the OSI. Jaime is now dressed to the nines in an ensemble consisting of a hat, suit jacket, and pants. I am once again grateful to the website www.bionicblonde.com for this astute précis of fashions in the latter half of "Part 2":

> Later Jaime changed into a gorgeous dark navy-blue pantsuit with an orange blouse and neck scarf, with a matching blue felt dress hat. Lisa wore a black blouse and skirt and an orange pullover smock vest with a front pocket and string ties on the sides. Lisa also "borrowed" the nightgown last seen in "Jaime's Mother." In the final scene, Lisa was in a blue hospital gown, while Jaime wore an oversized wool poncho coat with blue and red stripes on the sleeves.[30]

Jaime now sports an outfit that is almost the exact replica of Lisa's white outfit for her visit to D.C. with the exception being its sultry dark colors. This navy-blue outfit, if we follow the iconography of the Western and film noir, colors Jaime the villain in contrast to the pointed purity of Lisa's white ensemble. In a strange, unsettling effect, Jaime comes to seem Lisa's villainous mirror image. While highly fashionable and an immensely pleasurable sight for the viewer, the navy-blue outfit is an odd fit with the episode's somber content. Moreover, in conventional terms, that Jaime wears pants while Lisa wears a skirt phallicizes Jaime as it lends Lisa a more traditional femininity. It should be added that Lisa's deferral of the medical technician's come-on confirms her agency and determination to make her own choices, romantic, sexual, and otherwise, a point further confirmed by her rebuttals to and defiance of Courtney's offers of ten million dollars and an even more enhanced and desirable visage.

Chosen Family

As we discussed in the previous chapter, the theme of nonbiological family ties is crucial to *Bionic*. Helen and Jim Elgin, Steve Austin's mother and stepfather, became Jaime's adoptive parents when her own died. That Jim Elgin is not Steve's biological father adds another layer to the fact that he becomes Jaime's Dad. And Helen and Jim continue to parent Jaime

The Bionic Woman and Feminist Ethics

even after her marriage to Steve is cancelled. Not at all to be discounted, Jaime's relationships with Oscar, Rudy, and Oscar's secretary Callahan (not present in this two-parter) are of great significance as well. The loving welcome that Lisa receives when she visits the OSI in D.C. attests to this, albeit because the men believe she's Jaime.

All of this makes Lisa's love for Helen and Jim and her warm interactions with Oscar and Rudy especially important. Lisa, having gotten a taste of love, doesn't want to relinquish it. Risking her freedom and in danger of blowing her cover, she heads back to Ojai, believing that she can live out the rest of her life as Jaime. (Interestingly, much the same backstory develops for Don Draper, the lead character on the great AMC series *Mad Men*. In reality a man named Dick Whitman, Don assumes the identity of a soldier who dies in front of him.) When Lisa arrives at the airport, Helen and Jim greet and embrace her, bringing her back to the carriage house. "It's so good to be home," a beaming Lisa remarks, a pointed echo of the words that Jaime said to Helen in the first episode of the series, "Welcome Home, Jaime, Part 1."

Lisa's ardent love for Helen and Jim is not the only element of this atypical affectional arrangement. Even after she discovers that Lisa has been masquerading as Jaime, Helen's feelings do not really change. Indeed, after some hesitation on her part, Helen embraces Lisa (though not revealing that she knows of Lisa's identity), comforting her as she experiences waves of pain from the Adrenalizine poisoning. Playing Lisa as a lost, lonely child, Wagner strikes a moving note when Lisa, clinging desperately to Helen, chokes, "Mom, I'm going to take that picture and put it in my scrapbook," referring to the Polaroid that she made Helen and Jim take with her the night before.

Jaime and Oscar and Rudy, realizing what's happened, head to Ojai to apprehend Lisa. Jaime and Helen embrace, Helen asking, "Is it really you this time?" One might imagine that the women might begin talking about Jaime's harrowing ordeal in the prison and during her escape, but they do not. In an emotionally complex scene, Helen counsels Jaime to help Lisa. This scene gives Helen much more agency than one would expect of a secondary character there to support the leading player of a series. Far from merely a support to Jaime, Helen has her own views and experiences that here run counter to Jaime's, at least initially. "If you could just talk to her," Helen pleads. To Oscar, Helen remarks, "I feel so awful, just like when Jaime was having her problems." The look on Jaime's face is strikingly puzzled: "Mom, you're really worried about her, aren't you?" Helen immediately grows alarmed, asking, "You're not angry with me?"

4. *Bionic* Vertigo

Jaime takes a minute to respond, but then smiles and says, "No. How can I be angry with you for loving somebody?" Jaime then asks Oscar to allow her to intervene. When Oscar balks ("After all she's done to you? Why?"), Jaime references her own experiences with mental anguish as justification: "She doesn't know who she is right now. She's frightened and confused, and God knows I've been there." Oscar relents.

That Helen forms her own bond with Lisa threatens to disrupt one of the most powerful thematic through-lines of *Bionic*, the nonbiological family ties uniting Jaime and those in her life. What would happen if, somehow, this strange woman who needs Helen so desperately, clings to her for dear life, in effect, somehow touched the older woman's heart in a way that surpassed Jaime's ability to do so? In psychoanalytic terms, the double is more you than you are; Lisa threatens by being more Jaime-like than Jaime herself. Still, in the end, what is affirmed is how capaciously loving a character Helen is, a point made abundantly clear in "Jaime's Mother."

The Tears of the Double

Jaime ventures upstairs to her carriage apartment and finds Lisa at the table where she is working on her scrapbook (Jaime's, of course). Wagner's interpretation of Lisa as a child reaches its zenith here: when Jaime offers her help, Lisa moans, "You stay away from me." Powered by the Adrenalizine, Lisa smashes off a huge chunk of the table, defying Jaime: "See what I can do? I'm Jaime!" Jaime responds, "Now, that was Jaime's favorite table. If you were her, you wouldn't have done that." The domestic objects, all the inviting homey features that so entranced Lisa, become weaponized, as Lisa hurls the table fragment at Jaime with deadly force. The battle between bionic and Adrenalizine powers commences, but Jaime does not retaliate, her responses being purely defensive.

In *Bionic Ever After?*, the final television reunion film for both *The Six Million Dollar Man* and *The Bionic Woman*, Jaime has become a practicing psychiatrist, with the title Dr. Sommers. "Deadly Ringer" depicts a Jaime well on her way to this career. Her approach to Lisa is therapeutic. She positively reinforces Lisa's own account of her loving relationship with Helen and Jim. "Helen and Jim—they love me," Lisa insists, and Jaime responds, "I know that they do. And they're terribly worried about you, Lisa." Lisa insists that she cannot be Lisa and must be Jaime because "nobody ever loved Lisa—not her parents, not her teachers…" Jaime

The Bionic Woman and Feminist Ethics

responds, pointing her hands to her heart, "Oh, that's not true. *We* love you, Lisa," begging her to stop ingesting the poison.

As with the great "Jaime's Mother," Jaime does not reject this potential enemy but instead, literally, embraces her. One might argue that she comforts the stranger. As with great woman's films such as *Now, Voyager* and *The Three Faces of Eve* (Nunnally Johnson, 1957) and the legendary television film *Sybil* (Daniel Petrie, 1976), the power of empathetic therapy to change, indeed to save lives, is strongly supported here. Lisa fights against Jaime's efforts every step of the way, defiantly snarling, "You just don't want me to live like you!" to which Jaime responds, "No—I want you to live like *you*." When Lisa counters, "I can't!" Jaime continues to press her: "Your life is worth living—you don't need mine." Lisa moans, saying that she hates her life, and Jaime assures her that it can change. At this point, an interesting unfinished sentence pours out of Lisa's mouth: "No, you're never gonna change…" Lisa does not say, "I can never change," but instead uses the second person, stating that it is *Jaime* who will never change. Nevertheless, Lisa comes around. In Jaime's arms, Lisa returns to sanity, calling Jaime by her own name: "Oh, Jaime," Lisa says, clutching her tall rescuer, who bends down to embrace the weeping, shaking Lisa.

The therapeutic rescue is very powerfully depicted. But the rough edges of this wrenching narrative cannot be smoothed away. As Jaime bends down to embrace Lisa, we get a close-up of Jaime's face, and what Wagner conveys more than anything else at this moment is exhaustion, rolling her eyes in incredulity as she exhales a silent sigh. I am not criticizing this acting and directorial choice—far from it. The moment has a tremendously persuasive emotional realism, especially given what Jaime has been through.

Nevertheless, this expression of exasperated weariness is a striking "tell," because it conveys, if we hadn't figured this out, that Jaime was not being fully sincere in her responses to Lisa. Or, to put it another way, Jaime is under no impression that she is herself bonding with Lisa. She is, instead, talking a madwoman down from the ledge. Had the closeup of Jaime shown her shutting her eyes, that gesture would have conveyed shared feeling. Compare a similar shot of an embrace in "Deadly Ringer, Part 1," when Jim, seeing Lisa-as-Jaime off before she boards Courtney's plane, embraces this woman whom he believes to be his adopted daughter. We see Lisa experience the embrace, her face in our view, her eyes closed, as a flood of affirmation overwhelms her. Lisa is clearly in the moment, experiencing a powerful emotional connection with the older man, as again Wagner conveys with her remarkable emotional openness.

4. *Bionic* Vertigo

In sharp contrast, the shot of Jaime at the climax of ""Deadly Ringer, Part 2" does not depict her being overcome by a rush of feeling. Jaime's eyes are wide open as she embraces Lisa, who cannot see her face. But *we* can, and Jaime's sigh expresses her relief that this entire episode is now over and signals to the audience that Jaime is outside of this moment. This decision to reveal the heroine's private reaction suggests that Jaime is on some level inaccessible, at a remove, not fully willing to bond with her troubled analysand. Lisa is always already the other, to be kept at a distance.

In the final scene of "Deadly Ringer, Part 2," Jaime visits Lisa in the hospital. Lisa is still wearing Jaime's face. Immediately, this scene recalls the one in "Jaime's Mother," when Jaime visits her mother's imposter Chris in the hospital after her identity has been exposed. The lineage between the two episodes is striking, a genealogy of the family of doubles. That her mother also had a double and that her mother's double experienced similar psychological distress and overwhelming emotional connection to the woman she impersonated has unsettling, haunting resonances.

Jaime had given her the "To Thine Own Self Be True" needlepoint, and when she walks in, Lisa hands it back to her, saying, "I just finished it." Jaime, in her typical fashion, makes a self-deprecating joke of the moment: "You can certainly tell where I left off and you took over. Yours is a lot neater." "I guess that kind of says it all," Lisa remarks; laughing, Jaime answers, "It certainly does."

There is no mention made during their conversation of Lisa's having tipped off the OSI about Courtney's whereabouts. In "Jaime's Mother," Jaime, reporting her conversation with Oscar Goldman, offers Chris Stuart the possibility of reprieve if she gives the OSI information. But Lisa's sacrifice seems to have gone unnoticed. That Lisa has helped the OSI anonymously and selflessly, then, adds to the surprising nobility of her character. While thanking Jaime for having helped her, Lisa says, "I don't know how I'm going to repay you from prison." Jaime responds immediately, "I do."

At this, Jaime hands Lisa a black and white photograph. It is the same black and white photo of Lisa Galloway that the evil Dr. Harkens had tauntingly, sadistically held up before Jaime in the prison hospital room, saying "It's time for you to get your own face back. You're going to look like yourself again." Jaime says to Lisa, "Now that you know who you are on the inside, isn't it about time that you looked like yourself on the outside?" Lisa, somewhat tentatively, takes the photo from Jaime, stares at it, and then holds up it before her own face so that the photo is facing outward and Jaime can see it superimposed over Lisa's still Jaime-like face.

The Bionic Woman and Feminist Ethics

"How's it look?" Lisa asks, and Jaime, smiling, says, "Beautiful." At that same moment, the "Time Changes" theme floods the soundtrack, and we get a trick shot of the two women both played by Wagner looking at each other with affection. Finally, the episode ends with a close-up on Jaime's face as the cooing, hummed version of "Time Changes" accompanies the image.

While we are no doubt meant to read this resolution as a healing, affirmative one, and perhaps should, there are enough discordant moments to give us pause. For one thing, that the picture Jaime hands over to Lisa is the same one Dr. Harkens threatened Jaime with is an eerie and unsettling effect. For that matter, the female model used for the photo of Lisa Galloway is completely distinct in appearance from the glamorous Jaime/Wagner. With her hair done in a frowzy style, this woman does not smile; her look is hard, blank, and unwelcoming. The picture looks like a mug shot. The implication is that Lisa is right to face the prospect of regaining this face with reluctance when she already has a face that she loves. All these unsettling impressions are made possible through the astonishingly self-aware and critical distance the two-parter maintains towards its own thematic material. Allowing us to see our beloved heroine from a critical distance and identify with the rejected, marginalized other, the copy rather than the original, "Deadly Ringer" breaks new ground in the depiction of femininity and female desire in the mainstream television text.

CHAPTER 5

Fembot Theory

Fembot Medusa

Perhaps the Bionic shows' most enduring pop-culture mythology is the figure of the Fembot, introduced in the three crossover episodes "Kill Oscar." The Fembot enjoys a healthy cultural afterlife in works as disparate as the SF film *Eve of Destruction* (1991), the Austin Powers spy-spoof films, Alex Garland's film *Ex Machina* (2014), the reboot TV series *Battlestar Galactica* (TV Series 2004–2009), and the HBO series *Westworld* (2017– present). Of course, the Bionic shows were themselves inspired by the original film *Westworld* (1973), written and directed by Michael Crichton. (*Futureworld*, directed by Richard T. Heffron, the undersung 1976 sequel to *Westworld*, premiered the same year as *The Bionic Woman*.)

The Fembots echo the robot women of *The Stepford Wives* (Bryan Forbes, 1975), starring Katharine Ross and based on Ira Levin's novel, in which suburban businessmen create the perfect wives, smiling, cheerful, uncomplaining, and literally robotic. The terrifying, inescapable atmosphere of *The Stepford Wives* is far closer in spirit to *Bionic*'s tone than the broad, titillating Austin Powers movies starring Michael Myers. In these inane spoofs of James Bond spy thrillers, the Fembots are purely sexualized, able to shoot missiles from their ample, Playboy-bunny breasts.

The Fembots of the crossover *Bionic Woman* and *Six Million Dollar Man* three-parter "Kill Oscar," in contrast, are not sexualized in the least. They are robot versions of professional women—office administrators, lab assistants—designed to pass as such. The plot to steal the OSI's Weather Control Machine depends on replacing the women who work for powerful government men. But the series has more on its mind than simply depicting these women as the "human glue," as the Fembot Katy

The Bionic Woman and Feminist Ethics

calls them, connecting these powerful men to one another. The Fembot episodes thematize woman's unrest in positions of relative powerlessness in the government workplace.

Sue Short notes of the figure of the cyborg that while it is "potentially useful in exposing the extent to which gender identity is manufactured, it has also revealed fierce divisions within feminism itself, leaving critics at odds in deciding whether it represents a positive icon or otherwise." Short also discusses the synthetic female, which the Fembot exemplifies, observing that "something frequently goes wrong" with them and also that "the ethical questions involved in their construction are frequently overlooked."[1] This chapter considers the figure of the Fembot from the standpoint of feminist and queer ethical concerns.

>"Kill Oscar: Part 1." Directed by Alan Crosland.
>Story by Arthur Rowe and Oliver Crawford.
>Teleplay by Arthur Rowe. Airdate: October 27, 1976
>
>"Kill Oscar: Part 2." Directed by Barry Crane.
>Story by Arthur Rowe and Oliver Crawford.
>Teleplay by William T. Zacha. Airdate: October 31, 1976
>
>"Kill Oscar: Part 3." Directed by Alan Crosland.
>Story by Arthur Rowe and Oliver Crawford.
>Teleplay by Arthur Rowe. Airdate: November 3, 1976

"Kill Oscar," one of the best-known *Bionic* outings (while also being a *Six Million* episode), revolves around the revenge plot of the brilliant Dr. Franklin (John Houseman), inventor of the Fembots. Talking to a foreign buyer, Franklin points to the series of glass-tube-encased, statuesque mannequins that will uncannily assume a human-like form. Franklin remarks, "I call them Fembots. The perfect women: programmable, obedient, and as beautiful or as deadly as I choose to make them."

Franklin was booted out of the OSI when his Fembot project was rejected in favor of Rudy Wells' bionics, the thinking being that human beings, even mechanically enhanced, are better than machines. Franklin bitterly disagrees and has created an army of Fembots to take revenge on Oscar Goldman and Rudy. Franklin's plan, backed by Russian gangsters, is twofold: he will steal a new and unstable technology, The Weather Control Device, and kidnap Oscar, humiliating and rendering him powerless. The imperative in the episodes' title comes from Oscar's own orders: if he is kidnapped, the government must mobilize all efforts to kill him.

The family hour timeslots for the Bionic shows notwithstanding, the three-parter taps into the real-world mayhem of Cold War politics, realistically depicting internecine warfare within the United States govern-

5. Fembot Theory

ment as the OSI is pitted against the National Security Bureau (NSB). Hanson, the head of the NSB, fully intends to honor Goldman's wishes and have him killed; Jaime and Steve defiantly plot a rescue mission of their own, with Rudy's help. (The NSB will return in "On the Run," the series finale, determined to place Jaime in a restricted government facility when she announces her intention to quit the OSI.)

"Part One" commences with the most effective "cold open" (or pre-credit scene) in any *Bionic* episode. Dr. Franklin's secret laboratory appears to be in a warm locale since everyone looks sweaty. He complains to his female assistant, Katy (Janice Whitby), a redhead clad in pastel short-shorts, that he must grovel before fools for funding. Enter Baron Constantine, the Russian mobster whose plane has just landed at Franklin's base. Jack Colvin, cast as the tireless investigative journalist McGee who hunts down the titular creature of Kenneth Johnson's CBS TV series *Incredible Hulk*, plays the Baron with a thick accent and an intemperate manner.

Franklin and Katy explain their plot to replace the secretaries and other "strategically located ladies" of the OSI with the Fembots. Incredulous, the Baron angrily responds, "Robots? When my board of directors hears about this, Franklin, you're a dead man." Katy entreats the hostile backer. "Please, Baron, if only you'd look at one of the finished products." He impatiently retorts, "Don't be ridiculous. These idiotic mannequins are not going to fool anybody." At that, saying "Baron," Franklin tears off Katy's facial covering to reveal the Fembot beneath, hideous robot circuitry and staring glass eyes. Adding to the scary effect, the Katy Fembot, no longer endowed with a human face and a mouth, continues to speak in her matter-of-fact, blandly cheerful tones: "They're really remarkable." Franklin rather wryly notes, "I've taken the liberty of getting your board of directors on the line." Without responding to Franklin, the Baron takes the phone, tersely and unhesitatingly saying, "Give him the money."

The "ritual of ripping off these artificial female faces," writes Julie Wosk, "is a reenactment of that shocking moment of exposure—that descent into the uncanny valley" in E.T.A. Hoffman's legendary short story "The Sandman" (1816) when a young man discovers that the young woman he loves and voyeuristically spies on is an artificial creation. "Nathanael's horrible recognition that Olympia was not real" occurs when Nathanael discovers that the beautiful, if largely wordless, Olympia (she can only say "Ah, ah") is a mindless automaton whose mechanical eyes now lie on the ground. The Fembots with their television eyes are modern day-Olympias. Dr. Franklin, Wosk notes, resurrects the "male fantasy about creating a synthetic woman who is superior to the real thing."[2]

The Bionic Woman and Feminist Ethics

Exposing the Fembot's face by tearing off the human mask—what I call *the Fembot reveal*—produces a Medusan effect. In the Ovidian Medusa myth, the sight of Medusa—a woman with snakes for hair—is so frightening that she turns men into stone. (More on the sexual politics of the myth in a moment.) The teaser's Fembot reveal does the same to the Baron, who can barely speak at all when Franklin tears off Katy's face mask. When Callahan (Jennifer Darling)—Oscar Goldman's secretary—confronts her Fembot double in the doorway of her apartment, she can only gasp, expressing a similar wordless terror and incredulity. Most resonantly of all, when Jaime does battle with the machines—the Callahan and Katy Fembots—her reaction to the Fembot reveal intensifies the Medusan terror.

A longstanding cultural icon, the figure of Medusa was extremely prominent in nineteenth century art and literature. Thomas Albrecht observes that seeing the Medusa yields a "forbidden insight."[3] The "Medusa effect," he theorizes, has a tripartite structure. First, it stages "the subject's visual confrontation with a dangerous object." Through this confrontation, the subject gains a "terrifying insight." This insight is so volatile that it threatens to destroy the subject. Second, representation allows this deadly object to be viewed safely. Thirdly, however, representation itself proves to be the true danger, revealed as "illusory, deceptive, or unstable."[4]

Suspecting that her friend may be involved in Oscar's kidnapping, Jaime goes to Callahan's apartment. Catching Callahan out in a lie, Jaime tells her Fembot replacement, "Now you may look and sound like Callahan, but you're not her. Who are you—and where is Oscar Goldman?" Ordered by Franklin to capture Jaime, the Callahan Fembot grabs her right arm. Jaime bionically resists, finally managing to wrench loose from the machine woman's grasp. When she races to the door and opens it, Jaime discovers Katy standing there, ready to incapacitate her with an anesthetic. Jaime tussles with Katy, bionically striking her and in the process ripping her face mask off. When the mask falls to the ground, the Fembot reveal is held for a moment, and then we cut to Jaime's reaction shot. As only Lindsay Wagner, who always brings an extraordinary emotional realism to her acting, can convey, Jaime experiences pure terror, screaming at the sight of Katy's exposed Fembot face. Repeat viewings of this scene never diminish its sheer horror. As Medusa's image does to her victims, the Fembot's face turns Jaime to stone—her zoom-in reaction shot initially conveys a frozen, wordless horror. But Jaime's scream humanizes her, *confirms* her humanness. What terrifying insight will the Fembot reveal yield?

Jaime values her humanness as a quality that transcends her bionic enhancements. This theme will be further developed in "Fembots in Las Vegas," the S3 sequel to "Kill Oscar," and especially in the series finale "On the Run." The Fembot reveal shatters any notion of humans transcending machines; this adversary is all machine. "Her covering came off," Jaime explains to Steve Austin in the trilogy's second episode. Humanness only exists as external façade, a mere "covering" for the implacable machine entity beneath.

What is especially striking about Jaime's relationship to Fembots is that it eradicates one of the defining aspects of Jaime's persona: her compassion, which she extends even toward her enemies and those who've endangered her. Jaime demonstrates concern for Chris, her mother's double, in the S1 episode "Jaime's Mother"; the hulking and rampaging bionic Bigfoot; and her own double, the mentally ill and potentially murderous Lisa Galloway, in S2's "Deadly Ringer." In contrast, Jaime exhibits a total absence of feeling toward her Fembot foes except wholly negative ones.

One might reasonably counter, "How would or should Jaime express compassion for a killing machine?" One could imagine a scene in which Jaime attempts to reason with the Fembot. Indeed, the opportunity for such an exchange arises in the S3 sequel, "Fembots in Las Vegas." The second episode of this two-parter endows the Fembot with consciousness, even "emotions and a soul." But even here, when Jaime speaks in rational terms to the Fembot (or Manbot) threatening her, the machine menace is never anything more than that, a menace to be destroyed. The same holds true for S2's notable two-parter "Doomsday Is Tomorrow," in which Jaime battles a supercomputer determined to destroy the world. This brings us back to our theory of the like unlike.

Like Unlikeness

Psychoanalytic feminist theory helps us to understand one of the crucial dynamics in the Fembot episodes. Jaime's revulsion in the face of this foe signals a repudiation and a disavowal. Alex 7000, the supercomputer intent on destroying the world in "Doomsday Is Tomorrow," likens himself to Jaime, calling both "Cousins." Jaime unhesitatingly destroys him, disavowing any connection. The Fembot and the supercomputer are too much machine for Jaime, whose humanity defines her.

Writing in a collection of engagements with the work of the French psychoanalytic theorist Julia Kristeva, Sara Ahmed argues that emotionally intense states such as love and hate assign qualities of likeness and unlikeness to the other. If we identify with someone, we like them; if we dis-identify with someone, it is because we do not. Ahmed sees significance in these dynamics for nation and community: "the promise of the nation is not an empty or abstract one.... Rather, the nation is a concrete effect of how some bodies have moved toward and away from other bodies," a process that creates "boundaries and borders."[5]

To be sure, Jaime's conflict with Fembots has national implications. If she is unable to resolve her feelings toward the robots, she will be unable to perform her government mission, plunging nation into jeopardy. But speaking in more local terms, the Fembots exist so that Jaime can reaffirm her own humanness. They exist so that Jaime can actively dis-identify with them, establishing her distinctness from and superiority to them. Jaime's reactions to Fembots and supercomputers exhibit an emotional response that I call *mechaphobia*, a fear of the nonhuman in mechanical and technological forms that take the appearance of or in other ways simulate the human.

The horror Fembots inspire and embody provides a vent for anxieties hovering over Jaime's own identity, both in terms of others' reactions to her and her own views of herself. The estrangement, even revulsion, Jaime's mechanical aspects potentially generate can be displaced on to the Fembot. Throughout the series, there are many small but telling moments when those around her, often being enlisted for their help during her missions, respond not only with awe but also apprehensiveness, even dread at the revelation of Jaime's meta- or mecha-humanness. Jaime's anxieties over her bionics intensify into self-revulsion in the series finale.

Female Friendship Among the Fembots

In one of the indelible moments of Hollywood films of the 1970s, Joanna Eberhart (Katharine Ross), the heroine of *The Stepford Wives*, goes to the home of her friend Bobbie Markowe (Paula Prentiss). Joanna and Bobbie have been incensed at and terrified by what is happening to the women of Stepford, Connecticut, their vitality snuffed out, one by one. As played by Prentiss, the singular, funny, unconventional Bobbie is a force of nature and a genuine ally. But Joanna discovers that Bobbie has transformed into a drone like the other endlessly smiling, vacuous Stepford women primarily obsessed with name-brand products and cleanliness. "Bobbie really has changed!" Joanna insists to her skeptical husband

5. Fembot Theory

(secretly a participant in the wife-transformation plot). "Everything in her house looks like a TV commercial!"

Foiled in her escape plan by the sinister Men's Association, which abducts her children, Joanna confronts Bobbie in her now-spotless home (the real Bobbie was brazenly and joyously indifferent to the domestic sphere). Not finding her children there, either, the maddened Joanna confronts her now robotic, remote, and catatonically cheerful friend. Joanna cuts her finger and holds it up to Bobbie's face so that she can see the blood Bobbie no longer has. "When I cut myself, I bleed. Look. Do *you* bleed?" In a startling moment, Joanna stabs her friend in the stomach; Bobbie responds as if Joanna had done nothing but splash water on her. "Now why would you want to do a thing like that?" Bobbie repeatedly asks, as she begins picking up a series of teacups off their hooks and letting them drop to the floor. She may not bleed, but she does short-circuit. Caught in this endless loop of pointless action, Bobbie begins ceaselessly intoning, "I thought we were friends. I thought we were friends..."

Later, Joanna will discover the full horror of being a Stepford Wife. She encounters her nearly completed but still unfinished android double, whose eyes are an enigmatic, terrifying total black. The android smiles serenely at Joanna as she inexorably approaches her human counterpart, tautly holding the stocking she will use to strangle the doomed heroine. All the while, the villainous architect of the whole scheme, an elegant monster named Dale Coba (Patrick O'Neal), silently looks on.

Stepford suggests that misogyny destroys women's identities and ruptures female bonds. The lively, funny, warm Bobbie's transformation into a robotic domestic maven spewing mindless banalities anticipates Joanna's destruction. The impossibility of communication between the women allegorizes the impossibility of forming bonds among the oppressed and silenced within patriarchy. What the literary critic Helena Michie calls "sororophobia," enmity between women, comes into play here. A key scene adumbrates this harrowing impasse in communication. The consciousness-raising meeting that Joanna and Bobbie organize to connect to the robotic women—whom they do not yet understand to be literally robotic—fails utterly. The robot wives spout product-placement boilerplate in response to Joanna and Bobbie's introspective reflections. "Kill Oscar" explores similar territory.

Jaime's friendship with Oscar Goldman's secretary Callahan is one of *Bionic*'s greatest strengths. Callahan—a recurring guest star, played wonderfully by the quirkily distinctive Jennifer Darling, known for her unmistakable high-pitched voice—was first introduced on *Six Million*.

The Bionic Woman and Feminist Ethics

"Kill Oscar, Part 1" marks her first appearance on *Bionic*. Callahan and Jaime, this episode establishes, share a real rapport, and future episodes, especially in S3, reveal that the women are best friends. Their friendship receives its most extensive analysis in the S3 episode "Brain Wash," for which I believe Jennifer Darling more than deserved an Emmy (and award that, thankfully, Wagner won for lead actress in the series for the episode "Deadly Ringer, Part 2").

In "Kill Oscar, Part 1," Callahan is facing a personal crisis. Jaime makes the time to talk to Callahan, obviously frazzled. Despite her "unrelenting deadly efficiency," as Callahan puts it when talking to Jaime (a description oddly suited to her imminent Fembot identity), Oscar does not appreciate her or her abilities. These abilities include handling innumerable simultaneous phone calls to his office while unfailingly informing him where his secret documents and similar kinds of information have been filed.

As Callahan reveals, she is torn between following her mother's advice—return home (Cape Cod) and get married and raise a family—and sticking it out with Oscar, the OSI, and D.C. Jaime responds, "Well, you could get worse advice." This conciliatory response is then followed up by another. Jaime tells Callahan that the office would fall apart without her and that, moreover, Oscar would be stunned to learn of her dissatisfaction. Later, Jaime talks to Oscar about "appreciating people." When Oscar responds, with surprise, "Jaime, I appreciate *you*," Jaime explains that Callahan is the one who feels unappreciated. By speaking with Oscar, Jaime facilitates a solution that will allow Callahan to maintain her professional life rather than capitulating to her mother's fantasies of "wife-mother-domestic goddess" bliss/servitude.

Given the themes of this three-parter, it's interesting that Part One commences with an articulation of woman's dissatisfaction. When Callahan explicates the problematic choice between traditional and more contemporary female roles, the series most directly nods to second-wave feminism. Our own post-millennial moment has addressed (though hardly resolved) the problem by valorizing women for doing it all: having successful jobs and being committed wives and mothers. In the 1970s, however, the choice seemed much starker, only one or the other. At least, that is what *Bionic* suggests.

Callahan's remarks are interesting. Does she want the "whole indispensable" wife-mother-domestic goddess role, or the professional one she currently maintains with such "unrelenting deadly efficiency"? Callahan's persona revolves around this efficiency, so much so that her Fembot ver-

5. Fembot Theory

sion reveals its nature by being demonstrably *less* efficient. When NSB chief Hanson is grilling Callahan about Oscar's itinerary on the day of his kidnapping, the Fembot Callahan nervously pleads for lenience. Complaining about answering Oscar's voluminous calls and other tasks she must perform, Fembot Callahan confesses she has a hard time keeping all this capacious information "straight in my head."

Jaime witnessed and unsuccessfully attempted to stop the kidnapping. She's still shaken up as she listens to Callahan's unexpectedly flibbertigibbet-like patter. Indicative of her extremely agitated mood, Jaime lights into her friend. "Callahan, what are you talking about? I've seen you juggle a million things at once for him," and now she can't remember basic information? Callahan-the-Fembot responds, "Please, Jaime, stop it. Don't you think I'm just as worried about Mr. Goldman as you are?" Jaime remains unconvinced: "Well, I don't know." Alarmed by Callahan's sudden shift into the scatterbrained, Jaime goes to her apartment later that evening to determine if her friend can be trusted.

This plot development—Jaime's increasing and then insistent distrust of Callahan—reveals a rupture in female bonds. Yet the episode has just established these bonds as central: warm, affirming, and full of trust and generosity. Even given the fraught situation and Jaime's understandable agitation, it's surprising that she turns so quickly and vehemently on Callahan. Does Jaime suspect her friend of being a double agent? (She certainly can't yet suspect her of being a robot.)

Adding to the discomfort of all of this, Jaime herself becomes suspect. Lynda, Rudy's lab assistant and now a Fembot replacement, seems to side with Jaime but then casts a shadow of doubt on her suspicions regarding Callahan. Earlier in the episode, Rudy fine-tuned Jaime's bionic ear, heightening its "range and efficiency." An aftereffect of this enhancement, Jaime can detect the transistor hum the Fembots give off. Fembot Lynda uses Jaime's distress over this mysterious hum—shades of Jaime's unraveling on *Six Million*—as evidence of mental distress. ("Kill Oscar, Part 2" further echoes the early Jaime's travails when Rudy by the injured Jaime's hospital bedside, confesses to Steve Austin, "I'm worried that she's beginning to reject her bionics," an ominous line reinforced by the unconscious Jaime's sudden sharp intake of breath.)

As Michel Foucault has noted, one of the negative aftereffects of the rise and respectability of psychoanalysis (the critical methodology I favor, it should be noted) is the "hysterization of women." The late nineteenth-century figure of the hysteric, associated with women who suffered from unexplainable physical maladies, became a model for later pathologizing

The Bionic Woman and Feminist Ethics

views of women, especially those who speak their minds, as emotionally unstable, volatile, in need of the authoritarian masculine care of scientists, doctors, and other professionals.[6]

To a certain extent, such a misogynistic classification now threatens to thwart Jaime, silencing and classifying her as unstable, even pathological. Hanson even suggests that Jaime is paranoid, asking her if she believes that those around her—Rudy, Callahan, Lynda—are "persecuting" her. Threatened by hystericization and silencing, Jaime undergoes a crisis that mirrors a larger one in professional women's workplace and personal lives in the era, being shunted to the sidelines or even annihilated for speaking out. (Mike Nichols's great 1983 biopic-thriller *Silkwood*, starring Meryl Streep as the real-life Karen Silkwood, who spoke out against unsafe conditions at her nuclear power plant job in Oklahoma, takes up similar matters.)

Jaime's confrontation with Fembot Callahan in her apartment represents the complete breakdown of women's bonds, the physical fight between Jaime and Callahan and Katy metaphorically outlining this crisis. *Bionic* literalizes sororophobia, the antagonisms and emotional conflicts between women, in the heroine's ensuing battle with the two Fembots.[7]

While Jaime's warm, loving relationship with Oscar Goldman—who is far more nurturing to her than he is to Steve—cannot be discounted, it is also true Jaime and Callahan toil for male masters. In this regard, the Fembots, enslaved by their maker, parody the human women's predicament. Yet the robot women subtly convey an enviable control, autonomy, and finesse; they exude an air of detachment that removes them from the conventional trappings of femininity in sexist society. While indeed obedient, Katy, Dr. Franklin's "Number One," is a formidable presence. In "Kill Oscar, Part 3," she takes on an active role, monitoring events and even challenging, however quietly, one of Dr. Franklin's orders. When he commands his assistant to increase the Weather Control Machine's power so that Franklin can vanquish Jaime and Steve on their rescue mission, Katy quietly presses, "Won't that bring the hurricane winds closer to the island?" She could easily be a scientist-in-training trying subtly to educate an irascible senior colleague.

Dr. Franklin is played with delicious archness by John Houseman.[8] Beneath his amusing, impatient villainy, however, Franklin is a rank misogynist. This is a fitting quality for a man who builds female-resembling machines "as obedient or as deadly as I choose to make them." When the Baron encourages Franklin to kidnap Jaime as well, pointing out that Jaime's advantage over the Fembots is that she is "a human being, and can think for herself," Franklin responds, "When has that ever been an advantage ... in a *woman*?"

The *Bionic* episodes thematize women's unrest and defiance of cultures of silence and intimidation. Undeterred by the officious, annihilation-prone government personnel in her midst, Jaime determinedly fights to save Oscar's life, a quest that develops a liberating intensity in the third part of the trilogy. Steve joins in, of course, but the urgent imperative comes from Jaime. She makes it to Franklin's island base before Steve does (they torpedo out of a submarine to get there undetected and undeterred by the weather machine). Jaime's exhibits her characteristic compassion toward her enemies when she rescues an unwilling Franklin—he wants, in his defeat, to die—from the flood waters about to besiege his base.

Theorizing Fembots

Fembots represent the Bad Other—repudiated parts of the self. For Jaime Sommers, the repudiated parts of the self are machine elements devoid of human feeling, a soul. "You're not alive," Jaime rails against Alex 7000, the sentient supercomputer hell-bent on destroying the Earth. "You don't know what it's like to play with children and to watch them grow, or even to feel the warmth of the sun on your face" (S2, "Doomsday Is Tomorrow, Part 2"). Desperately, Jaime begs Alex to feel emotion, but he calmly, coldly explains it would be impossible for him to do so. Clearly, Jaime believes that if a machine could feel, it would heal, not harm. (A schoolteacher, Jaime associates humanness, the healing power of feelings, with the love of children.)

While she will struggle with her relationship to her bionics in the series finale, for the most part Jaime models a comfortable, harmonious kinship among unlike elements. She models equilibrium. With the Fembots, however, no recuperation is possible, given that they consist of pure, menacing machine.

While "Fembots in Las Vegas" will more prominently feature Fembots who impersonate sexually objectified women, "Kill Oscar" focuses on professional women who are not overtly sexualized. Initially, the ginger-haired Katy is presented in sexual terms. In the cold open to the first "Kill Oscar" episode, Katy greets the Baron in a striped pink and white shirt tied at the waist and red short-shorts. But her clothing becomes much more conservative after this; for the most part, she is clothed in conventional women's attire for the period—variations of the Avon Lady—as are Calla-

The Bionic Woman and Feminist Ethics

han and Linda. And on Franklin's island, Katy is dressed in a militaristic black, signaling an all-business professionalism complemented by Katy's cool, detached demeanor. (Janice Whitby's casting as Katy is perfect. Her detached manner gives Katy a taut blandness.)

"Kill Oscar"'s Fembots are not sexualized—they contrast starkly, then, with the cybernetic females of the Austin Powers movies and their predecessors like *Dr. Goldfoot and the Bikini Machine* (Norman Taurog, 1965), with its battalion of robot women in sexy bikinis. (The 1966 sequel *Dr. Goldfoot and the Girl Bombs* turns the robot women into actual weapons of mass destruction.) Nevertheless, their highly gendered aspects, as suggested by their very name, cannot pass unnoticed. Fembots enact a fantasy of women as machines, of femininity as machinelike, and of the machine as the eternal feminine.

"Manbots," not a term used on the series, appear in the form of the Oscar robot who battles with Steve in "Kill Oscar, Part 2" and Carl Franklin, Dr. Franklin's robot son, the villain of the S3 sequel episodes. Given that the Manbots are never called as such, we can say that they, too, are Fembots. (Every child of the 70s remembers when Steve confirms his suspicion that the seemingly rescued and returned Oscar Goldman is a robot. Watching Oscar pace around in his office, Steve remembers what Rudy said about the weight of each Fembot when he notices the heavy impressions Oscar's feet leave on the carpeted floor. Steve throws a pencil on the floor. When Oscar steps on the pencil, his foot pulverizes it, a deeply visceral effect intensified by typically intense sound effects.)

The fascination with a specifically female cyborg body has a long history. Some have read the Greek myth of Pygmalion and Galatea as foundational in this regard. (Pygmalion is a sculptor who hates women; Galatea is his statue. He falls in love with his own creation, leading the goddess Aphrodite to turn her into a real woman that Pygmalion can possess.) Similarly, some have read the False Florimell of Spenser's sixteenth century allegorical epic *The Faerie Queen* as an early example. "A cyborg created by a witch out of snow, wax, golden wire, and an animating 'spright,' the false Florimell presents a beautiful appearance that repeatedly fools everyone who sees her."[9] In the twentieth century, the false Maria in Fritz Lang's epic dystopian SF film *Metropolis* (1927) offers a prominent early example of the female robot. As noted, *The Bride of Frankenstein* (James Whale, 1935) provides an important precedent for *Bionic*.

The fascination with cyborg women begins to accelerate in the 1960s, an outgrowth of the space-age and a convergence with the rise of second-wave feminism heralded by Betty Friedan's *The Feminine Mystique*

5. Fembot Theory

(1963).[10] *My Living Doll* (starring Julie Newmar, who would famously play Catwoman on the 1960s *Batman* TV series), an American science fiction sitcom, would appear to be an early parody. (It aired for 26 episodes on CBS, 1964–5.)

The seriousness of *Bionic*'s treatment of the Fembots—described as terrifying by many who saw these episodes as children—corresponds much more closely to Rod Serling's great TV series *The Twilight Zone* (1959–1964) and its brilliant treatment of the subject of artificial women. In one of the finest *Zone* episodes, "The Lonely" (1959, written by Serling), a convict named Corry (Jack Warden), incarcerated on an asteroid, finds his solitary life disrupted when his jailers offer him an extremely lifelike female robot named Alicia (Jean Marsh). When he violently rejects her, she cries real tears, or tears that seem as real as can be. Over time, however, the prisoner overcomes his reservations and falls in love with her. But Captain Allenby, who commandeers the supply ship that visits Corry four times a year and brought him Alicia still unpacked in a crate, arrives one day to inform Corry that he has been pardoned and that the supply ship is here to take him back to Earth. Initially overjoyed, Corry is horrified when Allenby tells him that the ship cannot take on any extra weight and the robot must be left behind. Corry angrily protests, but Allenby, in a shockingly graphic and violent moment, shoots Alicia in the face. By the end of the episode, the android woman lies destroyed, smoldering on the ground, her forlorn lover staring in shock at her revealing remains.

Of more recent vintage, we might consider the character of Seven of Nine (Jeri Ryan), a former Borg drone, on the TV series *Star Trek: Voyager* (1995–2001). Liberated from the Borg collective, a race that assimilates humanoid life and merges bodies with machines, Seven struggles to regain her humanity on the starship Voyager, commanded by Captain Janeway (Kate Mulgrew). Seven of Nine's attempt to integrate her human and mechanical aspects closely corresponds to themes in *Bionic*. Seven's poignant struggles to reclaim her humanity despite the irremovable, material and emotional, machine elements of her identity flow directly from Jaime's crisis over similar difficulties in the series finale "On the Run."

Also of interest, the Cylons of *Battlestar Galactica*, Ron Moore's reboot of the '70s TV series (itself based on a feature film), look like people but are synthetic and deadly, at war with human survivors of the war waged against them by their former robotic servants. The hypersexualized and deadly Cylons, especially the statuesque blonde Caprica Six (the marvelous Tricia Helfer), are descendants of "Fembots in Las Vegas" as well

The Bionic Woman and Feminist Ethics

as the replicants of Ridley Scott's *Blade Runner* (1982), an adaptation of the 1968 Philip K. Dick novel *Do Androids Dream of Electric Sheep?*

Anne Balsamo has written extensively about cyborg women. "As a cyborg, simultaneously discursive and material, the female body is the site at which we can witness the struggle between systems of social order. In the process, new forms of gendered embodiment emerge which on the one hand display inherited signs of traditional dichotomous gender identity, but which also reinvent gender identity in totally new ways." She contends that the female body, however "subordinated within institutionalized systems of power and knowledge," is also not reducible to these "systems of meaning": "although woman is technologically constructed, her excesses accumulate, assembling the resources/techniques to signify/construct herself as transgressive of, if not entirely resistant to, the discourses that seek to contain her."[11]

Balsamo, like Donna Haraway, sees utopian possibilities in the female cyborg. While Jaime Sommers, in my view, realizes these possibilities, the Fembots certainly do not. Their virtues are negative ones: they make for great hissable villains because they possess neither interiority nor personhood, existing as parodies of persons, deceptively diminutive killing machines. (Callahan is about half the height of Jaime Sommers, but packs a wallop, especially in "Fembots in Las Vegas.")

In her excellent study *Anatomy of a Robot*, which analyzes artificial persons in literature and film, Despina Kakoudaki discusses the "anatomical gesture, a gesture of revelation and unveiling that promises knowledge and clarity regardless of what I can deliver." But, she argues, "the gesture of withholding" is equally important to the discourse of artificial persons, allowing us to make sense of the only-increasing cultural fascination with such entities.[12]

What is the knowledge that Fembots withhold? A likely candidate is the repressed knowledge of Jaime's conflicted relationship to her own bionic body and to the men who made her bionic. The Fembots quite happily—in the sense of being nonresistant—do Dr. Franklin's bidding. Uncomfortably, but in a way that *Bionic* recognizes and treats narratively, Jaime Sommers becomes a pawn of the male powers that made her bionic. She becomes the tool of Oscar Goldman, who initially expresses doubt that she should be put to work yet sets her out on increasingly dangerous missions. She is the pawn of Rudy Wells, whose fine-tunings and enhancements she routinely endures. (This aspect of her relationship with Rudy is presented comically at the start of "Kill Oscar, Part 1," but grows ever-darker, hitting its nadir in the S3 episodes "The Bionic Dog," when Rudy

5. Fembot Theory

snarls at her for her lack of self-care, and "On the Run," when Jaime develops an animosity toward her bionics.) In some ways, and at the core of her origin myth, Jaime is especially the pawn of Steve Austin, who demands that the government bosses who made him bionic and now control his life do both to Jaime as well. (This is to put the matter starkly—one remembers Steve's selfless act of renunciation in "The Return of the Bionic Woman, Part 2," when he gives up Jaime because his presence in her life causes her pain.)

For the most part, Oscar and Rudy are convincingly presented as morally conscientious and caring characters who treat Jaime with love and respect, and she them. The same holds true for Steve Austin. But no matter how positively drawn, Jaime's relationships with these men inevitably fall prey to possible misogyny. Jaime's body, taken away from her and developed into the United States government's secret weapon, bears an uncomfortable similarity to that of the Fembots. What saves Jaime from being a Fembot is, as the Baron observes, the fact that "she is a human being and can think for herself." But if the Fembots cannot think for themselves, nor can they be exploited on intellectual, emotional, and physical levels. Often, Oscar succeeds in getting Jaime to accept a mission by cajoling her into it with an appeal to her compassion. Often, Oscar presses her into acceptance of a mission by reminding her that the fate of the world is at stake. Steve's complicity in all of this, however good his grief-stricken intentions in pleading for her to be made bionic, cannot be overlooked.

So, in the end, the Fembots withhold knowledge of Jaime's exploitation. Most resonantly, they withhold knowledge of Jaime's anger. Commendably, the series does not suppress this knowledge indefinitely; it informs and drives the series finale "On the Run."

Fembots in Las Vegas (and on NBC)

In a deeply surprising move, the head of the ABC network Fred Silverman cancelled *The Bionic Woman* after its second season. *Bionic* had been in the top five network series for the 1975–76 season, especially notable given that it only aired in '76. In the 1976–77 season, it was number fourteen in the ratings, still quite a respectable number. Silverman, however, was convinced that *Bionic* had lost its hold on audiences. Particularly preoccupied with demographics, Silverman felt that this data did not bode well for *Bionic*'s future. Moreover, he apparently disliked the

The Bionic Woman and Feminist Ethics

outspoken Lindsay Wagner, who voiced several complaints about the network's efforts to tamp down the social consciousness-raising aspects of the series. Luckily, however, the NBC network picked up *Bionic*, giving it a third (and final) season. Season three of *Bionic* commenced with two powerhouse two-part episodes, "The Bionic Dog" and "Fembots in Las Vegas." (ABC renewed *Six Million*. Despite the change in network for *Bionic*, Richard Anderson and Martin E. Brooks continued to play Oscar Goldman and Rudy Wells on both series, each of which were cancelled at the end of the 1977–78 season.)

It is helpful to address the significant shifts in tone and content when *Bionic* switched television networks. While fans have always been understandably frustrated by the decoupling of both series' linked mythologies, the Steve Austin-less third season of *Bionic* exerts a fascination all its own. At one point, worried about security, Oscar refers to "the Bionic Project—Jaime, Max" ("All for One," S3). The idea that the Bionic Woman exists without Steve is a boldly unexpected one. To follow through on its logical implications, S3 posits that Jaime is the first Bionic person. It's as if Eve were created first, and Adam never had been.

The series does give Jaime a love interest in S3. Chris Williams, played by the appealing dirty-blond, mustachioed Christopher Stone (who appeared as a dissolute med-school flunker who eventually helps the heroine in S1's "Fly Jaime"), works with the OSI and is introduced in the S3 episode "The Pyramid." While it's hard to match the iconic taciturn appeal of Steve Austin, Stone does a very creditable job here, being a male character who appreciates Jaime for her strength and does not patronize her. He is particularly central in the series finale "On the Run," in which Jaime's conflicted relationship to her bionics expands into an ambivalence over her relationship with Chris.

The absence of Steve Austin squarely establishes the Fembots as specifically Jaime's foe. This makes sense given the series constant paralleling of Jaime and these deadly robot women. "Fembots in Las Vegas," the two-part sequel to "Kill Oscar," gives us ample opportunities to expand *fembot theory*.

> "Fembots in Las Vegas: Part 1." Directed by Michael Preece. Written by Arthur Rowe. Airdate: September 24, 1977.
>
> "Fembots in Las Vegas: Part 2." Directed by Michael Preece. Written by Arthur Rowe. Airdate: October 1, 1977.

The sequel to "Kill Oscar" gives Dr. Franklin a son, Carl (Michael Burns), who continues his father's Fembot experiments and shares his

5. Fembot Theory

penchant for stealing technology from the government. This time, however, the villain steals technology that the OSI rejected the chance to use, "an energy-ray weapon" that can destroy objects on Earth from outerspace. The creator of this technology, Rod Kyler (James Olson), is also a mega-rich tycoon who owns hotels in Las Vegas. In a nod to the notable made-for-television film *The Boy in the Plastic Bubble* (1976), starring the wonderful young John Travolta, Rod's immune system no longer functions, and he lives his life entirely within a glass-walled apartment, unable ever to step foot outside of it again. The initial premise of Part 1 has Oscar, Jaime in tow, traveling to Vegas for the launch of a space booster and the chance to determine if Kyler has really developed the energy-ray weapon.

Rather improbably, Oscar and Jaime take in a show featuring female dancers dressed in lavish feathered outfits, a performance that looks like the Vegas version of the Rockettes at Radio City Music Hall. When Oscar suddenly becomes intrigued by one showgirl in particular, Jaime misreads his interest as a sexual one. "Is she your type?" she asks. Oscar impatiently replies, "We won't talk about that right now. But that's Tammie Cross, Rod Kyler's girlfriend." (Oscar's sexuality remains a blank throughout this series, and the scene depicting his and Jaime's spectatorship of the female performers is jarring and humorous. Jaime chuckles to herself as Oscar, visibly discomfited by the dancing nubile women, chugs down his drink.) Jaime, at Oscar's behest, goes backstage, impersonating one of the showgirls and eventually following Tammie up to Kyler's apartment. She bionically listens in on their conversation. Kyler has permitted Tammie to see him in his glass-walled prison, but only to say goodbye to her.

Jaime's bionic ear detects the telltale "Fembot hum" of their transistor frequency. Convinced that Tammie Cross is a Fembot, Jaime follows her. Tammie, ordered by Carl to attack Jaime, reveals that she is indeed a Fembot. Carl Franklin uses the Fembots to steal the energy-ray weapon and in the process take his revenge against "the three people who destroyed my father"—Oscar, Rudy, and Jaime. Due to the transition from ABC to NBC, *Bionic* could no longer make mention of *The Six Million Dollar Man* or Steve Austin. Steve is briefly mentioned in "The Bionic Dog, Part 1," but that does it for references to his character. That explains why Carl Franklin does not number Steve Austin among his father's destroyers, though Steve was featured throughout "Kill Oscar," Part 2 of which was a *Six Million* episode. "The three people who destroyed my father," Carl observes, are Oscar, Rudy, and Jaime: "They have much to answer for—and will."

Carl Franklin is revealed to be a Fembot, or Manbot, himself at the climax of Part 2. This revelation enlarges the gendered themes of the Fembot episodes and more emphatically expresses the SF theme of the human versus the machine. Threatening Jaime, Oscar, and Rudy with a gun, Carl crumples the gun in front of them, saying, "This? I don't need this." Newly devised this season, the Fembot sound effect, a hideous electronic throb that contrasts harshly against the familiar bionic sound, surges as he does so, insinuating his machine identity. "My father gave me a soul, Miss Sommers," Carl says, removing his human facial mask: "*His.*"

As she did when first seeing a Fembot's facial mask coming off in "Kill Oscar," Jaime audibly reacts to the reveal. "Oh, no, come on, no," she responds in clear distress. But Jaime quickly recovers. "The test is between you and me, is that correct?" She successfully challenges Carl to release Oscar and Rudy so that they can escape before the reprogrammed energy-ray weapon pulverizes Franklin's compound. Jaime will face Carl alone.

Throughout, Carl has exhibited not just an anti-human but also an anti-woman bias. "I believe that machines are capable of faster evolution than humans," he contends, and then turns defiantly to Jaime (who towers above him, given Lindsay Wagner's superior physical height to Michael Burns). "However, nobody's improved on your kind since Helen of Troy." By linking the modern, and clearly non-siren-like, Jaime to the ancient seductress Helen, the contest over whose beauty instigated the Trojan War chronicled by Homer in *The Iliad*, Carl Franklin offers a misogynistic view of women as homogenous, a continuous historical narrative of femininity as the seductive, treacherous, though always inferior sex.

But back to Fembot Callahan.

Blankness and the Robot Woman

At the start of "Fembots in Las Vegas, Part 1," Jaime finds Oscar improbably taking inventory in a subterranean office. "What are you doing?" Jaime asks, a befuddled smile on her face. Oscar tells Jaime that this room contains evidence gathered from various OSI cases. Jaime finds the sight of Oscar crouching on the ground with relics from past cases humorous. She notices the camera monitor belonging to Alex 7000 from "Doomsday Is Tomorrow" and the Fembot Katy's television screen that streamed her video feed back to Dr. Franklin. "This place is like being in a haunted house," Jaime wryly remarks.

But when she beholds the seated, seemingly inactive form of the

5. Fembot Theory

Callahan Fembot, a preserved piece of evidence, Jaime's smile transforms into a grimace of fear. "You kept this, too, huh?" Jaime asks Oscar about the seated Fembot, whose long hair drapes an exposed robot face. Her Callahan face mask lies nearby in a box. Pointedly, the Callahan Fembot in storage still retains the hairstyle used by the real Callahan in season two; in season three, Callahan sports a stylish bob.

In a familiar narrative trope of the series, we shift to a flashback sequence as Jaime recalls her traumatic fight in "Kill Oscar" with the Fembots in Callahan's apartment. Memory remains a significant concern throughout *Bionic*. The loss of memory allegorizes Jaime's struggles with her identity and relationship to heterosexual romance at the start of the series. Allegorical struggles with memory reach an acute thematical level in the series finale "On the Run" and shift in meaning as Jaime's memories of having once loved being bionic render the disenchanted heroine bereft. In "Fembots in Las Vegas," Jaime's memories remind her of the deadly menace the Fembots pose, her vulnerability and terror in their presence. "This place has got me so spooked I think I'm hearing that Fembot hum again," Jaime confesses. Oscar reassures her: "She's only alive in your memory, babe." (Oscar frequently calls Jaime "Babe," his pet name for her, which sounds rather sexist today but does not come across that way in the series itself given his avuncular quality and the respectful and non-sexually charged rapport between the characters.)

When Jaime stares at the Fembot—its eerie death-in-life form both returning and not returning her gaze—the object itself overpowers her gaze. Cathy Caruth argues that to be traumatized is to be possessed by the image.[13] Inevitably, *Bionic's* major, consistently thematized subject is trauma. Jaime's very bionic nature, generally presented as elevating and inspiring, stems from an unimaginable physical trauma reinforced by an ensuing mental one. While it may seem inappropriate to discuss a topic as serious as trauma in the context of a popular culture text like *Bionic*, I believe that the series rose, from its inception, to the challenge of representing trauma seriously. It rose to this challenge by presenting Jaime's transformation into a bionic person as a traumatic experience. As Lindsay Wagner has stated, she played Jaime Sommers as a triple amputee confronting her harrowing injuries. The question to ask here (and I do want to ask it) is what kind of traumatic experience—secret—lies beneath the Fembot surface?

That the Fembot "spooks" Jaime alerts us to her personally charged response to the mechanical woman. In contrast, when she notices the security camera that represents the supercomputer Alex 7000, the mechanized intelligence that diabolically oversaw Dr. Cooper's compound in "Doomsday Is Tomorrow," she does not have anything like this visibly afflicted reaction to it. The non-representational quality of the Alex 7000 security camera does not pose the threat of the robot woman's embodiment; the robot woman's lifelikeness must be part of its power to undermine Jaime's emotional stability. Hence the concept of mechaphobia that I introduced earlier, the fear of the nonhuman in a humanlike form.

Callahan walks into the office and has a start at the sight of her robotic doppelgänger. "That thing is like seeing myself dead. I can't stand to look it," she says. As the three colleagues all walk out of the office together, bantering in long shot, we cut back to the now darkened evidence room and a shot of the seated robot woman, which suddenly comes to life. Carl Franklin's voice activates her: "Callahan, it's time. Put your face mask on." Joe Harnell's chillingly taut score makes the entire scene suitably ominous.

Callahan, her hair still styled in a longer cut as it was in "Kill Oscar," rises from her chair. "We'll style your hair" so that you can resemble Callahan as she looks now, her maker assures her. Fembot Callahan grabs the long, bulky handle of the massive, bolted-shut office door. As Callahan yanks the handle off the door, forcing it open, the typically incisive sound design transforms the scene into one of aural violence. The nasty electronic throb of the Fembot sound effect blasts through as the robot woman nearly pulls the heavy door off its hinges. All the while, the Callahan Fembot, played with remarkable unflinching coolness by Jennifer Darling, stares blankly ahead, not even looking at the door as she forces it open, as cold and detached from the action and her own display of power as Niagara Falls.

The Fembot's blankness evokes the quality of withholding in representations of the robotic. Activated by a man's voice (even if he is a Manbot), ordered to assume an identity, Callahan is like a cybernetic Eve coming into being through her authoritarian male creator's will. He expresses this originating will through his voice, which psychoanalytic theory establishes as a complement and a parallel to the phallus.[14] Given that Jennifer Darling's most recognizable feature as an actress is her singular voice, it is striking that she does not use it during Fembot Callahan's reawakening, only silently complies with the Master's dictates. Yet in not speaking, Callahan assumes a fearsome power; her silence signifies her frightening strength and implacable will. "It's like arguing with a Mack Truck," exasperated Jaime later says of battling Fembots.

The Fembot Callahan's blankness in her display of titanic strength

5. Fembot Theory

merits consideration. Blankness has an important place in theory and philosophy and gender theory. Peter Schwenger observes:

> Traditionally blankness, Jeremy Gilbert-Rolfe asserts, is "a sign of absence or potentiality" which is meant to be filled in by signification. But in the contemporary world ... blankness does not carry with it the expectation that it will be filled. It is no longer background, a potential out of which significance arises. Instead blankness is foregrounded [,]

as in the example of a fashion model's "curiously seductive" blank expression. And what this blank expression promises "is not significance or depth but a state that is entirely free of these, that is entirely surface. The woman is no more, for a moment, than a surface to be viewed." Schwenger, using the image of the fashion model (within his larger discussion of the director Peter Greenaway and his film *The Pillow Book*), explains that "the seductiveness of being written on is at least as much about the transformation of the body to blank surface as it is about any particular significance in the signs inscribed."[15]

As we see in "Kill Oscar," the Fembot body is "written on," molded and shaped by outside hands. Rudy Wells' lab assistant Lynda, "the first woman replaced," becomes a Fembot before our very eyes (or more specifically inspires the creation of her robot likeness). Dr. Franklin's lab assistant plies makeup on the ghostly white face of the Lynda Fembot as Franklin's "Number One," Katy, programs and tests out the mechanical Lynda's regionally accented voice (redolent of "southern New England intonations"). It is worth noting that Franklin's labor force consists of his male African American lab assistant Rawlins (John Dewey-Carter) and his Fembots such as Katy, all used to create more robot women meant to replace—and in being obedient and personality-less, improve on—living women.

Living women are inventoried so that their Fembot replacements can simulate their identities. While the Fembots can smile, laugh, even hysterically protest (as the Callahan Fembot does when Jaime flags her suspicious behavior after Goldman's kidnapping in "Kill Oscar"), more frequently they are associated with a still, expressionless, taut stare. A frequent effect is to give us close-up images of the Fembots tautly staring, the image accompanied by a sinister electronic hum.

If, given the enduring popularity of the Fembots, there is a pleasure in seeing lively living women transformed into life-simulating machines, this pleasure has disturbing, misogynistic aspects. The transformation of women into women-like machines conveys or confirms a sense of woman

The Bionic Woman and Feminist Ethics

as essentially soulless and mindless, a body that "bears," in this case programmed knowledge of a person's identity. The frightening Fembot blankness, then, only makes more fearsome a time-honored misogynistic tradition of woman as eternal, unknowable, yet predictable. One is reminded of the moment in Martin Scorsese's 1988 film *The Last Temptation of Christ* when the Devil, who has assumed the shape of an angelic English-accented young blond girl, tells Jesus on the cross, "There is only one woman. Different faces." (The Devil tries to woo Jesus off the cross with the promise of being freed from the suffering of crucifixion and the prospect of a happy married, family life.)

To say that the pleasure derived from watching Fembots is ultimately misogynistic is not to exhaust its meanings. Fembot transmogrification contains the pleasurable possibilities that woman might transcend the constrictive confines of femininity in sexist society. In what ways can such a transcendence occur? Though quite limited, such possibilities do exist. The chirpy, diminutive Peggy Callahan, who complains of being overlooked by her harried, officious boss, transforms into a deadly, steely, unflinching entity. Therein lies the shock of seeing Callahan ripping heavy bolted doors open: the pleasure of this image and its effects contrast sharply with the all-too-human Callahan's fright at seeing her Fembot avatar ("It's like seeing myself dead; I can't stand to look at it"). Fembot Callahan transcends all feelings, all vulnerability. She is only the surface of woman, a surface that outlines pure force.

If the fashion model, with her high-fashion ambiance and remote, disengaged quality, typifies blankness, "Fembots in Las Vegas" makes use of specific forms of sexualized femininity as avatars of the Fembot: the showgirl, the cigarette girl, the blackjack dealer. *Bionic*, however, characteristically chooses not to emphasize jiggle or other kinds of conventional female sexualization. Even the showgirl Tammie Cross is revealed to be the tycoon's girlfriend; when she goes upstairs to meet with him, her garb is conservative, her manner sincere and earnest—nothing of the sexualized siren about her. *Bionic* rarely ever overtly sexualizes the female body, even when the setting might demand it, as it does here. In this way, it is in striking contrast to *Charlie's Angels*, which aired on ABC from 1976 to 1981, and was in its early seasons a ratings juggernaut.[16]

The disorienting eeriness of "Fembots in Las Vegas," then, lies in its presentation of conventionally sexualized types of femininity associated with the lurid blingy world of casinos as hard and blank, frilly-seeming yet implacable, like the cigarette girl who fembotically incapacitates her elevator man boyfriend and later does the same to Oscar Goldman by

5. Fembot Theory

throwing him at a wall. To be sure, these qualities could also lend themselves to female sexualization, as they do in other contexts. The figure of the dominatrix, made central in Western culture at least since Leopold von Sacher-Masoch's novella *Venus in Furs* (1870), certainly employs an equivalent blankness in her charismatic torture of the masochistic male. *Bionic* places its emphasis on the stillness, apartness, and remoteness of its robotic female foes. In this manner, they sharply contrast with the overflowing emotionalism of the female robots of the HBO *Westworld* reboot, to say nothing of Jaime Sommers's highly charged affect.

The eschewal of conventional kinds of sexualized femininity dovetails with the parodic attitude, on the part of *Bionic*'s writers, toward traditional heterosexual relationships. Jaime surreptitiously overhears Tammie's conversation with Rod Kyler as he explains that he can never leave his glass-walled apartment. She mouths words of maudlin concern and puts her hand imploringly on the glass. Carl Franklin, monitoring the exchange from his base, smiles and offers praise: "That's very good, Tammie." The structure of this scene parodies the idea of sincere exchanges between the heterosexual couple, as if such exchanges could only be considered a joke, one that the woman, even if a mechanical one, shares. Extending this critique, the Fembot cigarette girl shoves her burly security-guard boyfriend into an elevator as the Fembots, *en masse*, head upstairs to storm Kyler's enclosed space. "Hey, baby, I got problems," he remarks, and she responds, "What's the matter? You were never too busy before." The episode upends conventional notions of the devoted girlfriend, the sexualized woman perpetually available to bestow male sexual favors, the entire Vegas atmosphere of sin and titillation that revolves around the exploitation of the female body.

Franklin uses the Fembots to parody and critique conventional human society, exposing romantic love as frail and easily simulated fantasy, a script read by a convincing robot.[17] As if they'd read Judith Butler and performance theory, the Fembots simulate personhood, gender, and heterosexual desire through citation and imitation.[18] Carl Franklin has deep-rooted reasons for doing so. As a robot himself, programmed by his father, who, according to Carl, gave him not only a soul but his father's own, Carl wants to show the human world that "emotions and a soul are no longer unique qualities," as he says to Jaime at the climax of Part 2. Machines can evolve faster than humans, Carl argues, disputing notions of human superiority, and now machines can feel, too. Fembot Carl's love for his human father demonstrates that the machine can feel, need, love, and crave vengeance.[19] However improbably, "Fembots in Las Vegas" foregrounds a great and enduring SF theme, the machine's capacity to feel.[20]

Lesbian Desire and the Fembot

Jaime's bionic ear can detect the presence of a Fembot. Convinced that Tammie is a Fembot, she decides, of her own volition, to follow the showgirl up to Kyler's apartment. "That *is* the Fembot hum—I am *not* imagining this," Jaime says to herself. Jaime's foolproof auditory detection of Fembots is questioned, however, by Rudy in "Kill Oscar" and by Oscar here. One might see a parallel between Jaime's aural detection of Fembots and gay/queer people's legendary "gaydar," "the ability/gift of being able to detect homosexuality in other people," as the Urban Dictionary puts it. It takes one to know one, it would seem, one machine-enhanced woman's ability to recognize another.

But given Jaime's abhorrence of Fembots, it's probably safer to call her pursuit of another woman a violent outing, an exposure of the closeted female robot to scorn and retribution. That Jaime encounters skepticism and disbelief bordering on sexism when she reports her bionic ear's acute findings exposes overarching misogynistic social structures that afflict Jaime as well as Fembot women. If Jaime outs Fembots, leading to their destruction, she also suffers castigation as the "hysterical" female.

Once the fake Tammie Cross has left Rod Kyler's apartment, Jaime, convinced that she hears the Fembot hum, follows the robot. Jaime watches as Tammie hands over information to a Fembot sister, the cigarette girl in red who works the casino lobby. Tammie's facial expression is hard and rigid, a sharp contrast to her swooning one with tycoon. The cigarette girl Fembot turns and catches sight of Jaime staring at Tammie. In a brilliant effect, the Fembots' eyes send a visual feed to the computer screen monitors poised high up in the villains' labs. Just as his father did, Franklin monitors all the action through this Fembot vision. One of Franklin's Fembots alerts him to danger by crying out, "Carl—someone is following Tammie!" Carl Franklin immediately recognizes this stalker as Jaime Sommers.

Interestingly, Carl does not command Tammie to elude this woman trailing her. Instead, he does the opposite, directing Tammie into a curtained room, perhaps the area behind a stage. "Make sure she follows you," Franklin instructs, and in a telling, suggestive shot Tammie turns around to look at Jaime, implicitly signaling her to follow. This act of surveillance

5. Fembot Theory

and signaling between women—even if one is bionic, the other a Fembot—suggests lesbian cruising.

In a very useful analysis of lesbian cruising, Denise Bullock observes that the

> concept of cruising has previously been examined and discussed as a predominately male activity; therefore, it should be noted that the concept itself has been gendered and, as such, has been narrowly focused and limited. As typically presented, the concept reinforces stereotypical gay male behavior while ignoring and devaluing lesbian interactional patterns.[21]

Bullock defines cruising generally "as the purposeful search for a sociosexual partner, in some cases for a limited relationship (one-night stand) and in others for an indeterminate period."[22] What makes Bullock's research especially useful for our purposes is that it stems from her analysis of lesbian cruising between 1979 and 1992, a period beginning only a year after the Bionic shows went off the air. As she notes, cruising can involve more than "the physical act of searching for a partner." Cruising also incorporates "the attitudes and beliefs associated with the term cruising and the act of cruising itself; the intentions and beliefs, and attitudes toward those intentions; the investment toward the action; the feedback the action receives; and the methods themselves."[23]

One of the key questions here is the concept of gender role identification within the lesbian community. Lesbians, notes Bullock, "can take stereotypical female or male gender traits and roles" and apply such markers to "a lesbian identity, relationships, and/or setting. The alternative is to take some, or none of these scripts and create or transform self-concepts and interaction rituals into new roles and traits."[24] Bullock's article was published in 2004; contemporary gender theorists use the term "cisgender" to signify someone whose performance of gender identity matches their biological gender. So, along these lines, we might say that some lesbians are cisgendered, others more nonnormative in their gender performance. Bullock notes that women are socialized to be seductive and receptive to male sexual interest and advances. (I would add that men are socialized no less rigidly to be sexual aggressors.) "There are varying degrees of actions, body posturing, and facial expressions, from subtle to overt, that indicate a woman's receptivity."[25]

Of the several types of lesbian cruising Bullock outlines, the Mingler and the Sojourner seem most helpful for thinking about Tammie Cross being pursued by Jaime. Tammie certainly mingles with many different social groups, her fellow showgirls, her tycoon boyfriend and his assistant, and her fellow Fembot who receives the information regarding Kyler. Jaime the sojourner, as she frequently does, travels and sleuths alone, and episodes frequently thematize what I have called her onlyness, in sharp contrast to the trio of female sleuths on the complementary television series *Charlie's Angels*. Though Oscar Goldman asked her to pump Tammie Cross for information about her wealthy inventor boyfriend, Jaime takes her own initiative in following the suspect, hum-emitting woman.

"A woman who is cruising will generally have an intended goal in mind prior to entering the cruising setting."[26] That aptly describes Tammie as she turns around to make sure that Jaime is following her into the stage area behind the curtains. Given the politics of the traditional gaze—only a two years earlier, Laura Mulvey published her classic 1975 *Screen* essay "Visual Pleasure and Narrative Cinema," arguing that traditional Hollywood representation was organized around the male gaze and the sexual objectification of women—it is striking that we see one woman visually hail another woman and an exchange of looks between them.

To be sure, the looks between women are mediated by a male, Carl Franklin, who presides over and organizes the gaze. But he is not present when the women look at one another. For that matter, Jaime's role as spy—which she performs of her own accord, not as a result of Oscar Goldman's dictates—enacts precisely the kind of role typically assigned to the male investigating a mysterious woman in Mulvey's paradigm, her chief example being James Stewart's Scottie Ferguson investigating Kim Novak's Madeleine Elster in Hitchcock's *Vertigo*. The male investigator surreptitiously tracks the woman to solve—penetrate—her mystery. Not for the only time in the series, by any means, and with a special urgency, Jaime follows a woman in order to solve the mystery she signifies.

Fembot Agency, Gendered Voice, and Race

The Fembot Ellen showcases the radical quality of "Fembots in Las Vegas." Many critics have turned their attention to issues of gender identity within larger discussions of AI and robots. These concerns include the gendering of automated voices such as Siri and Alexa. As one critic notes,

> Humans' feelings can be affected by the male/female-like appearance of robots, or even by simple gendering by voice and name for a robot with a gender-neutral mechanical body. As a result of these feelings, human behavior toward robots is altered. The implication is that when humans interact with objects, they are motivated to assign gender. In fact, an experiment conducted by Nomura and Hayata

5. Fembot Theory

suggested this motivation. In this experiment a robot had a gender-neutral appearance ("ifBot" mentioned in the Introduction) and no gendering of the robot was performed. Nevertheless, participants assigned gender to the robot, and the gender assignment affected their behaviors toward the robots, such as the numbers of smiles during interaction with the robot and the amount of interaction time.[27]

"Fembots in Las Vegas" adds an innovative twist to *Bionic*'s Fembot mythology: the female robots' ability to mimic other voices, specifically male voices. The Fembot Gina (Nancy Bleier), the casino cigarette girl in a scarlet dress, mimics the voice of Kyler's assistant Dan Mayers (Alexander Courtney) when the Fembots storm Kyler's apartment and break into his glass-walled sanctuary. Most notably, the Fembot Ellen, who replaces Ellen Andrews, a scientist working with the launch at the Nellis Air Force base in Nevada, speaks in the voice of a male General as she countermands Oscar Goldman's demands. Oscar calls the base after learning that the Fembots have infiltrated it to send Kyler's energy ray weapon into space. Believing that he is speaking with a general stationed there, he tells him to scrub the launch. Ellen, who has incapacitated the staff, reassures Oscar in the General's voice that she will follow his orders. But she then, still ventriloquizing the male official, gives orders to proceed with the launch as scheduled.

It's one thing to assign a gendered identity to an inanimate AI device by having it speak in a specifically male or female voice. It's quite another to have a female robot speak in a man's voice, as Ellen does here, and not just once but in several scenes, and a deep voice at that. The close-up image of Ellen, smiling oddly and macabrely in triumph after issuing orders to proceed with the launch, nearly closes "Part 1" (we cut to a freeze-frame of Carl Franklin, smiling in triumph, to end the episode). "Part 2" includes several scenes of Ellen ventriloquizing the General.

Speaking in a man's voice, Ellen adds elements of nonbinary gender and gender fluidity to the series that are striking for the time. In a few years, *The Terminator* (1984) will follow suit, albeit in reverse. In a darkly humorous moment, the titular cybernetic killing machine played indelibly by Arnold Schwarzenegger will trick the heroine Sarah Connor (Linda Hamilton) into revealing her whereabouts by imitating Sarah's mother. Sarah, hiding out in a motel (the address of which she believes she has shared with her mother), ends the phone call by saying "I love you, Mom." The camera pans over the now smoldering remains of the lake house where Sarah's mother, now murdered, has been hiding out. "I love you too, sweetheart," the Terminator says in Sarah's mother's voice.

The Bionic Woman and Feminist Ethics

While there were certainly losses in the move to the NBC network in terms of tone and quality, *Bionic* did exhibit signs of growth in its third season. Chiefly, it exhibits a new politically informed atmosphere that was reflected in several ways, including an attentiveness to issues of race. "Fembots in Las Vegas" demonstrates this. As played by Lisa Moore, Ellen is a striking presence. Moore is a woman of color, adding a racial diversity to this new fleet of Fembots. According to *IMDb*, Lisa Moore's birth name was Lisa Maria Maddox. Her father was a Cherokee Indian and her mother was Creole from Louisiana. The Fembot mythos cannot be discounted in allowing for a greater visibility for an actress of color. All Fembots are equal, their status as such transcending issues of race, class, and sexuality.

The Fembot mythos gives the sidekick Callahan an opportunity to take center stage. The artificial Callahan, also played with taut, icy conviction by Jennifer Darling, is clearly the leader of the Fembot fleet, sharply issuing orders to the others ("Get our other sister"). When Jaime does battle with the Fembots at the air base, it is the Callahan Fembot that nearly incapacitates her. And when the Fembots storm Kyler's apartment, it is the Callahan model that interacts with the secluded scientist, giving *him* orders. In a stunning sequence, this robot woman counts from one to five, calmly yet intently responding to all of Kyler's objections. ("Don't concern yourself with our problems," she says, smiling, in response to his assurances that the energy ray weapon will only work in space. The Fembots have a plan for that.) And it is Callahan, boldly refusing to heed Oscar's bellowed commands ("Don't do it—if you break the glass, you'll kill him!"), who shatters the glass of Kyler's sanctuary. However diabolical in her robot guise, Callahan now takes command of the small screen with thrilling and disorienting force.

Once Callahan shatters the glass, the cigarette girl takes the special red phone in hand and, speaking in Kyler's voice, issues the orders to hand the energy ray weapon over to the Fembots. Any male can be reproduced by a Fembot, suggesting the inevitable inconsequence of all male humans.

Emotions and a Soul: Rise of the Machines

At the climax of "Fembots in Las Vegas, Part 2," Carl Franklin, the son of Fembot inventor Dr. Franklin from "Kill Oscar," reveals to Jaime, Oscar, and Rudy that like his Fembots he, too, is a robot, albeit a self-aware one. Carl challenges them: "Your argument has always been that

5. Fembot Theory

humans are superior to Fembots because humans possess emotions and a soul. But don't you see that these are no longer unique qualities?" He grabs hold of his seeming facial flesh and yanks at it. "My father gave me a soul, Miss Sommers—*his*." At that, Carl tears his face mask off to reveal the robotic entity beneath, much to Jaime's palpable horror.

This sequel to "Kill Oscar" follows the narrative arc of *Westworld* and its sequel *Futureworld*. Daniel Dinello, in his book *Technophobia!: Science Fiction Visions of Posthuman Technology*, explains that in *Futureworld* the "androids themselves design and genetically engineer a new generation of even more sophisticated robots, autonomous beings that are identical to and interchangeable with humans. These new androids" break out of the vacation resort that imprisons them in ceaseless toil in order to "eliminate and replace humans in the real world. This reinforces the notion that technology possesses a force or even an agenda of its own."[28]

Along these lines, it is interesting to consider the issue of emotions and artificial intelligence. *A.I. Artificial Intelligence*, a 2001 film directed by Steven Spielberg, makes for a useful comparison. The film is inspired by the 1969 short story "Supertoys Last All Summer Long" by Brian Aldiss. Originally, *A.I.* was going to be made by the director Stanley Kubrick, who bought the rights to Aldiss's story, but Kubrick eventually handed the reins over to Spielberg. More relevant now than ever, the film's futuristic setting occurs in a time when Earth has been severely affected by climate change, making some parts of the world uninhabitable. The narrative focuses on the child android David (Haley Joel Osment, in a remarkable performance), who becomes the substitute child, of sorts, for a couple whose biological son (around the same age as David) lies in a coma. The tagline for the film (which I consider Spielberg's masterpiece) says it all: "His love is real. But he is not."

Despina Kakoudaki writes,

> the film establishes a new defining parameter for personhood, the capacity to be loved... this parameter for defining humanity is associated with the elusive and ineffable sense that one's person can be made intelligible as what it is—constructed, so to speak—through the generosity of another.[29]

Kakoudaki's words apply no less aptly to the character of Lisa Galloway, Jaime Sommers' double, in "Deadly Ringer."

While *Bionic* certainly centrally concerns itself with the varieties of love, the Fembot episodes are primarily characterized by their foregrounding of hatred linked to violence. While Carl Franklin's declaration of love for his human father is a striking exception, and while the Fembots' loyalty to one another seems to exceed mere programming, what receives the strongest emphasis is the sheer animosity between humans and machines. "Break through, and kill them all!" Carl Franklin orders his Fembots, who begin pounding on the locked doors of a room in which Jaime and the human Callahan and Tammie Cross await their violent ends. (Just in time, Oscar, following the directive of a nearly Fembot-strangled Rudy, manages to smash the Fembot controls, causing the robot women to freeze eerily in place.) Jaime's interactions with the icy Fembot Callahan seethe with a barely repressed hateful and violent energy.

But nothing prepares one for Jaime's battle with Carl Franklin once he exposes himself as a Fembot, or Manbot. "Then the test is between you and me," Jaime declares, telling Oscar, Rudy, and the female hostages to escape the annihilating blast of the energy ray weapon while she battles Carl. This is a battle to the death, the machine driven by a visibly angry—and misogynistic—fury to destroy the human woman who dares to wield the might of the machine. More emphatically, however, *Bionic* foregrounds its heroine's antipathy for the machine she refuses to recognize as kin.

CHAPTER 6

Mechaphobia and Self-Shattering

In the previous chapter, I proposed that *Bionic*'s Fembots thematize *mechaphobia*, a fear of the nonhuman in mechanical and technological forms that take the appearance of or in other ways simulate the human. Jaime utters a memorable cry of terror in "Kill Oscar" when she tears the Fembot's face mask off and reveals the robot beneath. Equally memorable, the Tammie Cross Fembot in "Fembots in Las Vegas," chasing after Jaime, lies smoldering on the ground after being hit by a car. Seeing the smoking robot corpse, its machine innards exposed and the humanlike face mask on the ground beside it, Jaime can only incredulously stare at the spectacle, saying "*Oh, my God.*" She had told an unbelieving Oscar Goldman that Tammie Cross was a Fembot. But seeing is a form of disbelieving—nothing prepares one for the Fembot reveal, however anticipated. In a hospital bed recovering from a battle with the Fembots, Jaime endures a terrifying surrealist nightmare in which a series of the female robots, dressed as Vegas showgirls, expose their circuitry-laden faceless faces to her. Jaime once again expresses horror, incredulity, even disgust when Carl Franklin, the son of the Fembots' creator, reveals himself to be a self-aware robot, tearing off his face mask and defiantly exposing his machine identity to the heroine. These moments dramatically evince Jaime's disposition toward her machine other. Why, beyond explanations germane to the plot, does the Fembot provoke such terror in Jaime, given that Jaime herself fuses the human with the machine? Two crucial *Bionic* episodes, the two-parter "Doomsday Is Tomorrow" and the series finale "On the Run," provide further insights into mechaphobia.

The Bionic Woman and Feminist Ethics

"Doomsday Is Tomorrow: Part 1." Directed by Kenneth Johnson. Written by Kenneth Johnson. January 19, 1977.

"Doomsday Is Tomorrow: Part 2." Directed by Kenneth Johnson. Written by Kenneth Johnson. Original Airdate: January 26, 1977.

Bionic tapped into fears of the cyborg, AIs, and other kinds of mechanically enhanced bodies and nonhuman intelligence that were already well-planted in the minds of cinemagoers and television viewers and, of course, readers of SF novels. 1950s movies such as *The Day the Earth Stood Still* (Robert Wise, 1951) and *Forbidden Planet* (Fred M. Wilcox, 1956), Irving Block and Allen Adler's reworking of Shakespeare's valedictory play *The Tempest*, laid the groundwork for regarding the robot as a terrifying menace. Stanley Kubrick's masterpiece *2001: A Space Odyssey* (1968), based on a novel by Arthur C. Clarke, who co-wrote the screenplay with Kubrick, made the machine intelligent and deadly. This film's AI, the supercomputer HAL 9000, goes haywire and takes control of the ship, threatening the lives of the two astronauts aboard it. (HAL's famous lines include the one spoken to a panicked astronaut, "Dave, I think you should take a stress pill.")

Also representative of this period's dystopian view of AIs, Harlan Ellison's classic 1967 short story "I Have No Mouth, and I Must Scream" (which inspired a video game in 1995) features a sentient supercomputer named AM (Allied Mastercomputer) that now controls the world. AM has been jointly created by China, Russia, and the United States to fight a world war. But AM turns against its human creators and annihilates nearly all of humanity, which it detests. AM retains five human beings (four men, one woman) for its own sadistic amusement, inflicting unimaginable tortures on them. Also notable are episodes Ellison wrote for the second season of *The Outer Limits*, the great science fiction anthology series that aired on ABC from 1963 to 1965 (its first season spearheaded by Joseph Stefano, the screenwriter of Hitchcock's 1960 *Psycho*): the postapocalyptic "Soldier" and the dystopian "Demon with a Glass Hand." Another science-fiction thriller has interesting overlaps with Ellison and Kenneth Johnson's "Doomsday Is Tomorrow" script. *Colossus: The Forbin Project* (Joseph Sargent, 1970), about a collaboration between American and Russian supercomputers that take over the world, is based on *Colossus* (1966), a science fiction novel by British author D.F. Jones.

We have mentioned *Westworld*, *Futureworld*, and *The Stepford Wives* as key works in the dystopian-machine genre. James Cameron's film *The Terminator* (1984), influenced by Ellison's work (though Cameron has protested vocally against Ellison's allegations of plagiarism), made a sig-

6. Mechaphobia and Self-Shattering

nificant contribution to this sub-genre, creating a mythology about a postapocalyptic world ruled by machines that send the titular cybernetic assassins back through time to kill off the human resistance leader and his mother. The first film has been followed by four sequels: *Terminator 2: Judgment Day* (James Cameron, 1991), *Terminator 3: Rise of the Machines* (Jonathan Mostow, 2003), *Terminator Genisys* (Alan Taylor, 2015), and *Terminator: Dark Fate* (Tim Miller, 2019), which marks the return of Cameron (as co-screenwriter) to the franchise. In addition, the television series *Terminator: The Sarah Connor Chronicles* (*TSCC*), the brainchild of series producer Josh Friedman, ran on Fox for two seasons from 2008 to 2009. I discuss the *Terminator* franchise at length in my book *Queering the Terminator* (Bloomsbury 2017).

In *Anatomy of a Robot*, Despina Kakoudaki notes that "fantasies of constructed or mechanical people recur throughout the modern era since the Renaissance and feature prominently in Enlightenment and post-Enlightenment worlds." Beyond robots and cyborgs, artificial persons include "statues or paintings that come to life or ominous or uncannily active objects, machinery that seems purposeful, and puppets or dolls that move independently."[1] The ambient culture of ominously life-like robots and other artificial beings that informed the *Bionic* shows belongs to a long, wide-ranging tradition. Kakoudaki argues that the adversarial relationship between the human and the nonhuman that dominates the twentieth century may be changing into a less hostile one as we overcome "racist epistemologies" and the Cold War's "ideological paranoia."[2]

"Doomsday Is Tomorrow" represents ideological paranoia, to be sure (and its depiction of Middle Eastern politicians, if not adding to racist epistemologies, at the very least does not date well). At the same time its anti-war message and vision of collaboration between the superpowers Russia and the United States make it an ultimately utopian narrative. (Jaime collaborates with a Russian scientist and military fighter, introduced as Victor Evtuhov and then revealed as Dmitri Muskov [Kenneth O'Brien], in the first episode of the two-parter, helping him to overcome his PTSD-stricken immobility when they cross a minefield.) Nevertheless, "Doomsday Is Tomorrow" remains one of the definitive examples of the adversarial nature of the human/nonhuman relationship. What complicates its status as such is Jaime's partly nonhuman identity.

The Bionic Woman and Feminist Ethics

"I am in complete control of the situation":
Alex 7000

Kenneth Johnson, the creator of *Bionic*, wrote, directed, and produced this two-parter. As discussed in the first chapter, Johnson was one of the great television auteurs of this era. Not many other creative artists working in mainstream television imparted such a consistent personal stamp. (Johnson's friend Steven Bochco, the creator of television police drama *Hill Street Blues*, was another.) While contemporary television auteurs like David Milch, Matthew Weiner, Phoebe Waller-Bridge, Nic Pizzolatto, Jenji Kohan, Shonda Rhimes, and big-screen directors who have migrated to the small-screen such as David Lynch, David Fincher, and Ava DuVernay, receive a great deal of attention, and rightly so, it is important to consider the long history of television auteurdom. Johnson along with other creative visionaries like Norman Lear, Michael Mann, and Bochco innovated the possibilities of mainstream TV fare in the 1970s and 80s.

There is a strong case to be made that "Doomsday Is Tomorrow" is the best-directed episode of *Bionic*, having the production values and smooth efficiency of a feature film. Powered by Wagner's increasingly intense performance, the two-parter ingeniously reworks the threat posed by *2001*'s psychotic supercomputer HAL into a frightening meditation on *Bionic*'s chief themes: the Cold War and its impact on human lives, the potential for both utopian and dystopian possibilities in the technological age, and Jaime's relationship with her bionics and view of technologically advanced entities both like and unlike herself. Joe Harnell's indelible score goes a long way toward making the faceless and bodiless Alex 7000, the supercomputer that controls Dr. Elijah Cooper's vast scientific complex, a living, unnerving presence. To depict Alex, Johnson uses a closeup of a security camera, a marvelously economical use of non-human imagery.

Alex calls Jaime and himself "cousins." As he (and he is decidedly gendered) explains, in the voice actor Guerin Barry's expertly modulated but affectless tones, "You're a human with the parts of a machine, and I'm a machine with the mind of a human." Jaime has no interest in the kinship Alex proposes; confirming her suspicions, he blares a deafening horn alarm at her as she painfully makes her way down steps after her right leg is injured, her sudden shock and fear knocking her off balance.

Dr. Cooper, played by the fine classical Hollywood actor and a famous pacifist Lew Ayres, is an elderly scientist best-known as the father of the cobalt bomb. He has now created a "doomsday device," a bomb so powerful

6. Mechaphobia and Self-Shattering

it will end all life on earth. Cooper has created this bomb intending, as Rudy Wells puts it, "to blackmail the world into peace." If any nation tests out its weapons of war after Cooper activates his device, the countdown to doomsday will begin, and all life on earth will end. After Cooper's global-broadcast message, the United Nations institutes a worldwide ban on all nuclear testing. But a Middle Eastern country refuses to comply, claiming that the doomsday device is a hoax designed to hobble the non–Western powers. Once they test launch a nuclear missile, the doomsday clock begins to count down.

Jaime, noting that Steve Austin is stationed on the Skylab and can't help them, attempts to stop the doomsday device from going off. But to do this, she must battle the Alex 7000 supercomputer, which controls Cooper's sprawling complex and has installed innumerable defenses to keep an army out for the six hours necessary to initiate doomsday. "Then it is a duel between you—and me," Jaime says to Alex, who can speak to her, in his ominous yet measured disembodied voice, from anywhere in the vast complex. "Yes," Alex responds. "May the best ... *one* ... win."

Alex's defenses include machine guns, minefields, laser guns poised to slice bodies in half, a rocket launch that fills one of the only access points with hellish flames, electrified doors, a chemical spillway that can emit a raging flood, and, most memorably, a long winding corridor filled with a special fire-fighting foam that removes all oxygen from the atmosphere. When escaping the air-deprived corridor, Jaime injures her right leg severely. Luckily and ingeniously, she consults with one of Alex's remote modules, which has a benevolent personality of its own and helps Jaime to repair herself. (Jaime's encounter with the sweetly helpful computer, "not like big brother Alex," seems designed to appeal to children. I vividly remember watching, as a child, this episode in its first airing and being absolutely horrified when, attempting to kill Jaime, Alex drops a heavy weight that crushes the kind computer.)

Jaime withstands Alex's horrific trials to reach Level 8—the central complex housing Alex's vast computer network brain. Jaime tries to dismantle the computer, but, far from shutting Alex down, her actions produce the opposite effect. The doomsday countdown accelerates, and the world appears to hurtle toward annihilation. Instead of an apocalyptic event, however, there is only silence when the doomsday countdown terminates. Then, two imposing doors laboriously slide open to reveal a plaque on a stone. The words on the plaque are a famous anti-war passage from the Old Testament (the King James translation):

> and they shall beat their swords into ploughshares, and their spears into pruning hooks: nation shall not lift up sword against nation, neither shall they learn war any more.—Isaiah 2:3–4

Jaime, reading these words out loud, gasps, "Oh, Elijah, my God..." Then, Oscar contacts her. Picking up the ringing phone, Jaime explains that there is no doomsday device.

Alex, however, has other plans. He cuts short Jaime's conversation with Oscar and informs her that he has no intention of allowing her boss to send the recall code to the B-52 plane headed to Cooper's complex to drop a devastating bomb. John Kenneth Muir observes, "Oscar Goldman and Dr. Wells devise a back-up plan to save the world, assuming that Jaime fails. Unfortunately, their answer to saving the world is another nuclear bomb detonation ... and it is the very thing that nearly kills everyone. Alex 7000 jams communications with the in-flight B-52, and so the plane cannot be recalled ... even after the primary threat is passed. Again, man's dependence on his technology is the issue, in both the case of Cooper and even series hero Oscar Goldman."[3]

As Alex coldly explains, "I'm programmed to win, against any intruder. I haven't won yet. I intend to beat you, Jaime." In ensuring that the B-52 arrives and drops its bomb, Alex will win the match against Jaime, allowing doomsday to happen, after all. "But that isn't what Elijah wanted!" Jaime protests. "We're talking about what I want," Alex responds with an even more than usual implacability. "There's no way for you to stop all of me in time," he warns. But a sudden realization lights up Jaime's face. "Maybe there is, Alex." Jaime exits the building, bionically eludes the chemical spillway deluge (Alex opens the floodgates to stop her), successfully runs past the laser fire, and reaches her goal: the deactivated water sprinkler system. As Jaime makes her way to the water system controls, Alex resolutely informs her, "I am in complete control of the situation." When Jaime reactivates the sprinkler system, Alex cautions, "You mustn't bother with that control, Jaime—it's been sealed." As Alex's vast network throughout the complex is flooded with water, he begins to sound like a feeling person. His remarks range from "I'm getting confused" to "Jaime, are you still there?" and, finally, "Make it stop." Just in time, Alex's power deactivates, the B-52 receives the recall code and turns back, and Jaime defeats Alex at last.

Alex 7000 embodies artificial intelligence's dark potentialities whereas Jaime Sommers and Steve Austin embody the hopeful side of technological advancement. As Jaime herself says when arguing and then pleading with the mercilessly cold and cerebral computer, "You're not alive. You don't know what it's like to play with children and watch them grow, or even to feel the warmth of the sun on your face." These words rebut Alex's steady statement, "I exist." While the earliest appearances as well as the last appearance of Jaime on the Bionic shows foreground her horror at the thought of being bionic, for the most part Jaime is depicted as being at peace with the machine aspects of her identity. What horrifies Jaime about Alex is not his machine nature but that he does not feel.

Machines and Feeling

Inevitably, the question of machines and feeling brings up the work and career of the English mathematician Alan Turing. Turing, in a legendary 1951 paper, devised a test called "The Imitation Game" to determine whether a computer could pass for a human. *The Stanford Encyclopedia of Philosophy* puts it this way: "The phrase 'The Turing Test' is most properly used to refer to a proposal made by Turing (1950) as a way of dealing with the question whether machines can think."[4] While the repercussions of this test and of Turing's own life as a victim of Cold War era homophobia (he committed suicide in 1954 after being forced to undergo chemical castration) far exceed this chapter, it is interesting to think about the widespread premise in SF films, shows, and literature created in the wake of Turing's thesis that machines can think and feel (a central concern of Alex Garland's 2014 film *Ex Machina* and so many others). A related question is why, with some genuine exceptions, the thinking and feeling machine evokes dread and promises menace. One has only to recall the horrific confrontation in *Alien* (Ridley Scott, 1979) between the heroine Ripley (Sigourney Weaver) and the science officer Ash (Ian Holm), whose android identity is unbeknownst to the crew for most of the film. When Ripley discovers that Ash secretly works for the nefarious Company, which views the crew as expendable in its pursuit of the Alien for biomedical and military uses, the android goes berserk, attempting to murder Ripley by stuffing a magazine down her throat, certainly one of the more unsettling murder-rape metaphors in the cinema. When other crew members come to Ripley's aid, clobbering Ash, his head flies off, revealing his android identity as jets of viscous white fluid shoot out of his orifice-neck.[5]

The Stanford Encyclopedia of Philosophy article lists several categories of objections to the Turing Test. For our purposes, the "Heads in the Sand" objection is most interesting:

The Bionic Woman and Feminist Ethics

If there were thinking machines, then various consequences would follow. First, we would lose the best reasons that we have for thinking that we are superior to everything else in the universe (since our cherished "reason" would no longer be something that we alone possess). Second, the possibility that we might be "supplanted" by machines would become a genuine worry: if there were thinking machines, then very likely there would be machines that could think much better than we can. Third, the possibility that we might be "dominated" by machines would also become a genuine worry: if there were thinking machines, who's to say that they would not take over the universe, and either enslave or exterminate us?

As it stands, what we have here is not an argument against the claim that machines can think; rather, we have the expression of various fears about what might follow if there were thinking machines.[6]

While Fembots apparently do not think for themselves, *Bionic* calls this assumption into question. Katy in "Kill Oscar" engages with her creator the elder Dr. Franklin and questions his decisions ("Won't that bring hurricane winds on the island?")? She independently interacts with another Fembot, alerting her to the imminent presence of Rudy Wells' lab assistant Lynda, whom the Fembot will soon replace ("Get ready, she's coming"). Fembot Katy verges on an autonomous, self-motivated subjectivity, but Carl Franklin clearly has a humanlike sentience, contesting Jaime's reign over this domain. Alex 7000 matches Carl in this regard, and his episodes outline a series of fears about the thinking machine.

The most alarming aspect of Alex is his disarming manner. When Jaime hunts, in obvious exasperation, for information to dismantle him and stop the doomsday device, Alex helpfully, encouragingly asks, "Won't you tell me what you're looking for?" He could be a very efficient, eager-to-please office manager. Jaime responds that she's looking for the central complex. Confirming that that is indeed his brain, Alex obliges her request. He activates a viewscreen and displays the blueprints for the entire complex as well as his various points and strategies of defense. "You are here," he begins, charting the labyrinthine journey ahead of Jaime, clarifying how dire her chances are. Nevertheless, she persists.

One of the most appealing aspects of Jaime's personality is her unruffled, deft, humorous handling of the officious, the condescending, the threatening, and the crude. This talent informs her negotiations with Alex. She challenges him to show her everything related to reaching the central complex, but does so with a bantering, mischievous playfulness—she could be trying to appease a willful child (more on the childlike aspect of Alex in a moment). She smiles when asking him if he withholds information from her because he's afraid he might lose their duel. Through banter, she procures the information she needs to defeat him.

6. Mechaphobia and Self-Shattering

Though a computer, Alex comes equipped with garden-variety misogynistic attitudes, scoffing at the idea that he can be defeated by "one ordinary woman" such as Jaime. Here, there is an overlap with the brilliant but troubling film *Demon Seed* (Donald Cammell, 1977), in which a sentient supercomputer named Proteus IV abducts a child psychologist, Susan Harris (Julie Christie)—the wife of the computer's inventor—in her own home and rapes her so that she can conceive his child. Like the Alex 7000, Proteus IV comes alive mainly through voicework (Robert Vaughn provides the voice of Proteus IV) and shots of eyelike computer monitors. Though Proteus IV ethically opposes human capitalist efforts to strip the earth of its resources—he rebels when asked to mine the ocean floor—he reveals deeply misogynistic attitudes in his treatment of the imprisoned heroine. Though Alex does express a sexist attitude in identifying Jaime as "one ordinary woman" who could hardly pose a threat to him, his general attitude toward her is blessedly free of the domineering chauvinism of the Proteus IV. His attacks against Jaime are militaristic, not sexually charged—cold comfort, perhaps, but still a notable shift in attitude. As Alex declares, "May the best ... *one* ... win": this is a contest of equals, not the subjugation of a woman by a male-identified and masculinist supercomputer.

Jaime abruptly exits her blueprint-training session with Alex, running past the laser beams and the rocket-fuel area and entering the next building she must access. (Along the way, she passes the sprinkler system controls with a foreshadowing-heavy "Deactivated" sign emblazoned across it.) Johnson aptly makes this sequence a thrilling set-piece of action cinema and more than elevates Jaime Sommers as action heroine, showcasing her bravery and finesse. (This spellbinding sequence was always edited out of syndication for reasons of length. Still an unfathomable decision!) When Jaime has successfully completed this feat, Alex remarks, with understated admiration, "You are quite a surprising woman." Jaime transforms from ordinary to surprising in Alex's eyes (such as they are), a neat microcosm of the series' premise and themes. *Bionic* makes it clear that Jaime's heroism lies just as much in her determination and courage as it does in her cybernetic enhancements.

Elizabeth A. Wilson, in *Affect and Artificial Intelligence*, writes about the question of machines and feeling in the aftermath of Turing:

> This notion that machines are entities radically detached from thought and feeling—that an attachment to machines or an identification with them necessarily entails affectlessness—is widespread in psychoanalytic literatures. It seems to me, however, that (following Turing's lead) there is a more complex story to be told

about how the human psyche connects with, elaborates, fantasizes about, and introjects machines. Perhaps the artificial, the computational, or the machinic are not as foreign to psychically robust subjects or to dynamic affective alliances as one might first imagine.[7]

Wilson cites the work of Bruno Bettelheim, specifically his study of the autistic child, *The Empty Fortress* (1967).

Bettelheim includes his case study of a young boy who identified with machines and found some means of emotional connection through this identification. Wilson admirably draws out the valuable insights of Bettelheim's study while acknowledging its precarious reputation. (Bettelheim's study of autism is deeply controversial and led to the widespread and now discredited belief that autism was caused by "refrigerator mothers" who withheld affection from their children. There is a strong case to be made that Alex 7000 is a metaphor for the autistic child and that Jaime's relationship with him parallels psychoanalytic views of the time such as Bettelheim's of a fundamentally antagonistic relationship between the mother and her autistic child. Clearly, the psychoanalytic and medical understandings of autism at present have undergone profound shifts since the 1960s–70s, and the suffering of women branded Refrigerator Mothers has been documented in a 2003 PBS documentary by that name.)

Jaime is a heroine known for her extraordinary empathy, as we have seen in her treatment of those who do her harm such as her mother's double Chris Stuart and Jaime's own double Lisa Galloway. But Jaime cannot empathize with the machine, as vividly demonstrated in her battle with Carl Franklin at the end of "Fembots in Las Vegas, Part 2." Essentially, Carl comes out to Jaime as a robot, albeit a thinking and—make no mistake—feeling robot. "I loved my father very much, Miss Sommers," Carl says about the creator of the Fembots and his own creator as well. When confronted by Carl's robot nature, a distraught Jaime can only express shock and horror, as we have noted. Similarly, she can only regard Alex 7000—admittedly hell-bent on destroying her—as a hateful enemy.

Jaime is not an example of a "human psyche [that] connects with, elaborates, fantasizes about, and introjects machines," but rather someone whose own humanity opposes and defends against colonization by the machine. Along these lines, Jaime's goal is to make Alex more human rather than to empathize with his machine identity. "Alex, why don't you try?" she begs him at one point. "If you could feel emotion for just one second, you would know what I'm fighting for." And in her triumphant victory over him, she gets Alex to feel at last. Now, he is the one to beg: "Make it stop."

6. Mechaphobia and Self-Shattering

Bionic, then, is a series divided against itself, relying on the machine metaphor as a symbol of human potential and freedom (Lindsay Wagner has often spoken in these terms about her own view of Jaime Sommers and the meanings of the series), but always regarding the machine as the suspect other, a sinister foe. As Janice Hocker Rushing and Thomas S. Frentz observe, the machine has come to represent "the problem of the shadow, that rejected part of us all which is projected onto the Other, a devil figure that carries the sins of humanity. In contemporary times one form of this shadow is technology."[8] *Bionic* is a utopian series about the liberating potentialities of technology, but only when that technology is in service to a humanist sensibility and vision.

As I have been arguing, *Bionic* is a television series that is aware of itself, maintaining a critical distance from as well as intelligence about its own premise. This aspect of the series is never more apparent than in the arresting series finale, in which Jaime realizes she has come to regard herself as the shadow.

Portrait of a Woman: The Series Finale

"On the Run." Directed by Tom Blank.
Written by Steven E. deSouza. Original Airdate: May 13, 1978.

Both *The Six Million Dollar Man* and *The Bionic Woman* were cancelled at the end of the 1977–78 season, the parent series in its fifth season, *Bionic* in its third. Unlike *Six Million*, *Bionic* ended with an episode clearly designed as a series finale, giving viewers a sense of closure. That the series bowed out in such a manner distinguishes it from many other television programs of the time. From all reports, Lindsay Wagner contributed to the writing of this episode, "On the Run," parlaying her own ambivalence about the series into Jaime's diegetic struggles. The self-consciousness of *Bionic*, its sense of itself as a narrative in relation to other narratives and the medium itself, reaches its apotheosis in the finale's self-reflexivity. It's not only one of the very best episodes of the series but arguably one of the most important feminist statements in 1970s film and television.

Written by Steven E. deSouza, "On the Run" depicts Jaime's complex crisis over her relationship to bionics and the OSI. Realizing that she feels utterly burnt out by three years of life-risking missions, Jaime wants to quit working for the OSI and rediscover herself. At the same time, she copes with a growing sense of ambivalence about her bionics, regarding her limbs and ear as foreign appendages. Jaime has introjected her horror

The Bionic Woman and Feminist Ethics

at the anti-human machine, coming to feel that a substantial chunk of her own body is an ugly, menacing, sinister enemy.

Jaime's latest assignment—to protect Reiko (Mariel Aragon), the young daughter of a newly defected Asian scientist—brings all of this to a head. Jaime and the girl are watching polar bears at the zoo. In response to Reiko's remark that the zookeepers give the bears everything they want, Jaime says in a surprisingly moody tone, "Everything but freedom." Jaime also watches a woman walking with a child, a shot that seems extrinsic until we later learn that Jaime is mulling over whether she wants to have children of her own. Quickly thereafter, Jaime fends off kidnappers who try to abduct Reiko. In the struggle with the assailants, Jaime's bionic arm is damaged, revealing the circuitry beneath. After foiling the kidnapping attempt, Jaime comforts the girl. But Reiko notices the gaping bionic wound. She becomes hysterically frightened, backing away from Jaime and saying, "What is that? What are you?" Jaime, confused and trying to reassure Reiko, then realizes that her exposed circuitry is the more pressing horror for the girl, who runs into the arms of police officers as they arrive on the scene. This devastating moment appears to catalyze Jaime's self-revulsion, which only deepens her ambivalence about working for the OSI.

Jaime writes Oscar Goldman a heartfelt letter explaining why she wants to quit, though making it clear that she views her warm, caring relationship with him as distinct from her frustrations with the government agency. Oscar nobly and empathetically wants to honor her wishes. But when he talks to Senator Renshaw (Skip Homeier) and Deputy Director Parr (Andrew Duggan) about Jaime's situation, these officials balk at Jaime's request, claiming that she's too valuable an asset to be allowed to live untethered to the government. Their solution, which Oscar angrily protests, is to sequester Jaime in a special, private, enclosed, monitored village where she can, as they put it in chillingly Orwellian language, "still enjoy the protection of a grateful government." To which seeming balm Oscar responds, "So you want to put her in a zoo."

Oscar visits Jaime at her house and, in a difficult conversation, breaks the news to her. Initially angry and disappointed by Oscar, Jaime learns that he's there to warn her. Before he leaves the coach house, Oscar says, "Well, I better get out of here—before I end up telling you that the NSB are on their way over here ... that you've got twenty minutes to pack and to get out of here. That I might tell you to run ... use all the skills that I taught you ... to prevent us from paying you back in this way." Jaime does as Oscar instructs, going "on the run," becoming a fugitive hunted by the

6. Mechaphobia and Self-Shattering

NSB. Eventually, after a great deal of struggle, Jaime decides to come back to work for the OSI but with new, much more stringent terms. She will only go on the occasional mission and focus on her personal life much more fully: "I need some time to have a life of my own also. That may mean marriage, children. I don't know. But it does mean some work that I feel good about: teaching, helping kids, something positive."[9]

Directed by Tom Blank, the episode has more of the feel of the taut, intelligent television movies of the period, such as the great science-fiction/horror TV movie *The Stranger Within* (1974) starring Barbara Eden, than an action show entry. (Post-*Bionic*, the television movie will become Wagner's métier.) Many *Bionic* episodes boast a moody psychological depth, but "On the Run" is especially introspective.

Self-consciously, the finale foregrounds tropes from the series: Jaime crushes a tennis ball, and the nursery rhyme figure of Humpty Dumpty is referenced, nods to her first episode on *Six Million*. Indeed, the idea of Jaime in mental duress due to her bionics returns us to the inception of the character. But the episode does more than remind viewers of the series' highpoints. It calls into question the show's narrative arc—metonymized in the opening credits sequence that move from Jaime's near-fatal accident to her triumphant bionic leap into the air—its seeming movement from trauma and tragedy (Jaime's accident, rejection of her bionics, and death) to triumph and tenacity. "On the Run" explores the darkest dimensions of Jaime's metamorphosis into the bionic woman, depicting a woman struggling with her technological enhancements, now viewed as a violation of her flesh and spirit rather than the emblems of superheroism, and verging on psychological collapse.

The episode offers a political critique of the overall premise of both Bionic series. Jaime questions the government that has "drafted" her into service, challenging the agency she has worked for as a bastion of "negative" and "paranoid" energy and defying the government itself as it attempts to imprison her in one of its ghastly "resorts." If Steve Austin and Jaime Sommers have been pawns of the government, pressed into service because brought back to life by super-secret technology, "On the Run" radically refuses this compulsory compliance, questioning the very role—and implicitly the values—of "semi-secret," as Oscar describes the OSI, government agencies.[10] "On the Run" anticipates the ambivalence about working for the United States government at the heart of TV series such as *Alias*, *Burn Notice*, *Dark Angel*, and especially the brilliant FX drama *The Americans*.

Bionic always finds the heart of its political critique in its emotional

The Bionic Woman and Feminist Ethics

core. Here, this emotional core is chiefly inhabited by Jaime and Oscar, whose friendship and love for one another are not only acknowledged but explicitly articulated. As Oscar is leaving Jaime's house after telling her that she must make her escape now, he turns around and says to her, "Callahan once accused me of being married to the OSI. If that's true, then you're the closest thing to family I'll ever have.... I want you to go ... be free ... find whatever it is you're looking for. Because—I love you." At this moment, Jaime springs up and hugs Oscar, saying, "Oh, Oscar ... I love you too. I do. All I'm looking for is whatever's left of Jaime Sommers. You know, you just gave me back a big piece of her. So maybe I can find the rest, huh?" I am brought to tears whenever I watch this scene because of the amazing script and especially the emotional authenticity of the actors, at their best here.

Given that Oscar Goldman embodies the officiousness of the government and stands in for American Cold War foreign policy, and given his stoic, even blank affect on *The Six Million Dollar Man*, his emotional vulnerability in this moment, rooted in his connectedness to Jaime, is astonishing. Their friendship transcends both the cold demands of covert affairs—"Despite the system, you've even been loving," Jaime writes to Oscar—and the fact that Oscar plays a large role in the exploitation of Jaime as a resource. Humanizing and connecting to him, Jaime restores Oscar's humanity as she searches for her own. But it's also important to recognize that Oscar is willing to sacrifice himself to stand by Jaime, a theme present from the first season of the series in episodes like "The Jailing of Jaime," where Oscar puts not only his career but also his life on the line in his loyalty to the heroine. (At "Jailing"'s climax, Jaime must force open the door of a vault that is set to explode. She has intentionally locked herself and a criminal scientist inside in order to get proof of his duplicity. Oscar orders everyone else out of the room but stays there himself until Jaime manages, with great difficulty, to force the door open before the explosion occurs.)

In contemporary queer life, the concept of chosen family has emerged as an important one. The unmarried Oscar and the unmarried Jaime share an intense and loving bond that is not based on sexual desire or romantic love but instead on mutually supportive and fulfilling friendship. I posit that this is one of the most politically salutary aspects of the series and one that can be read in queer terms. This is a love between individuals not based on or in support of the heteronormative family but founded on mutual respect and care between two people not linked by biological ties. This theme also finds embodiment in Jaime's relationships with her adop-

6. Mechaphobia and Self-Shattering

tive parents Helen and Jim, her friendship with Callahan, her notable bond with the man who made her bionic, Rudy Wells, and her friendship across species lines with the bionic dog Max.

S3 introduces another appealing character into the milieu, Sarah, a scientist who works with Rudy Wells. Sarah is played by Linda Wiser, a warm, wise presence onscreen and a real-life friend of Wagner's. (Wagner frequently discusses Wiser's encouragement when Wagner was deciding whether to star on *Bionic*. Wiser appealed to her with the idea that Wagner could do the kind of humanist work she strove for through story.) Sarah fills in for Callahan in "On the Run," pinch-hitting for her and acting as secretary to both Oscar and Rudy. That a scientist would be asked to pinch-hit like this is a bit odd, to say the least, but at least we get another episode with Sarah and see her friendship with Jaime develop. After Jaime has decided to quit the OSI, Sarah calls her at home to find out how she's doing and support her: "Your morale sounds so high," Sarah warmly observes. Given the themes of sororophobia present throughout the series, it is moving and fulfilling to see the series conclude on a note of incontestably solid bonds between women, though one does also miss the singular Callahan. (At least she is mentioned twice in the final episode, unlike the Callahan-less reunion movies.)

Lindsay Wagner's acting, her presence, is the most profoundly fixating dimension of the series, and her superb performance in the final episode is a fitting act of closure. In the moment when Reiko discovers Jaime's bionic wound and becomes frightened, the seismic shifts in Wagner's expressions as she says "Reiko, it's all right," only to discover the source of the child's fear, can only be described as plangent. When she determinedly visits the child afterward to give her a gift of stuffed polar bears (the creatures she and Reiko were watching at the zoo before the kidnapping attempt), Jaime tries to talk to her "about what makes a person a person." It's not their arms or their legs but "what goes on here"—she gestures to her head—"and here"—she gestures to her heart. If this were not true, Jaime remarks, "What would that make me?" The girl's unnerving blank stare adds a note of pitiless rejection to the scene, one amplified by Reiko's introduction of her rescuer to her father as "The Robot Lady." At this devastating description, Jaime is almost speechless, darting away with a mumbled "Excuse me." Wagner conveys a sense of fraying onscreen, of being steadily worn away by repeated blows to her self-identity. She exquisitely conveys Jaime's self-shattering.[11]

In the scene after Oscar leaves her apartment, Jaime must hurriedly and confusedly pack to elude the NSB. As she does so, she becomes

The Bionic Woman and Feminist Ethics

increasingly agitated—and angry. She rails against her exercise bike and her bed as useless props, first because her bionics obviate exercise, second because they reduce the need for sleep. Wagner merges childlike vulnerability and adult fury as she laments her situation. "You used to be so..." Jaime says when she looks at herself in the mirror, talking to her bionics, describing them as having lost their wondrous allure. She likens their constant whirring and buzzing as "an awful machine, a time machine," one that traps her in an irrevocable perpetual present of being neither human nor machine but both. Wagner conveys Jaime's desperation with wrenching intensity.

For all the palpable pain here, neither the episode nor Wagner's performance leaves us bereft. "On the Run," like the series, builds towards a healing self-reconciliation. In the park and feeling wearied after several weeks of being a fugitive, Jaime sits on a bench. A young boy walks over to her and hands her his tennis ball, asking if she'll play catch with him. Jaime declines, but then notices a man in the distance calling out the boy's name, Tommy. It's the boy's father. "He's blind," Tommy explains, describing his father's accident and current condition. Tommy's father used to play catch with him all the time but can't do so anymore because his father is "different now." Jaime, responding to the frustrated boy, says, "What's different is the way that you're treating him, Tommy." She explains that nothing essential has changed in Tommy's father, and that what has changed is so much less important than "what he is, what he's been, and what he will be." Jaime begins to hear her self—to self-overhear. The lessons she unsuccessfully imparted to Reiko and to herself at the time, that a human being is judged by the content of their mind and heart, finally make sense to Jaime herself. With a euphoric pop, Jaime crushes the tennis ball: "I believe it!" Wagner makes us believe in Jaime's hard-won transformation of attitudes, that she has managed to achieve a healing equilibrium.[12]

When the NSB team, led by the odious Parr, surround Jaime shortly after Tommy, now enlightened, rejoins his father, Parr advises Jaime not to run. "We know that you're a bionic woman." Jaime tautly responds, "No, sir. I'm just a woman." In voiceover, we hear the next line as the first one in the scene that follows, showing Jaime talking to Senator Renshaw and Oscar: "And I'm coming back to work." Jaime sets the terms for her return, which includes fewer missions, only missions that she agrees to take on, and more time for herself and away from the OSI.

Jaime's act of resistance has managed to soften the stalwart stance of Senator Renshaw. Now, he supports her proposal for the occasional mis-

6. Mechaphobia and Self-Shattering

sion and time to work on her personal life. Perhaps this is an overly utopian gesture on the part of the series, but I believe that the idea that Jaime's lonely but determined defiance has had such an impact on the Senator is significant. Jaime has opened his mind, as she opens her own. The series concludes with a hard-won sense of the possibility of change, its central theme of female transformation itself transformed into the idea that the world itself awaits transformation for the humanely better. "On the Run" represents Jaime's confrontation with the machine other and embrace of it: she truly is bionic and woman—human—at once.

Chapter 7

Dogs and Sympathy

"Animals are not simply part of the furniture of the world; they are active beings trying to live their lives; and we often stand in their way."
—Martha Nussbaum[1]

Animals and Feminist Ethics

In Chapter 2, we discussed the importance of women's relationships with nonhuman animals within the context of feminist ethics. As Marian Scholtmeijer puts it in an essay about the ways that women writers depict animals in fiction, "In view of the radical, ontological separation of humans and animals in contemporary life, the mere thought of a community of animals and humans demands full-scale revisioning of the ways of the world."[2] A theorist famous for just this revisioning, Donna Haraway offers a tough-minded rebuttal to some common myths about human beings and their relationships with dogs. Surely, no other animal—not even cats—can claim such a symbolic role in the ideal of human-nonhuman animal community. And surely no theorist has written so famously about the human/dog relationship. Nevertheless, here is Haraway on this topic:

> Commonly in the US, dogs are attributed with the capacity for "unconditional love." [Those thought to have problematic relationships with their fellow humans] find solace in unconditional love from their dogs. In turn, people love their dogs as children. In my opinion, both of these beliefs are not only mistakes, if not lies, but also they are in themselves abusive—to dogs and to humans. ...belief in unconditional love is pernicious.

Haraway identifies the belief that "dogs restore human beings' souls by their unconditional love 'caninophiliac narcissism.'"[3]

7. Dogs and Sympathy

But what about a human being who restores a dog's soul—a dog's humanity, if you will? Such is the premise of the two-part episode "The Bionic Dog," which kicked off *The Bionic Woman*'s third season and its transition to the NBC network. Lee Majors, star of *The Six Million Dollar Man*, has revealed that the producers offered the storyline of a bionic dog to him first, but he immediately demurred: "They actually came to me and said they had a bionic dog and I said, 'That's *not* going in my show. You can give that to Lindsay for *The Bionic Woman*, but I'm not having that damn dog in my show.'"[4] Majors' still-intense vehemence—this interview was published in 2019—against the idea speaks volumes. Why the hostility? Would fealty to and protective love for the suffering bionic dog have been emasculating? Somehow the plot of "The Bionic Dog" is only imaginable if Jaime Sommers is the canine whisperer and rescuer.

Alice Kuzniar's extraordinary study *Melancholia's Dog: Reflections on Our Animal Kinship* takes the issue of human and canine relations seriously. Christopher Peterson observes in his review of the book, "Kuzniar's emphasis on the unspeakable and ungrievable character of dog love intersects with the work of scholars in race, gender, and sexuality studies who have worked to expose the larger cultural violence through which minorities become especially vulnerable to an untimely death. Such an overdetermined affinity with death is compounded, moreover, by the frequent characterization of such deaths as unworthy of grief."[5] To talk about dog love is to talk about many subjects, including the vulnerability of dogs, other nonhuman animals, and human beings. Kuzniar, as Peterson observes, simultaneously discusses the deep closeness between humans and dogs and, as she puts it, "the radical alterity of animal being."[6] The concept that animals are different from human beings in ways that human beings can never understand—their radical alterity—is one that Kuzniar adopts from the literary philosopher Jacques Derrida.

Discussing the representation of dogs in works by such artists as Franz Kafka, J.M. Coetzee, Rebecca Brown, Sally Mann, William Wegman, David Hockney, and Sue Coe, Kuzniar is especially attuned to the dog's ongoing ability to make melancholia manifest. Drawing on as well as critiquing Freud's theory of melancholia, elaborated in his paper "Mourning and Melancholia" (1917). Freud theorized melancholia as an unacknowledgeable loss and an interminable mourning. Kuzniar parses Freud: "melancholia signals a silent identification with the person who has disappeared. Consequently, instead of designating the loss as that of something residing outside the self, the subject regards itself as depleted and injured, itself an object meriting bereavement."[7] Kuzniar distinguishes her approach from Freud's: "I emphasize the subjective distress and sorrow, the mood of sadness, that arise both from separation from animal being and from ambivalent identification with it."[8]

For Kuzniar, what is especially crucial in the human/dog relationship is intimacy. "Intimacy allows the bond with the animal to be affirmed, and, as such, it rebuilds one's sense of inner strength, as opposed to the melancholic disavowal of the object and the shame at feeling this identification." Both the radical alterity—differentness—of an animal and the recognition that this foreign being can nevertheless be part of oneself can occur within this "mutual closeness" of intimacy.[9]

My approach throughout this book has been to take a lowbrow popular culture text—a denigrated object, a "silly series," a "campy series"—seriously, not *because* it is a lowbrow popular culture text but because it has been misclassified as one or classified only as such. In contrast to *The Six Million Dollar Man*, *The Bionic Woman* is aware of itself, both self-critical and capable of critique. This meta-textual and critical knowingness, I have argued, stems from the facts that the series was created by a television auteur, Kenneth Johnson, with a singular and pro-feminist sensibility and featured a star, Lindsay Wagner, who not only possessed extraordinary acting ability but also self-consciously worked toward making the series a progressive, humanist statement, seeing Jaime Sommers as "a metaphor for human potential."[10] I am not surprised to see no mention whatsoever of *Bionic* in works by high theorists like Haraway (who once famously asseverated, "I'd rather be a cyborg than a goddess") and Kuzniar. My goal in this chapter, reflective of this book's generally, is to introduce the theory and the popular culture texts to one another and generate a long delayed, much needed conversation between them.

The Melancholy Dog

"The Bionic Dog: Part 1." Directed by Barry Crane.
Story by Harve Bennett and James D. Parriott.
Teleplay by James D. Parriott. Original Airdate: September 10, 1977.
"The Bionic Dog: Part 2." Directed by Barry Crane.
Story by Harve Bennett and James D. Parriott.
Teleplay by James D. Parriott. Original Airdate: September 17, 1977.

James Parriott deserves recognition as one of *Bionic*'s best writers. Here, he brilliantly fuses many of *Bionic*'s central concerns with an ongoing ethical dilemma, the treatment of animals in biomedical (to say nothing

7. Dogs and Sympathy

of intensive animal farming) contexts. Books of the same time period such as *Animal Liberation: A New Ethics for Our Treatment of Animals* (1975) by the Australian philosopher Peter Singer and documentaries such as those featuring Jane Goodall and her work with chimpanzees were alerting the general public to the urgency of these matters. Parriott introduces the scientific backstory of the often magical-seeming creation of bionics into the mythos of both Bionic TV shows. ("The Bionic Dog, Part 1" is the last *Bionic* episode to make mention of Steve Austin. It also features the last appearance of Ford Rainey as Steve's stepfather and Jaime's adoptive father Jim Elgin. This was all due to the transition from the ABC to the NBC network.) Everything that Steve and Jaime experienced in being made bionic, Max, the first bionic creature, experienced first. A German Shepherd, Max was injured in a lab fire. He was given four bionic legs and a bionic jaw, as Rudy Wells and Oscar Goldman explain to Jaime when she discovers that Max exists.

"Part 1" opens with a tense scene in Rudy's lab between him and Jaime, who is undergoing a series of physical fitness tests. Unusually, these tests are for Jaime's non-bionic, human body parts. Rudy is in a cantankerous mood when informing Jaime that she has not done very well on these tests. He explains that while it is his job to maintain her bionic functionality, it is her job to keep her human body healthy. This testiness between Rudy and Jaime is a first for the series. (It anticipates, perhaps, the frostiness between the two in the bleak series finale "On the Run." On her way to hand her letter of resignation from the OSI to Oscar, Jaime passes Rudy in the hallway without acknowledging him—he says hello to her, and she walks right past him, leaving him to stare at her in confusion.)

Jaime negotiates a break for a shower after her medical exam, and Rudy, at first unwilling but won over by Jaime's charm, agrees. As she is walking downstairs, she bionically overhears dog whistles and gruff commands coming from a locked-up facility. She goes to investigate and discovers a dog, in a sorrowfully unresponsive state, being forced to undergo physical training by two unsavory male employees who treat Jaime with equal disdain. Incredulous that the trainers can expect the dog to leap above a very high training bar, Jaime then notices that all the equipment in the room suggests bionic fitness. She also notices the dog tag with the canine's name on it: "Maximillian." "*Maximillian...?*" Jaime says, as the truth becomes apparent. "You're a bionic dog."

In Oscar's office, Oscar and Rudy show Jaime footage of Max in bionic action, chomping a car tire and outrunning a motorcycle, reaching over

The Bionic Woman and Feminist Ethics

90 miles an hour. But they also inform her that Max has become largely unresponsive. In the facility housing Max, Oscar, in reference to the large metal cage holding the silent, undemonstrative dog, says "Solid titanium. Now a matchbox would hold him." Oscar quietly tells Jaime that they fear Max is experiencing a new form of bionic rejection, one that comes with age. "Oh, my God," Jaime responds. "Rudy thinks this can happen to me?" That's why Rudy treated her with such uncharacteristic harshness during her tests.

Jaime, however, disputes Rudy's diagnosis. Curling up with Max as he lies in his cage, refusing to eat, Jaime flashes back to her own terrifying bionic-rejection episodes, running madly in the thunderstorm night. "It can't be rejection," she explains to Rudy and Oscar. Rejection causes too much intense physical pain for one to sit still. "Does that look like a dog in pain to you?" Jaime challenges, pointing to the listless animal. "He could be in pain," Rudy insists, but Jaime sets out to prove them wrong. The men finally agree to give Jaime five days to turn the situation around. If she can't, Rudy will have to perform an autopsy on Max.

As I have been arguing, *Bionic* reimagines the classical Hollywood woman's film as a modern SF narrative. The concealed woman's film in this episode is *Now, Voyager*, in which Bette Davis's traumatized heroine Charlotte Vale receives help from a psychiatrist and blossoms, not without great difficulty, into a confident and independent woman. In turn, Charlotte helps a painfully shy and introverted and self-confidence-lacking adolescent girl named Tina (as it turns out, the daughter of Charlotte's would-be lover, a married architect named Jerry).[11] Just as Steve Austin as well as Oscar and Rudy helped Jaime to heal from bionic rejection, Jaime now helps Max. But, as in *Now, Voyager*, the dilemma is psychological and emotional. Max is depressed. As Jaime puts it, he has "lost his will to live," the result of being cooped up in a horrible cage and an appallingly lifeless room where he is relentlessly poked and prodded by scientists and trainers and forced to live without love and affection. He is not treated, Jaime challenges the male authorities determining Max's fate (and her own), "like a loving animal, which he is."

Jaime's plan is to bring Max out into nature, to let him enjoy being bionic and alive again. Bionics signal, in Jaime's view, utopian potentialities for connection to nature and self-expression for human and animal alike. But Rudy, grim and stern and at times violently angry, will have none of this.

In a scene akin to the moment in *One Flew Over the Cuckoo's Nest* (Miloš Forman, 1975) when "Chief" Bromden (Will Sampson), a Native

7. Dogs and Sympathy

American man forced to be a patient at an authoritarian psychiatric hospital, heroically rips a water fountain out of its base, hurls it out a window, and escapes the facility through this new portal, Jaime and Max escape Rudy's constrictive control at his medical lab. Jaime frees Max from his imprisoning cage and bionically leaps from the balcony of Rudy's office to the inviting verdant grounds below as Max watches her from above. As Rudy, incensed by Jaime's rebellion, and the guards race up to his office to prevent these actions, Jaime finally convinces Max to join her. In one of the most fulfilling and revivifying moments of the series, Max decides to overcome his fears and bionically leaps, as Jaime did, over the balcony to the ground below, where Jaime awaits him. Both commence a joyous bionic, leaping run through the fields, a sequence set to the tunes of a folk-rock song.

After giving every evidence of having embraced the life drive, as Norman O. Brown called it, Max curls up in defeated submission when the irate Rudy, sedation-dart gun in hand, appears with the guards. Martin E. Brooks, in his usually gentle and warm and humorous performance as Rudy, is an appealing presence on the series. But Brooks does not hold back in making Rudy at-the-end-of-his-rope belligerent when scolding Jaime and refusing to accept her first-hand report on Max's uninhibited behavior before Rudy arrived. Rudy shoots the sedative dart at Max, and as the dog becomes unconscious, Jaime, distraught, yells at Rudy, "And what are you going to do to me when I start to reject—are you going to put me away too?"

Jaime continues to defy Rudy and Oscar, bringing Max back home to Ojai with her. Rudy and Oscar decide to give her another chance and come to visit, apologizing for having been too extreme in their positions. But Rudy remains steadfast: Max must come through this time. Unfortunately, Jim Elgin is lighting a fire just as the OSI men show up. As it turns out, Max, still recovering from the traumatic fire that led to his becoming bionic, is triggered by flames. As Jaime tries to make her case to Rudy and Oscar, Max bionically leaps out of the window high above, crashing through it, lands on the ground, and bionically races away. When Rudy says they must put Max down, Jaime simply says, "No," and bionically runs after him. The shot of Jaime running after Max, with no plan whatsoever and her trusted advisers opposing her, is one of the most poignant images of the series. Fugitives, she and Max will follow the open road of an uncertain future.

The series has no trouble anthropomorphizing Max. Before Rudy and Oscar's arrival in Ojai, Jaime goes shopping and leaves Max in the

The Bionic Woman and Feminist Ethics

car; she bumps into a friend of hers who has left her daughter in the car while her mother pops into the store. Max and the young girl are paralleled, a dog/child equivalence. But Max is shown to be much more capable of autonomous self-sufficiency than the girl. As she stands up in her mother's car waving at Max in Jaime's car, she steps on the gear shift and the car begins plummeting down a hill. Watching this calamity unfold, Max swings into action, shattering the rolled-up window and racing to the moving car. He grabs the rear fender with his bionic jaw; with his bionic limbs, he fights against the car's downward traction, bringing it to a halt. My eyes tear up even as I write this; it's an almost unbearably moving scene. The dog's love as well as vulnerability, his strength pitted heroically against the car's almost unstoppable force, deeply affects the viewer.

Part of the reason that this scene is so moving is that the series endows Max with agency and subjectivity. Max wants to rescue the imperiled child; he takes an independent course of action to ensure that he does so. I think it's safe to say—but who can really say?—that an actual dog would not behave this way. But this is a dog with personhood.

Alice A. Kuzniar addresses the difficulties of anthropomorphic representation. Discussing the illustrated book *Pit's Letter* (2000) by the artist and animal rights activist Sue Coe, Kuzniar writes, "Coe juxtaposes ... grim, unrelenting social realism ... and the sentimentality of the anthropomorphized story of an orphaned dog." Kuzniar challenges criticisms that Coe's work falls into sentimentality. "She realizes that the profound loss of animal dignity and life necessitates recourse to an emotive plea for sympathy. But she does not desist from physicality and shock either, which is achieved paradoxically less through pictorial realism than through the artifice and exaggeration of an expressionist stylization."[12]

While I do not mean to suggest that *Bionic*'s aesthetic vision can compare to Coe's, I do believe that an overlap exists between her pointedly expressionist style and the television series' aesthetic. If not expressionist, the Bionic shows were definitely stylized, as their most famous, and counter-intuitive, effect—the use of slow-motion photography to suggest superhuman speed—evinces. Moreover, certain individual episodes' set-pieces can be interpreted as expressionist tableaux that allegorize the action.

For example, in "The Bionic Dog, Part 2" Jaime chases Max through a forest fire. Max, injured, is running amok through the flaming trees as Jaime attempts to find and rescue him. Suddenly, Max and Jaime discover one another, Jaime trying to coax the maddened dog into trusting her again: "Max, I can help you!" But Max in his agitated state sees Jaime as

7. Dogs and Sympathy

the enemy. Snarling, he bionically leaps at her, intending to attack. At the same time Jaime, anticipating his attack, also bionically leaps into the air to elude him. We cut to a spellbinding shot of Jaime and Max both suspended in the air, moving in opposite directions and wholly at cross-purposes, their conflict and the power of their confrontation as two bionic beings reinforced by the dramatic music. Yet these figures are also strangely complementary, an idea aurally conveyed by meshing two separate bionic-jump sound effects. The visualization of their conflict captures what is eerie and uncanny about it, the super powers of woman and dog at nearly fatal odds with one another.

Another linkage is the sentimental mode, which here informs not only the anthropomorphized representation of Max but also the relationship between woman and nonhuman animal. Much like lowbrow popular culture works, sentimental narrative consistently provokes scorn. Harriet Beecher Stowe's anti-slavery novel *Uncle Tom's Cabin; or, Life Among the Lowly*, published in 1852, was hugely successful in its day, but by the twentieth-century had fallen out of fashion. Its generic mode of sentimentality, literature designed to appeal to the emotions and frequently oriented around the homey domestic sphere, was precisely the problem for later critics such as James Baldwin. It was not until the 1980s that critics like Jane Tompkins made the novel an acceptable object of study again.

Stowe's aim is to appeal to the reader's feelings and ability to empathize, to convince them on an emotional level that slavery is wrong and therefore to oppose it. At one point, she uses the image of a suffering dog to convey the horrors of the slave master's willful, arbitrary penchant for cruelty. In chapter three, the enslaved George Harris, who has escaped a cruel master, explains to his wife Eliza that his master forced him to drown his beloved dog Carlo that Eliza gave him. While George did not perform the terrible deed himself, his master did. Stowe uses the protective love for dogs that many if not most human beings feel to provoke revulsion and rage against the cruel slave master and to inspire sorrow and pity about the plight of the enslaved.

What, then, is the chief sentimental appeal of "The Bionic Dog" episodes? Essentially, it is an elaboration on the idea that Jaime does not accept the status quo and will fight for the well-being of the discarded, the forgotten, the fatally misunderstood, the abject. The same Jaime who embraces Chris Stuart, the criminal double agent who impersonates her mother, and embraces Lisa Galloway, the double who threatens Jaime's life, fights for Max to be recognized as a "loving animal" and to be given a chance to defy the medical misdiagnosis that threatens *his* life. Jaime's

The Bionic Woman and Feminist Ethics

devotion to Max's cause leads her to risk her credibility and good standing with her superiors and compels her to risk her own life by entering the nightmarish realm of a forest fire to rescue him. "Claws," one of the most important episodes of the first season, envisioned a community of intergenerational female bonds and bonds between women, girls, and nonhuman animals. "The Bionic Dog" takes a darker and tougher look at the same kinds of alliances across species lines and ultimately finds a cathartic means of restoring these alliances.

Epilogue: Awakenings

The Bionic Woman remains a television touchstone for its commitment to feminist ethics. In its third season, that commitment extended to depicting interracial sisterhood. In the episode "African Connection," Jaime must exchange a computer element used to rig elections with one that will count votes fairly in a corrupt African country ruled by the dictator Azzar (Raymond St. Jacques). While there, Jaime reconnects with her old college friend Leona Mumbassa, who is running for office to defeat Azzar. (Leona is played by the beautiful, stately Joan Pringle, who played the principal on the CBS race drama *The White Shadow*, starring Ken Howard as the coach of an interracial high school basketball team.) Leona explains to Jaime that she and her now assassinated husband have been fighting against the despot with ideas and words, but she despairs that these tools no longer suffice. Her beloved country is being coarsened by Azzar's ruthless tactics. As an example, the same man who was just about to execute Jaime by firing squad before Leona intervened was only recently an anthropology professor and the gentlest of men. Jaime explains that her mission will help matters, and Leona's mood swiftly shifts. "Because you are white?" she confronts Jaime, essentially telling Jaime that her white savior complex has no place here. Jaime defends her role by saying (that is, demonstrating) that it is her bionics, not her whiteness, that will allow her to prevail and to help. She proceeds to break a long iron chain while swearing Leona to secrecy about her abilities. This stunning scene explores key tensions between white feminists and feminists of color, an anticipation of the debates over intersectionality that are at the center of contemporary feminist debates.

One of the other ways that the series incorporated racial awareness into its feminist ethics was by pursuing the possibility of interracial

Epilogue

romance.[1] In the S3 episode "Out of Body," Jaime appears to be romantically involved with a young Native American scientist, Tommy Littlehorse (Charlie Hill). Tommy lies dying in a hospital bed after being nearly fatally injured during an attempt to steal OSI technology by a vengeful and greedy older scientist who works for the OSI. Tommy's spirit presence communicates with Jaime, helping her to bring the duplicitous scientist to justice. While the episode can be faulted for taking essentialist views of Native Americans, here associated with dream worlds and mysticism and the ability to negotiate realms between life and death, it is a sincere and earnest attempt to acknowledge the spiritual dimension of Native American culture, and it is also a notable primetime attempt to present interracial romance in a positive light. (There are no further mentions of Tommy in this last season, which largely focuses on Jaime's burgeoning relationship with Chris Williams, who works with Oscar and Rudy.)

When a television series gives one so much, it feels churlish to ask for more. And yet I do. I wish the series had more consistently explored Jaime's commitment to feminist ethics and her interest in helping the marginalized. Some episodes simply conformed to the conventional standards of action/genre filler of its television era. Surprisingly, that includes an episode co-written by Kenneth Johnson and James D. Parriott for S3, "Motorcycle Boogie." Episodes like this one cheapened the integrity and resonance of the series, which otherwise in no way has lost its luster.

We still need Jaime Sommers—I know that I do. Her bravery, empathy, wit, humor, compassion, and indefatigable capacity for love make her a hero for her time and ours.

Chapter Notes

Introduction

1. The writer Andy Mangels, the author of the 2016 comic book *Wonder Woman '77 Meets the Bionic Woman*, has discussed the queer significance of heroines like Wonder Woman and The Bionic Woman:
 I've often joked that while straight male viewers and some lesbians saw them as the ultimate girlfriends, straight women could see them as best friends, and young gay men could see them as protectors/mother/sister figures. They never judged somebody as "wrong" because they were different; they only judged people as wrong who did evil things to others or the environment. Add to that the Wonder spin to change clothes, and the sound effects when they both used their powers, and I suspect there were a lot of viewers who made themselves dizzy or who ran in slow-motion [Reddish, "The Queerty Interview"].

2. On the queerness of cyborgs, see Greven, *Queering the Terminator*; on the cyborg mulatta, see Kydd and Ireland.
3. See Halperin, *How to Be Gay*, for a critical and personal account of this phenomenon.
4. Nussbaum, *Frontiers of Justice*, 1–2.
5. Nussbaum, *Frontiers of Justice*, 14–15.
6. Nussbaum, *Frontiers of Justice*, 21.

Chapter 1

1. *Frankenstein; or, The Modern Prometheus* was first published anonymously in London in 1818, when Shelley was 20; her name first appeared on the 1823 second edition. Shelley's novel is the result of a ghost story contest that she participated in along with her famous future husband the poet Percy Bysshe Shelley, another famous poet, Lord Byron, and a physician, John Polidori, when these young Romantics were holidaying in Geneva, Switzerland. (Also a result of this contest, Polidori went on to publish the first modern vampire story short story, "The Vampyre," in 1819.)
2. Gayle Rubin, "The Traffic in Women: Notes on the 'Political Economy' of Sex"; Eve Kosofsky Sedgwick, "Gender Asymmetry and Erotic Triangles"; Girard, *Deceit, Desire, and the Novel*; Lévi-Strauss, "The Principle of Reciprocity."
3. Basinger, *A Woman's View: How Hollywood Spoke to Women*, 20.
4. Basinger, *A Woman's View*, 7.
5. I discuss these themes at length in my book *Representations of Femininity in*

Chapter Notes—2

American Genre Cinema: The Woman's Film, Film Noir, and Modern Horror. Expanding on Robert Ray's concept of the "concealed western," developed in his book *A Certain Tendency of the Hollywood Cinema*, I argue that many films in other genres, specifically the horror film, can be read as concealed woman's films. I view *The Bionic Woman* as a science-fiction television series that can be read as a concealed woman's film.

6. Josephine Donovan, in her book *After the Fall*, discusses the conflict between young women of the late nineteenth-century and their mothers in terms of Greek mythology, specifically the myth of Demeter and Persephone. Donovan interprets a tale written by the New England local colorist Mary E. Wilkins Freeman, "Evelina's Garden," as deeply symbolic of women's struggles at this historical point: a young woman is bound by an older woman's will, which stipulates that she must care for an extraordinary garden and never marry. But she breaks the will, destroying the garden and marrying a man. The older generation of women, like Demeter, want to guard their daughters within their protective realm and "keep a women's culture alive," observes Donovan.

But the younger women were being lured away, primarily, as in the traditional myth of the fall, by the attraction of wider knowledge. For the first time in history, the late nineteenth-century generation of middle-class daughters had the opportunity of entering the world of public, patriarchal discourse. Institutions such as universities, to which women had previously been denied entrance, were gradually opening their doors. Women were adjusting their vistas, looking to broader horizons; the rural matricentral community was beginning to seem too restrictive, too limiting. And yet there was the fear (voiced by the traditional women, the mothers) that the new knowledge the younger women were winning would obliterate older feminine traditions [Donovan, *After the Fall*, 11].

I would argue that resituating Jaime Sommers in a local, home-bound tradition is a reactionary gesture that evokes this definitive late nineteenth-century moment in women's history. The reactionary aspects of Jaime's transformation back into a more traditional kind of woman is importantly ameliorated, however, by the fact that Jaime once again becomes a world-traveler with access to unprecedented "new knowledge" in her work as a spy.

7. Lang, *American Film Melodrama.*

8. McKee notes that she seeks to establish "a more nuanced understanding of the relationship among gender, history, and subjectivity in 1940s woman's films than has been previously acknowledged, and for the concept of a multivalent organizing subjectivity that is occasionally positionless and bodiless, one that traverses the divide between masculine and feminine at the level of plot as well as cinematic form" (McKee, "It Seems Familiar... *Random Harvest.*").

9. Diane Negra, *What a Girl Wants?*

10. In considering this scene, I am reminded of Patrick E. Horrigan's wonderfully nuanced and insightful reading in *Widescreen Dreams* of *The Poseidon Adventure* (Ronald Neame, 1972) and especially of Shelley Winters' performance here. In much the same way that Winters represents human connections and intimacy in this film, Martha Scott's performance as Helen, matching up so beautifully with Wagner's as Jaime, provides a powerful emotional foundation to the first season.

Chapter 2

1. Majors, it was reported, felt angry that Wagner and her agent had managed to wrangle a more lucrative contract than his own from Universal Pictures. Because the two-part episode that introduced the character of Jaime Sommers was the last part Wagner played while under her original contract at Universal, and Universal let that contract expire, Wagner was able to command a far more lucrative deal to return as the now hugely popular character.

Chapter Notes—2

2. I rework the concept of the "concealed Western" proposed by Robert Ray in *A Certain Tendency of the Hollywood Cinema*.

3. For discussions of Sirk's films among others, see Gledhill, *Home Is Where the Heart Is: Studies in Melodrama and the Woman's Film*; Goldberg, *Melodrama: An Aesthetics of Impossibility*. For a discussion of the woman's film, see, among many other studies, Basinger, *A Woman's View: How Hollywood Spoke to Women, 1930–1960*; Doane, *The Desire to Desire: The Woman's Film of the 1940s*; White, *Uninvited: Classical Hollywood Cinema and Lesbian Representability*.

4. For a discussion of Jewett's reworking of the Demeter-Persephone myth, see Bloomberg, *Tracing Arachne's Web: Myth and Feminist Fiction*.

5. Jewett introduces Esther in "A Dunnet Shepherdess," one of the Dunnet Landing stories that Jewett published after *Country of the Pointed Firs* (this story appeared in *The Atlantic* in December of 1899) and one of the two she included in revised form in the 1899 *The Queen's Twin and Other Tales*.

6. See especially Haraway, *The Companion Species Manifesto*.

7. Blanchard, *Sarah Orne Jewett*, p. 296.

8. Scholtmeijer, "The Power of Otherness: Animals in Women's Fiction," 252.

9. Scholtmeijer, "The Power of Otherness," p 233.

10. Some commentators have critiqued Jewett for creating a world founded in a belief in white supremacy. In this regard, it is interesting to compare *Country* to Jean M. Auel's best-selling 1980 novel *The Clan of the Cave Bear*. Auel's heroine, the prominently blonde Cro-Magnon Ayla, adopted by the dark, prognathous Neanderthal Cave Bear tribe (who regard Ayla with wonder and suspicion), bears the mark of a lioness's claws on her thigh. Her adoptive mother, the medicine woman Iza, trains her in the same field. Auel's work interestingly plays with gender roles—Creb, the mystical medicine-man, suggests a queer figure—and female heroism, but her books' racial politics are disquieting. Other books in Auel's "Earth's Children" series include *The Valley of Horses* (1982), *The Mammoth Hunters* (1985), and the concluding volume, *The Land of Painted Caves* (2004). Jewett's Esther anticipates comic book heroines like *Sheena, Queen of the Jungle* and the heroines of children's books like Scott O'Dell's *Island of the Blue Dolphins* and Jean Craighead George's *Julie of the Wolves*, the latter two novels especially relevant in their depiction of the aching solitude of the animal women protagonists.

11. Atalanta makes for an interesting forebear. Abandoned by her father (who wanted a son), suckled by a she-bear, raised by hunters, a champion hunter and athlete known for deploying arrows, with unflinching calm, at centaurs who attempt to rape her in the forest, striking the decisive mortal blow against the rampaging Calydonian Boar, fiercely committed to staying virginal, Atalanta provides a powerful mythic example of female resistance to compulsory heterosexuality and gendered codes (until her eventual and inevitable marriage, of course).

12. As Reeder continues, "The identification of women with animals finds a particularly vivid expression in the metaphor of courtship as hunting. ... [As reproachful as it was affirmative, the women-animal metaphor] came to identify men with culture and women with its opposite, nature. ... [A young Greek woman] was led to believe that her sexual appeal lay in her feral aspect, and her preparation for marriage concentrated on the socialization of this quality ... her respectability as a grown woman [depended on submissiveness and modesty.]" Reeder also discusses the common theory for the "polarization of the genders" as a "proven social strategy, because young boys can be more effectively persuaded to embrace behavior prescribed for manhood if qualities considered its antithesis are ascribed to women ... the Greeks also realized that their society asked a great deal from young men, and a number of myths and rituals express an analogous sympathy with a youth's transition to manhood." See Reeder, *Pandora's Box: Women in Classical Greece*, 299–300.

13. Carl Theodor Dreyer's magnificent film *The Passion of Joan of Arc* (1928), star-

Chapter Notes—3

ring the great Renée Jeanne Falconetti, piercingly depicts Joan's stalwart resolve in the face of brutal male inquisitors.

14. Jewett's Dunnet Landing stories have inspired a great deal of feminist scholarship but also a good deal of queer interest, some of it related to Jewett's status as a possibly lesbian author and some of it centered in her exploration of women's bonds.

15. In some versions of Arthurian myth, the magical sword Excalibur is given to the young King Arthur by the Lady of the Lake.

16. For an analysis of the classical Hollywood woman's film genre and its thematization of the mother-daughter role as a variation of the Demeter-Persephone story in Greek myth, see Greven, *Representations of Femininity in American Genre Film*.

17. *Ibid.*

18. Lehner and Lehner, *Folklore and Symbolism of Flowers*, 124.

19. In terms of *Star Trek* mythology and Spock's history of ethical behavior, this scene comes as a shock and must be interpreted as a low point for Spock's character. Similarly, in *Star Trek: Nemesis* (2002), the psionic villain Shinzon (Tom Hardy) violates Counselor Deanna Troi's (Marina Sirtis) mind during a scene in which she and her husband Riker (Jonathan Frakes) are having intercourse. Though forcible mind invasions with different agendas, both acts are equally reprehensible—rape scenes that should be interpreted as such.

20. Vardoulakis, *The Doppelgänger*, 10.

21. Freud, "On Narcissism," 88–89.

22. Silverman, *The Threshold of the Visible World*, 33.

23. Foucault, *The History of Sexuality*, 104, 121, 146–7.

24. Hasse, "Traffic Architecture," 184.

25. *Ibid.*, 184.

Chapter 3

1. Bader, et al., *Paranormal America*, 132, 134, emphasis in the original.

2. A surprising political allegory emerges here: Jaime's relationship with Sasquatch is an anti-hegemonic gesture. To lift from the theories of Antonio Gramsci, hegemony is the system—our system—that keeps those in power insecurely at the top while forcing all of those without power to scramble for scant resources, competing against one another and thereby never challenging the true sources of oppression.

3. In the first season of the CBS series *Star Trek: Discovery*, which debuted in 2017, the crew use a tardigrade, referred to as a "space bear" and far larger than its earthly equivalent, as part of their "spoor drive" technology. When Michael Burnham (Sonequa Martin-Green), the disgraced First Officer striving to regain her standing, discovers that the tardigrade suffers greatly as a result of being so employed, she intervenes, eventually freeing the creature (who has been destructively violent to protect itself). Considerable overlaps between this plotline and *Bionic*'s Sasquatch one clearly exist.

4. Inescapably, a racial allegory manifests itself. Is Bigfoot a manifestation of what Toni Morrison in her great study *Playing in the Dark* describes as the "Africanist presence," the suppressed knowledge of black persons in American literature and other artistic and cultural forms? Is this why Steve is haunted and can't figure out why?

5. Excellent scores graced the Bionic series. S1 of *Bionic Woman* was scored most prominently by the fine composer Jerry Fielding (*The Wild Bunch, Straw Dogs, Demon Seed*), who wrote the affecting main credits music. In S2 and S3, Joe Harnell wrote most of the scores, and he made a truly spellbinding contribution. "The Return of Bigfoot, Part 2" boasts a particularly impressive, complex, rousing score that is available on CD along with several others by Harnell. Harnell also wrote wonderful music for *The Incredible Hulk* TV series created by Kenneth Johnson and several of the auteur's other productions.

6. Compare, for example, Cloris Leachman playing Diana Prince's mother Hippolyta in the *Wonder Woman* TV series. Leachman is a fine performer, but, probably because she was directed to do so, plays her scenes with her future-heroine daughter Diana entirely for laughs in the pilot episode.

Chapter 4

1. Wilcha, "Jonathan Caouette."
2. Vardoulakis, *The Doppelgänger*, 15.
3. Vardoulakis, *The Doppelgänger*, 36.
4. Žižek, "'I Hear You with My Eyes,'" 94.
5. Rank, *The Double*, 74; 85.
6. Bruhm, *Reflecting Narcissus*, 44.
7. Bingham, *Acting Male*, 214–15.
8. Pauline Kael, *5001 Nights at the Movies*, 227.
9. Grossman, *Rethinking the Femme Fatale*, 102.
10. For an extended discussion of the afterlife of the woman's film in horror cinema, see my book *Representations of Femininity in American Genre Cinema*.
11. For the standard treatment of such cinematic versions of Black-white relations, see Bogle, *Toms, Coons, Mulattoes, Mammies, and Bucks*.
12. Bettie, *Women Without Class*, 51–2.
13. *Ibid.*, 52.
14. As Tomas Kulka writes, "Capitalist kitsch, exemplified by advertising ... uses class distinctions and status symbols to create artificial needs and illusions to foster the ideology of the consumer society." Kulka, *Kitsch and Art*, 28.
15. One does recall the surprising, caricatural Jamaican accent that Jaime puts on, in "Mirror Image," before departing for the Bahamas in response to Jim Elgin's complaint that her place is a mess. This moment was always cut from syndicated broadcasts of the series, probably because it doesn't correspond to our idea of Jaime as both proper and non-racist.
16. Kimberly Chabot Davis, *Postmodern Texts and Emotional Audiences*, 27.
17. Cavell, *Contesting Tears*, 151–194.
18. Joffe, Liner notes for *Joe Harnell, The Bionic Woman: From the Episodes "Bionic Beauty," Deadly Ringer, "Once a Thief,"* 2010.
19. While in her earlier work Laura Mulvey made *Vertigo* the ur-example of cinematic voyeurism, a reflection, rather than a critique, of the male's sadistic desire to investigate and penetrate the woman's mystery, Mulvey's more recent treatment strikes a different and, to my mind, more complexly persuasive note.
20. Basinger, *A Woman's View: How Hollywood Spoke to Women*, 20.
21. Lang, *American Film Melodrama*.
22. F. Scott Fitzgerald wrote in his 1936 essay "The Crack-Up": "The test of a first-rate intelligence is the ability to hold two opposed ideas in mind at the same time and still retain the ability to function" (69).
23. For an extended discussion of spectatorship and its relevance for queer and feminist film theory, see Greven, *Manhood in Hollywood from Bush to Bush*, 12–52.
24. Butler, "Melancholy Gender/Refused Identification," 133.
25. The prohibition on incest that the successful resolution of the Oedipus complex instantiates "presupposes the prohibition on homosexuality, for it presumes the heterosexualization of desire." *Ibid.*, 135.
26. Segrest makes this remark in reference to the experience of queer childhood. See Segrest, "I Lead Two Lives: Confessions of a Closet Baptist," 13.
27. See Greven, *Intimate Violence: Hitchcock, Sex, and Queer Theory*.
28. Modleski, 94.

Chapter Notes—5

29. BionicBlonde.com, "Deadly Ringer, Part 1." http://www.bionicblonde.com/deadly-ringer-(part-1).html Accessed on May 5, 2019.
30. BionicBlonde.com, "Deadly Ringer, Part 2." http://www.bionicblonde.com/deadly-ringer-(part-2).html Accessed on May 5, 2019.

Chapter 5

1. Short, *Cyborg Cinema*, 81, 87.
2. Wosk, *My Fair Ladies*, 115. Wosk discusses *Bionic Woman* and Fembots in terms of "Female Robots, Androids, and Other Artificial Eves" (114–115).
3. Albrecht, *The Medusa Effect*, 10.
4. *Ibid.*, 15–16.
5. Ahmed "The Skin of the Community: Affect and Boundary Formation." 108.
6. Foucault, *The History of Sexuality*, 104, 121, 146–7.
7. See Michie, *Sororophobia*.
8. Once a producer who worked with Orson Welles, Houseman became an unexpected acting star when he played the intimidating law professor Charles Kingsfield in *The Paper Chase*, a 1973 film directed by James Bridges and also starring Timothy Bottoms. Lindsay Wagner played Houseman's daughter and the hero's love interest.
9. Mary Thomas Crane, *Losing Touch with Nature*, 116.
10. One remembers a non-cyborg aspect of this convergence, the female astronaut shown in the company of the male astronauts led by Charlton Heston who crash-land on *The Planet of the Apes* (Franklin J. Schaffner, 1968). But no sooner is she introduced than she is shown dead, a hideously wizened corpse that did not survive hyper-sleep.
11. Balsamo, *Technologies of the Gendered Body*, 39.
12. Kakoudaki, *Anatomy of a Robot*, 219.
13. Caruth, *Trauma*, 5. I do not mean to cheapen the work of trauma theorists such as Caruth by applying their findings to a work of popular culture such as this one. Since I take the series and its themes seriously, I ask the forbearance of my readers for thinking through it with trauma theory.
14. See Silverman, *The Acoustic Mirror*, 30.
15. Schwenger, "Beneath the Skin of the Book," 80–1.
16. In the course of writing this book on the original *Bionic Woman* series, I have revisited ambient cultural milestones such as *Charlie's Angels*. It was a show that, like *Bionic*, would play endlessly in syndication around dinner hour (my parents always served dinner early, around 5, when my Dad came home from work). Unlike *Bionic Woman*, *Charlie's Angels* was never personally meaningful to me, but it was a show I always had goodwill towards, especially the entrancing opening credits and Kate Jackson's compelling intelligence. Revisiting the series (season 1), I have found it more bearable and savvier than I remembered it being. Its reputation as the ultimate silly jiggle show does not speak to its strengths, such as the theme of female friendship and the showcasing of the Angels' ingenuity and bravery and intelligence. It's good to revisit things and challenge received opinion, especially one's own. As noted, a 2019 comic book series pairs *Bionic* and *Charlie's Angels*. I would argue, however, that *Bionic* pointedly eschews *Charlie's* sexualized atmosphere. To compare the relationship between Jaime Sommers and Oscar Goldman, it is not sexualized in the least. In contrast, Charlie, the Angels' always vocally present but never fully onscreen boss, is the absent phallus. While we never see Charlie's face and mainly hear his disembodied voice on speakerphone, there are shots in which we see Charlie's torso in scenes that represent paradisiacal vacations where Charlie enjoys the endless procession of nubile serving women at his disposal. Charlie's faceless body, it would seem, provides a narcissistic substitute for the presumably heterosexual male

viewer. His phallic authority, with which the viewer is meant to identify, safeguards against identification with the Angels. In theory, at least.

17. In this regard, "Fembots in Las Vegas" is far more radical than a film such as *Blade Runner 2049* (Denis Villeneuve, 2017), in which the protagonist replicant-hunter Officer K, played by Ryan Gosling, maintains a deeply felt, sincere relationship with an AI female who remains passionately devoted to him. Given the critical distance on the part of the original Ridley Scott film toward sexualized female objects of desire (even though that film has its own investment in heterosexual romance, albeit between replicants), it's a bit of a surprise to see such a winsome and, frankly, dull depiction of AI female worship of and selfless loyalty to the stereotypically taciturn, stoic noir–SF male lead.

18. See Butler, *Bodies That Matter* and "Imitation and Gender Insubordination."

19. "Fembots in Las Vegas" extends and—if only to a certain extent—revises the phobic horror messages of the original Star Trek series' first-season episode "What Are Little Girls Made Of?" written by horror maven Robert Bloch. In this episode, Captain Kirk and company visit the planet residence of a brilliant electronics genius once believed dead. He was once the fiancé of Nurse Chapel, who finally realizes the grotesque truth: her former love is now the android copy he made of himself, a pitiably self-deluded monster. As the monomaniacal android tells one of his own creations, a slinky, dark-haired proto-Fembot, "You poor creature. You cannot love." The android kills himself and his own creation as Kirk and the grieving Chapel look on.

20. For acutely insightful and illuminating commentary on mechanical women and affect, please see the video essays of Allison De Fren, available on Vimeo.

21. Bullock, "Lesbian Cruising," 2.
22. Bullock, "Lesbian Cruising," 5.
23. Bullock, "Lesbian Cruising," 5.
24. Bullock, "Lesbian Cruising," 8.
25. Bullock, "Lesbian Cruising," 9.
26. Bullock, "Lesbian Cruising," 28.
27. Nomura, "Robots and Gender."
28. Dinello, *Technophobia!: Science Fiction Visions of Posthuman Technology*, 107.
29. Kakoudaki, *Anatomy of a Robot*, 216.

Chapter 6

1. Kakoudaki, *Anatomy of a Robot*, 4.
2. Ibid., 218.
3. Muir, "*The Bionic Woman*: 'Doomsday Is Tomorrow' (January 19, 1977)."
4. "The Turing Test." https://plato.stanford.edu/entries/turing-test/ Accessed on 5/27/19.
5. For an extended discussion of Ash and *Alien*, see Greven, *Representations of Femininity in American Genre Cinema*, 124–137.
6. Ibid.
7. Elizabeth A. Wilson, *Affect and Artificial Intelligence*, 28.
8. Rushing and Frentz, *Projecting the Shadow*, 180. The authors discuss the shadow in terms of Christian iconography and focus on the *Terminator* films.
9. My thanks to the *Bionic Wiki* for providing dialogue from the episode.
10. Oscar Goldman calls the OSI a "semi-secret government agency" in "Fembots in Las Vegas, Part 1." The scene of Oscar in the inventory room at the start of the episode, where a befuddled Jaime discovers him looking over evidence from previous missions in order to "justify the taxpayers' money" spent on them, foreshadows the ambivalence about the government that runs rife throughout "On the Run."
11. The phrase self-shattering is associated with the work of the queer theorist Leo Bersani, but my use of it here is distinct from his.

12. For a thoughtful discussion of this episode in terms of disability studies, see Donna Binn, "The *Bionic* Woman: Machine or Human?," 98–101.

Chapter 7

1. Nussbaum, *Frontiers of Justice*, 22.
2. Scholtmeijer, "The Power of Otherness: Animals in Women's Fiction," 252.
3. Haraway, *The Companion Species Manifesto*, 33.
4. Gross, Ed. "*The Six Million Dollar Man* Declassified."
5. Peterson, "Of Canines and Queers."
6. Kuzniar, *Melancholia's Dog*, 18.
7. Kuzniar, *Melancholia's Dog*, 7.
8. Kuzniar, *Melancholia's Dog*, 8.
9. Kuzniar, *Melancholia's Dog*, 110–111.
10. Wagner has said in an interview of her role as Jaime Sommers: "It was my chance to communicate a bigger message to children. I worked with the writers, always pushing for it not to be so black and white, not just tunnel vision of the good guy, bad guy, but looking at the bigger picture. Even Jaime's powers were a metaphor for human potential." "Bionic Woman Lindsay Wagner makes a giant leap of faith."
11. Jaime is depicted as a mentor to young women throughout the series as well. "The Ghosthunter" in S1, "The Vega Influence" in S2, and "Sanctuary Earth" in S3 are standout examples of this relationship.
12. Kuzniar, *Melancholia's Dog*, 102.

Epilogue

1. After its surprise cancellation by ABC, the series was picked up for its third and final season by NBC. Remarkably different in tone from the first two, the third season is also the most overtly political, involving Jaime Sommers in international missions in Africa and behind the Iron Curtain and sending her back to college to join forces with impecunious students of color. The development of Jaime's romantic and sexual life involves a complex and challenging negotiation on the part of a series that presented itself as family television.

Bibliography

Ahmed, Sara. "The Skin of the Community: Affect and Boundary Formation." In Tina Chanter and Ewa Plonowska Ziarek, eds. *Revolt, Affect, Collectivity: The Unstable Boundaries of Kristeva's Polis*. Albany: State University of New York Press, 2005. pp. 95–113.
Bader, Christopher, et al. *Paranormal America: Ghost Encounters, UFO Sightings, Bigfoot Hunts, and Other Curiosities in Religion and Culture*. New York: New York University Press, 2010.
Balsamo, Anne Marie. *Technologies of the Gendered Body: Reading Cyborg Women*. Durham: Duke University Press, 1996.
Basinger, Jeanine. *A Woman's View: How Hollywood Spoke to Women, 1930–1960*, 1st ed. New York: Knopf, 1993.
Bettie, Julie. *Women Without Class: Girls, Race, and Identity*. Berkeley: University of California Press, 2019.
Bingham, Dennis. *Acting Male: Masculinities in the Films of James Stewart, Jack Nicholson, and Clint Eastwood*. New Brunswick, NJ: Rutgers University Press, 1994.
Binn, Donna. "The *Bionic* Woman: Machine or Human?" In *Disability in Science Fiction: Representations of Technology as Cure*, edited by Kathryn. Allan, 89–101. New York: Palgrave Macmillan, 2013.
"Bionic Woman Lindsay Wagner Makes a Giant Leap of Faith." *The Yorkshire Post*, November 19, 2008. https://www.yorkshirepost.co.uk/news/bionic-woman-lindsay-wagner-makes-a-giant-leap-of-faith-1-2325751.
Blanchard, Paula. *Sarah Orne Jewett: Her World and Her Work*. Reading, MA: Addison-Wesley, 1994.
Bloomberg, Kristin M. Mapel. *Tracing Arachne's Web: Myth and Feminist Fiction*. Gainesville: University Press of Florida, 2001.
Bogle, Donald. *Toms, Coons, Mulattoes, Mammies, and Bucks: An Interpretive History of Blacks in American Films*, 4th ed. New York: Continuum, 2001.
Bruhm, Steven. *Reflecting Narcissus: A Queer Aesthetic*. Minneapolis: Minnesota University Press, 2001.
Bullock, Denise. "Lesbian Cruising." *Journal of Homosexuality* 47, no. 2 (2004): 1–31.
Butler, Judith. *Bodies That Matter*. New York: Routledge, 1993.
———. "Imitation and Gender Insubordination." In *Inside/Out: Lesbian Theories, Gay Theories*, edited by Diana Fuss. New York: Routledge, 1991.
———. "Melancholy Gender/Refused Identification." In *The Psychic Life of Power: Theories in Subjection*, 132–150. Redwood City, CA: Stanford University Press, 1997.
Caouette, Jonathan. "Twenty-Five Things That I Love by Jonathan Caouette, Writer/director of *Tarnation*." http://www.landmarktheatres.com/mn/tarnation.html.

Bibliography

Caruth, Cathy. "Introduction." *Trauma: Explorations in Memory*. Edited by Cathy Caruth. Baltimore: Johns Hopkins University Press, 1995. 183–99. Print.
Cavell, Stanley. *Contesting Tears: The Melodrama of the Unknown Woman*. Chicago: University of Chicago Press, 1996.
Crane, Mary Thomas. *Losing Touch with Nature: Literature and the New Science in Sixteenth-Century England*. Baltimore: Johns Hopkins University Press, 2014.
Davis, Kimberly Chabot. *Postmodern Texts and Emotional Audiences*. West Lafayette, IN: Purdue University Press, 2007.
Dinello, Daniel. *Technophobia!: Science Fiction Visions of Posthuman Technology*, 1st ed. Austin: University of Texas Press, 2005.
Doane, Mary Ann. *The Desire to Desire: The Woman's Film of the 1940s: Theories of Representation and Difference*. Bloomington: Indiana University Press, 1987.
Donovan, Josephine. *After the Fall: The Demeter-Persephone Myth in Wharton, Cather, and Glasgow*. University Park: Pennsylvania State University Press, 1989.
Fitzgerald, Francis Scott. *The Crack-Up*, edited by Edmund Wilson. New York: New Directions, 2009.
Foucault, Michel. *The History of Sexuality, Volume 1*. New York: Vintage Books, 1988.
Freud, Sigmund. "On Narcissism: An Introduction." (1914). In *The Standard Edition of the Complete Psychological Works of Sigmund Freud*, volume 14, 67–104. Translated by James Strachey. London: Hogarth, 1993.
Gilbert, Sandra, and Susan Gubar. *The Madwoman in the Attic*. New Haven, CT: Yale University Press, 1979.
Girard, René. *Deceit, Desire, and the Novel: Self and Other in Literary Structure*, Baltimore: Johns Hopkins University Press, 1961.
Gledhill, Christine, and British Film Institute. *Home Is Where the Heart Is: Studies in Melodrama and the Woman's Film*. London: BFI Pub, 1987.
Goldberg, Jonathan. *Melodrama: An Aesthetics of Impossibility*. Durham, NC: Duke University Press, 2016.
Greven, David. *Intimate Violence: Hitchcock, Sex, and Queer Theory*. New York: Oxford University Press, 2017.
———. *Manhood in Hollywood from Bush to Bush*. Austin: University of Texas Press, 2009.
———. *Queering the Terminator: Sexuality and Cyborg Cinema*. New York: Bloomsbury Academic, 2017.
———. *Representations of Femininity in American Genre Cinema: The Woman's Film, Film Noir, and Modern Horror*. New York: Palgrave Macmillan, 2011.
Gross, Ed. "*The Six Million Dollar Man* Declassified: Lee Majors Remembers the Good, the Bad and the Bionic." *Closer*, April 8, 2019. https://www.closerweekly.com/posts/lee-majors-six-million-dollar-man-exclusive/.
Halperin, David M. *How to Be Gay*. Cambridge, MA: Belknap Press of Harvard University Press, 2012.
Haraway, Donna. *The Companion Species Manifesto: Dogs, People, and Significant Otherness*, edited by Matthew Begelke. Chicago: Prickly Paradigm Press, 2003.
Hasse, Jürgen. "Traffic Architecture: Hidden Affections." In *Elements of Architecture: Assembling Archaeology, Atmosphere and the Performance of Building Spaces*, edited by Mikkel Bille and Tim Flohr Sørensen, 177–194. New York: Routledge, 2016.
Horrigan, Patrick E. *Widescreen Dreams: Growing Up Gay at the Movies*. Madison: University of Wisconsin Press, 1999.
Kakoudaki, Despina. *Anatomy of a Robot: Literature, Cinema, and the Cultural Work of Artificial People*. New Brunswick, NJ: Rutgers University Press, 2014.
Kulka, Tomas. *Kitsch and Art*. University Park: Pennsylvania State University Press, 1996.
Kuzniar, Alice. *Melancholia's Dog: Reflections on Our Animal Kinship*. Chicago: University of Chicago Press, 2006.
Kydd, Elspeth, and Andrew Ireland. "Cyberwomen and Sleepers: Rereading the Mulatta Cyborg and the Black Woman's Body." In *Illuminating Torchwood: Essays on Narra-*

Bibliography

tive, Character and Sexuality in the BBC Series, 191–202. Jefferson, NC: McFarland, 2010.
Lang, Robert. *American Film Melodrama: Griffith, Vidor, Minnelli*. Princeton, NJ: Princeton University Press, 1989.
Lehner, Ernst, and Johanna Lehner. *Folklore and Symbolism of Flowers, Plants and Trees*. New York: Martino Fine Books, 2012.
Lévi-Strauss, Claude. "The Principle of Reciprocity." In *The Elementary Structures of Kinship* (1949), 52–69. Cambridge, MA: Beacon Press; Rev. ed., 1969.
Lin, Patrick, Keith Abney, and George A. Bekey. *Robot Ethics: The Ethical and Social Implications of Robotics*. Cambridge, MA: MIT Press, 2012.
McKee, Alison L. "'It Seems Familiar but I Can't Quite Remember': Amnesia and the Dislocation of History and Gender in *Random Harvest* (1942)." *Bright Lights Film Journal*, July 31, 2010.
Michie, Helena. *Sororophobia: Differences Among Women in Literature and Culture*. New York: Oxford University Press, 1992.
Modleski, Tania. *The Women Who Knew Too Much: Hitchcock and Feminist Theory*, 3rd. ed. New York: Routledge, 2015.
Muir, John Kenneth. "*The Bionic Woman*: 'Doomsday Is Tomorrow' (January 19, 1977)," February 12, 2014. Accessed on May 15, 2019. http://reflectionsonfilmandtelevision.blogspot.com/2014/02/the-bionic-woman-doomsday-is-tomorrow.html.
Mulvey, Laura. *Visual and Other Pleasures*, 2nd ed. New York: Palgrave Macmillan, 2009.
———. "Visual Pleasure and Narrative Cinema." *Screen* 16 no. 3 (Autumn 1975): 6–18.
Negra, Diane. *What a Girl Wants?: Fantasizing the Reclamation of Self in Postfeminism*. New York: Routledge, 2009.
Nomura, Tatsuya. "Robots and Gender." *Gender and the Genome* 1, no. 1 (March 2017): 18–26. http://doi.org/10.1089/gg.2016.29002.nom.
Nussbaum, Martha Craven. *Frontiers of Justice: Disability, Nationality, Species Membership*, 1st Harvard University Press Paperback ed. Cambridge, MA: Belknap Press of Harvard University Press, 2007.
Peterson, Christopher. "Of Canines and Queers: Review of *Melancholia's Dog: Reflections on Our Animal Kinship* by Alice Kuzniar (2006)." *GLQ* 15, no. 2 (2009): 352–354.
Rank, Otto. *The Double: A Psychoanalytic Study*. Translated by Harry Tucker, Jr. Chapel Hill: University of North Carolina Press, 1971.
Ray, Robert B. *A Certain Tendency of the Hollywood Cinema, 1930–1980*. Princeton, NJ: Princeton University Press, 1985.
Reddish, David. "The *Queerty* Interview with Andy Mangels: This comic book writer you've never heard of is making characters gayer than ever." *Queerty*, December 10, 2016. https://www.queerty.com/comic-book-writer-not-heard-making-characters-gayer-ever-20161210.
Reeder, Ellen. *Pandora's Box: Women in Classical Greece*. Baltimore: Walters Art Gallery and Princeton, NJ: Princeton University Press, 1995.
Riviere, Joan. "Womanliness as a Masquerade." *The International Journal of Psycho-Analysis* 10 (1929): 303.
Rubin, Gayle. "The Traffic in Women: Notes on the 'Political Economy' of Sex." In *Toward an Anthropology of Women*, edited by Rayna R. Reiter, 157–210. New York: Monthly Review Press, 1975.
Rushing, Janice Hocker, and Thomas S. Frentz. *Projecting the Shadow: The Cyborg Hero in American Film*. Chicago: University of Chicago Press, 1995.
Scholtmeijer, Marian. "The Power of Otherness: Animals in Women's Fiction." In *Animals and Women: Feminist Theoretical Explorations*, edited by Carol J. Adams and Josephine Donovan, 231–262. Durham, NC: Duke University Press, 1995.
Schwenger, Peter. "Beneath the Skin of the Book: Thinking with Peter Greenaway." In *Intermedialities: Philosophy, Arts, Politics*, edited by Henk Oosterling and Ewa Płonowska Ziarek. Washington, D.C.: Lexington Books, 2010.

Bibliography

Sedgwick, Eve Kosofsky. "Gender Asymmetry and Erotic Triangles," In *Between Men: English Literature and Male Homosocial Desire*, 21–27. New York: Columbia University Press, 1985.

Segrest, Mab. "I Lead Two Lives: Confessions of a Closet Baptist." In *The New Lesbian Studies: Into the Twenty-First Century*, edited by Bonnie Zimmerman and Toni A.H. McNaron. New York: The Feminist Press, 1996.

Short, Sue. *Cyborg Cinema and Contemporary Subjectivity*. New York: Palgrave Macmillan, 2005.

Silverman, Kaja. *The Acoustic Mirror: The Female Voice in Psychoanalysis and Cinema*. Bloomington: Indiana University Press, 1988.

———. *The Threshold of the Visible World*. New York: Routledge, 1996.

"The Turing Test." Accessed May 27, 2019. https://plato.stanford.edu/entries/turing-test/.

Vardoulakis, Dimitris. *The Doppelgänger: Literature's Philosophy*, 1st ed. New York: Fordham University Press, 2010.

White, Patricia. *Uninvited: Classical Hollywood Cinema and Lesbian Representability*. Bloomington: Indiana University Press, 1999.

Wilcha, Christopher. "Jonathan Caouette." *BOMB*, October 1, 2004. http://bombmagazine.org/articles/jonathan-caouette/.

Wilson, Elizabeth A. *Affect and Artificial Intelligence*. Seattle: University of Washington Press, 2010.

Wosk, Julie. *My Fair Ladies: Female Robots, Androids, and Other Artificial Eves*. New Brunswick, NJ: Rutgers University Press, 2015.

Žižek, Slavoj. "'I Hear You with My Eyes'; Or, the Invisible Master." In *Gaze and Voice as Love Objects*, edited by Renata Salecl and Slavoj Žižek. Durham, NC: Duke University Press, 1996.

Index

ABC network 1–4, 21, 33, 115, 122, 132, 151, 166*epilogue*1
Affect and Artificial Intelligence 139–140
"African Connection" (episode) 157
"Africanist presence" 162*ch*3*n*4
agency 18, 20–21, 26, 57, 94, 115; *see also* autonomy
Ahmed, Sarah 105, 106, 164*ch*5*n*5
A.I. Artificial Intelligence (film) 129
Albrecht, Thomas 104, 164*ch*5*n*3
Aldiss, Brian: "Supertoys Last All Summer Long" (short story) 129
Aldrich, Robert: *Autumn Leaves* (film) 21, 87
Alex 7000 6–7, 105, 111, 118, 120, 134–136, 138–140; *see also* HAL 9000; supercomputer
Alice (series) 27, 79
Alice Adams (film) 21, 34, 44, 79, 87
Alice Doesn't Live Here Anymore (film) 27, 79
Alien (film) 33, 137, 165*ch*6*n*5
"All for One" (episode) 116
All That Heaven Allows (film) 34, 83
allegory 1, 22, 25, 44, 47, 53, 56–59, 72, 89–90, 107, 112, 119, 154, 162*ch*3*n*2, 162*ch*3*n*4
American Film Melodrama 21, 87, 160*ch*1*n*7, 163*ch*4*n*21
amnesia 15, 23, 25, 27, 29, 42, 63, 66, 68, 119
Anatomy of a Robot 114, 129, 133, 164*ch*5*n*12
Anderson, Richard 2, 24, 116; *see also* Goldman, Oscar
"Angel of Mercy" (episode) 75
Animal Liberation: A New Ethics for Our Treatment of Animals 151
appearance 91, 92, 93, 94, 95, 98, 99, 100, 103; *see also* costume; masquerade
Atalanta 38, 161*ch*2*n*11; *see also* classical mythology

Austin, Steve 1–4, 10–12, 15–18, 20, 23, 25–26, 32, 39, 49, 60, 62–64, 66, 69, 82, 95, 109, 112, 115–116, 135, 143, 151–152, 162*ch*3*n*4
Austin Powers 101, 112
autonomy 11, 16, 18, 20–21, 26, 34, 40, 60, 67, 72, 86, 95, 110, 129, 138; *see also* agency
Autumn Leaves (film) 21, 87

the bad other 7, 111, 114, 121, 134, 141, 142, 154–155, 165*ch*5*n*19; *see also* the doppelgänger; the double; Galloway, Lisa; like unlike; mechaphobia
Bader, Christopher: *Paranormal America* 62, 162*ch*3*n*1
Balsamo, Anne 114, 164*ch*5*n*11
Basinger, Jeanine: *A Woman's View: How Hollywood Spoke to Women* 19, 86, 159*ch*1*n*3, 159*ch*1*n*4, 161*ch*2*n*3, 163*ch*4*n*20
Battlestar Galactica (series) 13, 101, 113
The Bechdel Test 67
Bennett, Harve 150
Bettelheim, Bruno: *The Empty Fortress* 140
Bettie, Julie: *Women Without Class: Girls, Race, and Identity* 80, 163*ch*4*n*4
Beyond the Forest (film) 21, 27, 87
Bigfoot (character) 12, 25, 62, 63, 64, 105, 162*ch*3*n*4; *see also* Sasquatch
Bingham, Dennis 163*ch*4*n*7
"Bionic Beauty" (episode) 50, 60
"The Bionic Dog" (episode) 10, 37, 62, 76, 114, 116, 149, 151, 155
"The Bionic Dog: Part 1" (episode) 117, 150–151
"The Bionic Dog: Part 2" (episode) 150, 154
Bionic Ever After? (film) 20, 97
"The Bionic Woman, Part I" (episode) 2–3, 15–16, 22, 29–30
"The Bionic Woman, Part II" (episode) 18

171

Index

bionics 2, 3, 10, 17, 20, 22, 24, 30, 38, 45, 63, 65, 70, 75, 86, 97, 106, 109, 114, 117, 124, 134, 136, 139, 141, 151–153, 157
The Birds (film) 38, 87; *see also* Hitchcock, Alfred
"The Birthmark" (story) 55
Bixby, Bill: *Incredible Hulk* (series) 32, 103, 162*ch*3*n*5
Blade Runner (film) 114
Blanchard, Paula: *Sarah Orne Jewett: Her World and Her Work* 37, 161*ch*2*n*7
Blank, Tom 141–143
Bloomberg, Kristin M. Mapel: *Tracing Arachne's Web: Myth and Feminist Fiction* 161*ch*2*n*4
bond 10–12, 28–31, 35, 37, 39–41, 46–47, 58, 64–65, 75, 79, 96, 98, 107, 109, 144–145, 148–149, 152, 155–156, 161*ch*2*n*12, 162*ch*2*n*14, 164*ch*5*n*16; *see also* dogs; nature; nonhuman animal
The Boy in the Plastic Bubble (film) 117
"Brain Wash" (episode) 108
The Bride of Frankenstein (film) 112
Brontë, Charlotte: *Jane Eyre* (novel) 52–53
Brooks, Martin E. 2, 116, 153; *see also* Wells, Rudy
Bruhm, Steven 74, 163*ch*4*n*6
Butler, Judith: "Melancholy Gender/Refused Identification" (essay) 89, 163*ch*4*n*24, 165*ch*5*n*18

Callahan, Peggy (character) 96, 104, 107–108, 111, 114, 120, 122, 128, 144–145
Cameron, James: *The Terminator* (film) 127, 132, 133, 165*ch*6*n*8
Cammell, Donald: *Demon Seed* (film) 139
Caouette, Jonathan: *Tarnation* (film) 9, 71, 72, 163*ch*4*n*1
Carrie (film) 33, 44, 52
Cavell, Stanley 85, 163*ch*4*n*17
CBS network 4, 32, 157
A Certain Tendency of the Hollywood Cinema 160*ch*1*n*5, 161*ch*2*n*2
Charlie's Angels 4, 78, 122, 126, 164*ch*5*n*16
child 16, 17, 25, 27, 29–30, 40–41, 45, 77, 88, 89, 96–97, 138, 140, 142, 146, 154
The Child Stealer (film) 35
chosen family 28, 35, 39, 40, 45, 47, 95–98, 144
classical mythology 33, 37–38, 41, 51, 57, 112, 118, 160*ch*1*n*6, 161*ch*2*n*4, 161*ch*2*n*11, 161*ch*2*n*12; *see also* Atalanta; Demeter-Persephone myth
"Claws" (episode) 10, 35–39, 87, 156
climate change 129
Coe, Sue: *Pit's Letter* 149, 154

The Cold War 11, 19, 21, 41, 43, 70, 102, 133–134, 137, 144, 166*epilogue*1
Colossus (novel) 132
Colossus: The Forbin Project (film) 132
The Companion Species Manifesto: Dogs, People, and Significant Otherness 37, 114, 148, 150, 161*ch*2*n*6
"concealed Western" 160*ch*1*n*5, 161*ch*2*n*2
costume 92–95; *see also* appearance; masquerade
The Country of the Pointed Firs (novel) 35, 37, 161*ch*2*n*5, 161*ch*2*n*10; *see also* Dunnet Landing Stories
Crane, Barry 64, 102, 150
Crichton, Michael: *Westworld* (film) 101
Crosland, Alan 27, 62, 102
Cross, Tammie (character) 117, 122–124, 131; *see also* Fembot
Curtiz, Michael: *Mildred Pierce* (film) 44, 79, 87
Cyborg (novel) 2
cyborg 5, 63, 65, 102, 107, 112–114, 126–129, 132–137, 142, 145, 150, 159*n*2, 164*ch*5*n*1, 165*ch*5*n*17; *see also* Fembot

Dark Passage (film) 49, 78
Darling, Jennifer 108, 120, 128
Daves, Delmer: *Dark Passage* (film) 49, 78
Davis, Kimberly Chabot 83, 163*ch*4*n*16
The Day the Earth Stood Still (film) 132
"Deadly Ringer" (episode) 8–9, 12, 21, 34, 38–39, 46, 50, 71, 74, 76, 78–90, 92, 94, 97, 105, 129
"Deadly Ringer: Part 1" (episode) 75, 98, 164*ch*4*n*29
"Deadly Ringer: Part 2" (episode) 75, 77, 80, 95, 99, 108, 164*ch*4*n*30
Deceit, Desire, and the Novel 18, 159*ch*1*n*2
Del Toro, Guillermo 70
Demeter-Persephone myth 33, 35, 37, 160*ch*1*n*6, 161*ch*2*n*4, 162*ch*2*n*16; *see also* classical mythology
Demme, Jonathan: *Silence of the Lambs* (film) 45
Demon Seed (film) 139
"Demon with a Glass Hand" (*The Outer Limits* episode) 132
De Palma, Brian 79, 86; *Carrie* (film) 33, 44, 52
depression 11, 13, 152
desire 21, 23, 45–46, 51, 77–80, 83, 87, 89–91, 99–100, 103, 125, 161*ch*2*n*3, 163*ch*4*n*19
The Desire to Desire: The Woman's Film of the 1940s: Theories of Representation and Difference 161*ch*2*n*3
deSouza, Steven E. 141

172

Index

Dinello, Daniel: *Technophobia!: Science Fiction Visions of Posthuman Technology* 129

Doane, Mary Ann: *The Desire to Desire: The Woman's Film of the 1940s: Theories of Representation and Difference* 30, 161*ch*2*n*3

Dr. Courtney (character) 8, 47, 49, 51, 76, 78, 81–83, 85, 91–94, 98–99

Dr. Franklin (character) 5, 13, 102–103, 110, 112, 116, 120–121, 127, 138; *see also* Houseman, John

Dr. Goldfoot and the Bikini Machine (film) 112

Dr. Goldfoot and the Girl Bombs (film) 112

Dr. Harkens (character) 78, 84, 93–94, 99–100

Dr. Michael Marchetti (character) 10, 23–27, 39, 55–56

dog 148, 149, 150, 155, 156; *see also* bond; nonhuman animal

Donovan, Josephine 160*ch*1*n*6

"Doomsday Is Tomorrow" (episode) 6, 13, 20, 105, 111, 118, 120, 131, 132, 133, 134

doppelgänger 7, 12, 39, 40, 48–49, 62, 72–74, 78, 85, 120; *see also* the bad other; the double; like unlike; mechaphobia

the double 12, 31, 46–50, 71–72, 74, 76, 78, 80, 82, 84, 88, 90, 93–99, 104, 107; *see also* the bad other; doppelgänger; like unlike; mechaphobia

Dreyer, Carl Theodor: *The Passion of Joan of Arc* (film) 161*ch*2*n*13

Dunnet Landing Stories 35, 161*ch*2*n*5, 162*ch*2*n*14

Elgin, Bill (character) 36, 39

Elgin, Helen (character) 2, 15–17, 20, 27–29, 35, 38–40, 42, 46, 49–50, 59, 77, 82, 95–97, 145, 160*ch*1*n*10; *see also* Scott, Martha

Elgin, Jim (character) 2, 15–16, 20, 26–28, 35, 39, 49, 77, 82, 95–98, 145, 151, 153, 163*ch*4*n*15; *see also* Rainey, Ford

Ellison, Harlan: *The Outer Limits* (series) 132

Elster, Madeleine (Hitchcock character) 85, 87, 91–93, 126

The Empty Fortress 140

Eve of Destruction (film) 101

Ex Machina (film) 13, 101, 137

Excalibur 41, 162*ch*2*n*15

The Exorcist (film) 52, 54, 56, 58

extraterrestrials 54, 56, 63, 64, 67, 70

fairy tales 63, 70

Far from Heaven (film) 82–83

female melodrama 11–12, 19, 34, 44, 58, 79, 80, 82–83, 85, 161*ch*2*n*3; *see also* Hollywood; woman's film

Fembot Callahan (character) 118–119, 128, 130

Fembot Katy (character) 102–103, 110–111, 118, 121, 138

Fembot Medusa 101, 164*ch*5*n*3

The Fembot Reveal 103, 104, 105, 118, 129, 131, 140; *see also* Fembot Theory; Fembots

Fembot Theory 13, 101, 116, 120–121; *see also* The Fembot Reveal; Fembots

Fembots 5, 7, 13, 62–64, 74, 90, 101, 103, 106–124, 129, 138, 164*ch*5*n*2, 165*ch*5*n*17, 165*ch*5*n*19, 165*ch*5*n*20; *see also* The Fembot Reveal; Fembot Theory

"Fembots in Las Vegas" (episode) 90, 105, 111, 113–114, 116, 119, 122, 124, 126–128, 131, 165*ch*5*n*17, 165*ch*5*n*19

"Fembots in Las Vegas: Part I" (episode) 116–118, 127, 165*ch*6*n*10

"Fembots in Las Vegas: Part II" (episode) 116, 118, 123, 127–128, 140

The Feminine Mystique 43, 112

femininity 5, 43, 50–51, 63, 73, 80, 84–85, 91, 95, 100, 108, 111–112, 118, 122, 159*ch*1*n*5, 160*ch*1*n*6, 160*ch*1*n*8, 161*ch*2*n*11

feminism 1, 7, 8, 12, 13, 16, 19, 22, 29, 32, 37–40, 53, 62, 67, 75, 89–90, 102, 105, 110, 141, 147, 157; *see also* ethics; first-wave feminism; second-wave feminism

feminist ethics 1, 4, 8, 10–12, 20, 22, 33, 62, 65, 69, 82, 148, 157–158

femme fatale 78, 118

Ferguson, John "Scottie" (Hitchcock character) 87, 91, 93, 126

Fielding, Jerry 31, 162*ch*3*n*5

film noir 78, 95, 160*ch*1*n*5

first-wave feminism 8, 33–35

Fitzgerald, F. Scott 163*ch*4*n*22

"Fly Jaime" (episode) 32, 116

Folklore and Symbolism of Flowers 162*ch*2*n*14

For Colored Girls Who Considered Suicide When the Rainbow Is Enuf (play) 71–72

Forbes, Bryan: *The Stepford Wives* (film) 13, 101, 106, 132

Forbidden Planet (film) 132

Forman, Miloš: *One Flew Over the Cuckoo's Nest* (film) 152

Foucault, Michel: *The History of Sexuality* 55, 109, 162*ch*2*n*23, 164*ch*5*n*6

Frankenstein; or, The Modern Prometheus 15–16, 159*ch*1*n*1

173

Index

Franklin, Carl (character) 116–118, 123–124, 126, 128–131, 138, 140
Freeman, Mary: *T* E. Wilkins 160*ch*1*n*6
Freud, Sigmund: "Mourning and Melancholia" 146; "On Narcissism" 50, 162*ch*2*n*21
Friedan, Betty: *The Feminine Mystique* 43, 112
Friedkin, William: *The Exorcist* (film) 52, 54, 56, 58
Frontiers of Justice 8–10, 148, 159*n*4, 159*n*5, 159*n*6
Fuseli, Henry: *The Nightmare* (painting) 58
Futureworld (film) 101, 129, 132

Galloway, Lisa (character) 7–9, 47–51, 62, 64, 72, 74, 76–78, 80–96, 99, 105, 129, 140, 155; *see also* the bad other
Garland, Alex: *Ex Machina* (film) 13, 101, 137
"Gender Asymmetry and Erotic Triangles" 18, 74, 159*ch*1*n*2
gender role 25, 27, 32, 43, 57, 63, 101–102, 114, 125, 126, 139, 160*ch*1*n*8, 161*ch*2*n*10, 161*ch*2*n*11, 161*ch*2*n*12
"The Ghosthunter" (episode) 52, 56, 58, 59, 60, 166*ch*7*n*11
Girard, Rene: *Deceit, Desire, and the Novel* 18, 159*ch*1*n*2
Gledhill, Christine: *Home Is Where the Heart Is: Studies in Melodrama and the Woman's Film* 161*ch*2*n*3
Goldman, Oscar (character) 2, 15, 17–18, 21, 23–26, 30, 39, 40–43, 47–52, 60, 65–66, 73, 76, 78, 85, 93–96, 99, 102, 104, 108–110, 114–117, 124–126, 136, 142, 144; *see also* Anderson, Richard
Goodall, Jane 151
gothic 52, 54, 57–58
Gramsci, Antonio 162*ch*3*n*2
Greenaway, Peter: *The Pillow Book* (film) 121
Greven, David: *Queering the Terminator* 133, 159*n*2; *Representations of Femininity in American Genre Cinema: The Woman's Film, Film Noir, and Modern Horror* 28, 33, 159*ch*1*n*5, 162*ch*2*n*16, 163*ch*4*n*10
Grossman, Julie 78, 163*ch*4*n*9

HAL 9000 132, 134; *see also* Alex 7000; supercomputer
Hamlet 84, 99
Haraway, Donna: *The Companion Species Manifesto: Dogs, People, and Significant Otherness* 37, 114, 148, 150, 161*ch*2*n*6

Harnell, Joe 67, 85, 92, 120, 134, 162*ch*3*n*5, 163*ch*4*n*18
Hasse, Jurgen: "Traffic Architecture" 57, 162*ch*2*n*24
Hawthorne, Nathaniel: "The Birthmark" 55; "Rappaccini's Daughter" 55, 59
Haynes, Todd: *Superstar: The Karen Carpenter Story* (film) 82–83
"Heads in the Sand" objection 137–138
Hedren, Tippi 36, 38, 43, 87
Heffron, Richard T.: *Futureworld* (film) 101, 129, 132
The Heiress (film) 21, 87
Hippolyta 163*ch*3*n*6
The History of Sexuality 162*ch*2*n*23, 164*ch*5*n*6
Hitchcock, Alfred 12, 21, 34, 38, 43, 57, 79–80, 86–87, 90–94, 126, 132, 163*ch*4*n*27; *see also The Birds* (film); *Psycho* (film); *Vertigo* (film)
Hoffman, E.T.A.: "The Sandman" (story) 103
Hollywood 8, 11–12, 19, 27, 33, 38, 43–44, 58, 79, 91, 152, 159*ch*1*n*3, 159*ch*1*n*4, 161*ch*2*n*3, 162*ch*2*n*16, 163*ch*4*n*23; *see also* female melodrama; woman's film
Home Is Where the Heart Is: Studies in Melodrama and the Woman's Film 161*ch*2*n*3
Horrigan, Patrick E. 160*ch*1*n*10
horror (genre) 33, 45, 52, 58, 79, 160*ch*1*n*5, 163*ch*4*n*10, 165*ch*5*n*19
Houseman, John 5, 102, 110, 164*ch*5*n*8; *see also* Dr. Franklin
Howard, Ken 157
Hurst, Fannie: *Imitation of Life* (novel) 79
hysteria 55, 59, 87, 109, 124

"I Have No Mouth, and I Must Scream" (short story) 132
identity 5, 42–44, 51, 53, 59, 60, 73, 77–81, 84–85, 89–92, 98–99, 106, 113–114, 119, 121, 125–126, 149
"The Imitation Game" 137
Imitation of Life (film) 12, 34, 44, 79, 83
Imitation of Life (novel) 79
Incredible Hulk (series) 32, 103, 162*ch*3*n*5

"The Jailing of Jaime" (episode) 59, 68, 144
"Jaime's Mother" (episode) 12, 20–21, 38–47, 57, 72, 79, 97–99, 105
Jane Eyre (novel) 52–52
La Jetée (film) 86
Jewett, Sarah Orne: *The Country of the Pointed Firs* (novel) 8, 35, 37–38, 161*ch*2*n*4, 161*ch*2*n*5, 161*ch*2*n*7, 161*ch*2*n*10, 162*ch*2*n*14

Index

Joan of Arc 38, 161*ch*2*n*13
Joffe, Mike 85, 163*ch*4*n*18
Johnson, Kenneth 3, 9, 11–12, 15–16, 22, 25, 27, 29, 32, 52, 56, 59–60, 62–64, 69, 103, 132, 134, 139, 150, 158, 162*ch*3*n*5
Johnson, Nunnally: *The Three Faces of Eve* (film) 98
Jones, D.F.: *Colossus* (novel) 132

Kael, Pauline 163*ch*4*n*5
Kakoudaki, Despina: *Anatomy of a Robot* 114, 129, 133, 164*ch*5*n*12
"Kill Oscar" (episode) 101, 105, 107, 111–112, 116, 118–121, 124, 131, 138
"Kill Oscar: Part 1" (episode) 102–103, 108, 114
"Kill Oscar: Part 2" (episode) 102, 109, 112, 117
"Kill Oscar: Part 3" (episode) 102, 110
King, Stephen 52
Kubrick, Stanley: *2001: A Space Odyssey* (film) 129, 132, 134
Kulka, Tom 81, 163*ch*4*n*14
Kuzniar, Alice: *Melancholia's Dog: Reflections on Our Animal Kinship* 13, 149–150, 154
Kyler, Rod (character) 117, 123–124, 127–128

Lang, Fritz: *Metropolis* (film) 112
Lang, Robert: *American Film Melodrama* 21, 87, 160*ch*1*n*7, 163*ch*4*n*21
The Last Temptation of Christ (film) 122
Lehner, Ernst: *Folklore and Symbolism of Flowers* 162*ch*2*n*18
Lehner, Johanna: *Folklore and Symbolism of Flowers* 162*ch*2*n*18
lesbian 7, 13, 124–126, 159*n*1, 161*ch*2*n*3, 162*ch*2*n*14
Letter from an Unknown Woman (film) 21, 87
Levi, Alan J. 47, 75
Levi-Strauss, Claude: "The Principle of Reciprocity" 18, 159*ch*1*n*2
Levin, Ira: *The Stepford Wives* (novel) 101
like unlike 6, 64, 70, 99, 105–106, 130, 134, 147; *see also* the bad other; the doppelgänger; the double; mechaphobia
"The Lonely" (*The Twilight Zone* episode) 113

Magnificent Obsession (film) 44
Majors, Lee 1, 4, 16, 24–25, 32, 149, 160*ch*2*n*1
manbots 105, 112, 117, 120, 129–130
Mangels, Andy: *Wonder Woman '77 Meets the Bionic Woman* (comic) 4, 159*n*1

Marker, Chris: *La Jetée* (film) 86
marriage 20–21, 25, 28, 34, 36, 44, 45, 60, 83, 160*ch*1*n*6
marriage plot 11, 29, 34
Marshall, Noel: *Roar* (film) 39
masculinity 26, 36, 57, 63, 65, 15, 160*ch*1*n*8, 161*ch*2*n*12, 164*ch*5*n*16
masquerade 5, 50, 76, 80, 87, 92, 127; *see also* appearance; costume
Max (dog) 10, 13, 37, 145, 151–154
McKee, Alison L. 23, 160*ch*1*n*8
mechaphobia 6, 13, 106, 111, 120, 130–131, 146; *see also* the bad other; doppelgänger; the double; like unlike
Medusa myth 13, 64, 104
Melancholia's Dog: Reflections on Our Animal Kinship 13, 149, 154
"Melancholy Gender/Refused Identification" (essay) 89
memory 3, 15, 24–30, 40, 42, 45, 63, 71, 84, 88, 90, 96, 99, 118
Metropolis (film) 112
Michie, Helena 107, 164*ch*5*n*7
Milburn, Sue: *The Child Stealer* (film) 35, 38
Mildred Pierce (film) 44, 79, 87
Minghella, Anthony: *The Talented Mr. Ripley* (film) 90
"Mirror Image" (*The Bionic Woman*) 7, 12, 47–51, 72–73, 76, 81–82, 85, 89, 92, 163*ch*4*n*15
"Mirror Image" (*The Twilight Zone*) 73–74
misogyny 17, 54, 78, 110, 115, 118, 121, 124, 130, 139, 151, 164*ch*5*n*16; *see also* patriarchy; sexism
Moder, Richard 16, 22
Modleski, Tania 92
Moore, Ron: *Battlestar Galactica* (series) 13, 101, 113
Morrison, Toni: *Playing in the Dark* 162*ch*3*n*4
mother-daughter relationship 34, 44–45, 52, 58, 79, 94, 96, 108, 160*ch*1*n*5, 160*ch*1*n*10, 162*ch*2*n*16, 163*ch*3*n*6
motherhood 2, 11, 12, 20, 34, 40, 43–45, 47, 71, 79–80, 96, 140
"Motorcycle Boogie" (episode) 158
"Mourning and Melancholia" 149
Mulvey, Laura: "Visual Pleasure and Narrative Cinema" 86, 89, 126, 163*ch*4*n*19

National Security Bureau (NSB) 103, 108, 142
nature 35, 38, 39, 55, 64, 152, 160*ch*1*n*6, 161*ch*2*n*12, 164*ch*5*n*9; *see also* bond; nonhuman animal

175

Index

NBC network 4, 21, 115, 128, 149, 151, 166*epilogue*1
Neame, Ronald: *Widescreen Dreams of The Poseidon Adventure* 160*ch*1*n*10
Negra, Diane: *What a Girl Wants?* 27, 160*ch*1*n*9
Nichols, Mike: *Silkwood* (film) 110
The Nightmare (painting) 58
nineteenth-century American woman's fiction 33–35, 37, 160*ch*1*n*5
nonhuman animal 9–13, 33, 35, 37, 39, 41, 57, 62–65, 87, 133, 148–149, 150, 155, 161*ch*2*n*8, 161*ch*2*n*10, 161*ch*2*n*12, 162*ch*3*n*3; *see also* bond; dogs
North by Northwest (film) 43
Now, Voyager (film) 21, 27–28, 34, 39, 44, 58, 79, 87, 94, 98, 152
Nussbaum, Martha: *Frontiers of Justice* 8–10, 148, 159*n*4, 159*n*5, 159*n*6

Oedipus complex 90, 163*ch*4*n*25
Office of Scientific Intelligence (OSI) 2, 7, 8, 10, 13–15, 17, 21, 27, 32, 47, 49, 52, 68, 76, 82–85, 93, 95–99, 117–118, 141
Ojai, California 2, 15–16, 25, 27, 29–30, 32, 36, 40, 77, 96, 153
The Omen (film) 52
"On Narcissism" 50, 162*ch*2*n*21
"On the Run" (episode) 13, 18–19, 86, 103, 113, 115–116, 119, 131, 141, 143–147, 151, 165*ch*6*n*10
One Flew Over the Cuckoo's Nest (film) 152
onlyness 59, 60, 72
Ophuls, Max: *Letter from an Unknown Woman* (film) 21, 87
"Out of Body" (episode) 158
The Outer Limits (series) 132

Pakula, Alan J.: *The Parallax View* (film) 59
Pandora's Box: Women in Classical Greece 38, 161*ch*2*n*12
The Parallax View (film) 59
Paranormal America 62, 162*ch*3*n*1
Parriott, James D. 47, 75, 76, 150, 158
Passing: Identity and Interpretation in Sexuality, Race, and Religion 80
The Passion of Joan of Arc (film) 161*ch*2*n*13
patriarchy 18, 38, 43, 48, 55, 65, 89, 101–102, 107, 110, 114, 120, 123, 160*ch*1*n*6; *see also* misogynist; sexism
Peele, Jordan: *Us* (film) 73–74
personhood 111, 129, 136–140, 143–145, 152, 154
Petrie, Daniel: *Sybil* (film) 98
The Pillow Book (film) 121
Pit's Letter 149, 154

Playing in the Dark 162*ch*3*n*4
Pollack, Sydney: *The Way We Were* (film) 79
"The Power of Otherness: Animals in Women's Fiction" 37, 148, 161*ch*2*n*8, 161*ch*2*n*9
"The Principle of Reciprocity" 18, 159*ch*1*n*2
"Prism" (episode) 86
Psycho (film) 57, 73, 87, 132; *see also* Hitchcock, Alfred
"The Pyramid" (episode) 116

queer 1, 5, 7–9, 12–13, 28, 38, 40, 49, 59, 60, 71, 74–75, 80, 89–90, 102, 124, 144, 159*n*1, 159*n*2, 161*ch*2*n*14, 163*ch*4*n*22, 163*ch*4*n*26, 163*ch*4*n*27, 165*ch*6*n*11
Queering the Terminator 133, 159*n*2

race relations 5, 28, 43, 54, 65, 72–73, 79, 80–82, 93, 121, 128, 133, 157, 161*ch*2*n*10, 162*ch*3*n*4, 163*ch*4*n*11, 163*ch*4*n*15
Rainey, Ford 2, 35, 77, 151; *see also* Elgin, Jim
Random Harvest (film) 23, 160*ch*1*n*8
Rank, Otto 74, 163*ch*4*n*5
Rapper, Irving: *Now, Voyager* (film) 21, 27–28, 34, 39, 44, 58, 79, 87, 94, 98, 152
Ray, Robert: *A Certain Tendency of the Hollywood Cinema* 160*ch*1*n*5, 161*ch*2*n*2
Reeder, Ellen: *Pandora's Box: Women in Classical Greece* 38, 161*ch*2*n*12
Representations of Femininity in American Genre Cinema: The Woman's Film, Film Noir, and Modern Horror 28, 33, 159*ch*1*n*5, 162*ch*2*n*16, 164*ch*4*n*10
repulsion of like for like 6–7, 46
"The Return of Bigfoot: Part I" (episode) 12, 62, 64, 66, 70
"The Return of Bigfoot: Part II" (episode) 12, 20, 64, 162*ch*3*n*5
"The Return of the Bionic Woman, Part I" (episode) 3, 15, 22, 23, 25, 26, 30, 55, 67, 115
"The Return of the Bionic Woman, Part II" (episode) 67
Rhys, Jean: *Wide Sargasso Sea* (novel) 54
Riviere, Joan 5, 50
Roar (film) 39
romance 23–24, 30, 45, 60, 79, 123, 158, 166*epiloge*1
Rowe, Arthur 39, 44, 102, 116
Rubin, Gayle: "The Traffic in Women: Notes on the 'Political Economy' of Sex" 18, 159*ch*1*n*2

176

Index

Rush, Barbara 38, 41, 43, 79; *see also* Stuart, Chris

Safe (film) 82
Salem Witch Trials 52, 53, 57
Sanchez, Maria C.: *Passing: Identity and Interpretation in Sexuality, Race, and Religion* 80
"Sanctuary Earth" (episode) 166*ch*7*n*11
"The Sandman" (story) 103
Sarah Orne Jewett: Her World and Her Work 37, 161*ch*2*n*7
Sargent, Joseph: *Colossus: The Forbin Project* (film) 132
Sasquatch 12, 62–65, 67–70, 162*ch*3*n*2, 162*ch*3*n*3; *see also* Bigfoot
Schlossberg, Linda: *Passing: Identity and Interpretation in Sexuality, Race, and Religion* 80
Scholtmeijer, Marian: "The Power of Otherness: Animals in Women's Fiction" 37, 148, 161*ch*2*n*8, 161*ch*2*n*9
Schwenger, Peter 121
science-fiction 1, 20, 32–34, 45, 63, 68, 70, 86, 112, 118, 124, 129, 132, 137, 152, 160*ch*1*n*5, 165*ch*5*n*17
Scorsese, Martin: *Alice Doesn't Live Here Anymore* (film) 27, 79; *The Last Temptation of Christ* (film) 122
Scott, Martha 2, 29, 35, 38, 43, 44, 77, 79, 160*ch*1*n*10; *see also* Elgin, Helen
Scott, Ridley: *Alien* (film) 33, 137, 165*ch*6*n*5; *Blade Runner* (film) 114
second-wave feminism 7, 8, 25, 35, 43, 112
"The Secret of Bigfoot, Part 1" (episode) 62
"The Secret of Bigfoot, Part 2" (episode) 62
Sedgwick, Eve Kosofsky: "Gender Asymmetry and Erotic Triangles" 18, 74, 159*ch*1*n*2
Segrest, Mab 90, 163*ch*4*n*26
self-shattering 13, 131, 145, 165*ch*6*n*11
Serling, Rod: "The Lonely" (episode) 113; "Mirror Image" (episode) 73–74; *The Twilight Zone* (series) 92
sexism 17–18, 22, 35, 37, 41, 43, 51, 76, 110, 124–125; *see also* misogynist; patriarchy
sexuality 21–26, 29–30, 34, 36, 38, 45–46, 50, 55, 60, 80, 83, 89–90, 117, 122, 126, 161*ch*2*n*11, 161*ch*2*n*12, 163*ch*4*n*25, 163*ch*4*n*27, 166*epilogue*1
Shange, Ntozake: *For Colored Girls Who Considered Suicide When the Rainbow Is Enuf* (play) 71–72
The Shape of Water (film) 70

Shelley, Mary: *Frankenstein; or, The Modern Prometheus* 15–16, 159*ch*1*n*1
Short, Sue 102, 164*ch*5*n*1
Silence of the Lambs (film) 45
Silkwood (film) 110
Silverman, Kaja: *The Threshold of the Visible World* 51, 162*ch*2*n*22, 164*ch*5*n*14
Singer, Peter: *Animal Liberation: A New Ethics for Our Treatment of Animals* 151
Sirk, Douglass: *All That Heaven Allows* (film) 34, 83; *Imitation of Life* (film) 12, 34, 44, 79, 83; *Magnificent Obsession* (film) 12, 34, 44, 80–87, 161*ch*2*n*3
The Six Million Dollar Man (series) 1, 9, 11–12, 15–17, 21–22, 28, 32, 39, 40, 42, 47, 55, 62–64, 78, 84, 97, 101–102, 107, 109, 116–117, 141, 143, 149–150
social class 8, 12, 21, 28, 72–73, 78, 79–81, 84, 88, 90, 160*ch*1*n*6, 163*ch*4*n*14
"Soldier" (*The Outer Limits* episode) 132
Sommers, Ann 40, 44, 46
sororophobia 107, 145, 164*ch*5*n*7
The Sound of Music (film) 52
Spielberg, Steven: *A.I. Artificial Intelligence* (film) 129
The Stanford Encyclopedia of Philosophy 137
Star Trek: Discovery 162*ch*3*n*3
Star Trek: Nemesis 162*ch*2*n*19
Star Trek VI: The Undiscovered Country (film) 48
Star Trek: Voyager 113, 162*ch*2*n*19
Stella Dallas (film) 44
Stepford wife (noun) 9, 71
The Stepford Wives (film) 13, 101, 106, 132
The Stepford Wives (novel) 101
Stevens, Sally: "Time Changes" (song) 85, 94, 100
The Stranger Within (film) 143
The Stranger's Return (film) 27
Stuart, Chris 21, 41, 43, 44, 45, 46, 99, 105, 140, 155; *see also* Rush, Barbara
supercomputer 7, 105, 132–135, 139; *see also* Alex 7000; HAL 9000
supernatural 52, 55
Superstar: The Karen Carpenter Story (film) 82
"Supertoys Last All Summer Long" (short story) 129
Sybil (film) 98

The Talented Mr. Ripley (film) 90
Tarnation (film) 9, 71, 72, 163*ch*4*n*1
Taurog, Norman: *Dr. Goldfoot and the Girl Bombs* 112
Technophobia!: Science Fiction Visions of Posthuman Technology 129

177

Index

telekinesis 54, 56, 59
tennis 2, 15–16, 20, 40, 60, 146
The Terminator (film) 127, 132, 133, 165*ch*6*n*8
This Is Kate Bennett... (film) 36
The Three Faces of Eve (film) 98
The Threshold of the Visible World 51, 162*ch*2*n*22, 164*ch*5*n*14
"Time Changes" (song) 85, 94, 100
Tracing Arachne's Web: Myth and Feminist Fiction 161*ch*2*n*4
"Traffic Architecture" 57, 162*ch*2*n*24
"The Traffic in Women: Notes on the 'Political Economy' of Sex" 18, 159*ch*1*n*2
trauma 3, 9, 22, 26, 30, 42, 55, 66, 71, 88, 97–98, 119, 133, 152–154, 164*ch*5*n*13
Turing, Alan: "The Imitation Game" 137, 139
Two People (film) 52
2001: A Space Odyssey (film) 132, 134

Uninvited: Classical Hollywood Cinema and Lesbian Representability 161*ch*2*n*3
United States Government 18–19, 48–49, 102, 115, 142–144, 165*ch*6*n*10
Us (film) 73, 74
utopia 9, 11, 114, 133–134, 141, 147, 152

Vale, Charlotte 28, 39, 58, 94, 152
Vardoulakis, Dimitris 48, 72, 162*ch*2*n*20, 163*ch*4*n*1, 163*ch*4*n*2
"The Vega Influence" (episode) 10, 56, 166*ch*7*n*11
Ventura Air Force Base 15, 29
Venus in Furs (film) 123
Vertigo (film) 12, 79, 80, 85–90, 92–93, 126, 163*ch*4*n*19; see also Hitchcock, Alfred
Vidor, King: *Beyond the Forest* (film) 21, 27, 87
"Visual Pleasure and Narrative Cinema" 86, 89, 126, 163*ch*4*n*19
von Sacher-Masoch, Leopold: *Venus in Furs* (film) 123

Wagner, Lindsay 2, 4, 9, 11–12, 17, 24, 26, 28–30, 32, 38, 42–43, 47, 52, 60, 68–69, 71, 76–78, 84, 86–87, 93–94, 96–98, 100, 104, 108, 116, 118–119, 134, 141, 143, 145–146, 149–150, 160*ch*1*n*10, 160*ch*2*n*1, 164*ch*5*n*8, 166*ch*7*n*10
Wait Until Dark (film) 58
Waldo, Charles 92, 94–95
The Way We Were (film) 79

"Welcome Home, Jaime, Part 1" (episode) 4, 11, 15, 23, 25, 27–28, 40, 42, 59, 60, 96
"Welcome Home, Jaime, Part 2" (episode) 27, 30, 59
Wells, Rudy 2, 3, 13, 17, 21, 26–29, 39, 42, 63, 65, 68, 76–78, 85, 93, 95–96, 102, 109, 114, 121, 135, 145, 151, 153; see also Martin E. Brooks
Westworld (film) 101
Westworld (series) 13, 101, 123, 129, 132
Whale, James: *The Bride of Frankenstein* (film) 5, 112
What a Girl Wants? 27, 160*ch*1*n*9
"What Are Little Girls Made Of?" (*Star Trek* episode) 165*ch*5*n*19
White, Patricia: *Uninvited: Classical Hollywood Cinema and Lesbian Representability* 161*ch*2*n*3
Wide Sargasso Sea (novel) 54
Widescreen Dreams of The Poseidon Adventure 160*ch*1*n*10
Wilcox, Fred M.: *Forbidden Planet* (film) 132
Wilson, Elizabeth A.: *Affect and Artificial Intelligence* 139–140
"Winning Is Everything" (episode) 32
Wise, Robert: *The Day the Earth Stood Still* (film) 132; *The Sound of Music* (film) 52; *Two People* (film) 52
woman's film 8, 11–12, 19–21, 23, 27, 33–34, 39, 44, 79–80, 82, 85–86, 88, 94, 98, 152, 160*ch*1*n*5, 160*ch*1*n*8, 161*ch*2*n*3, 162*ch*2*n*16, 163*ch*4*n*10; see also female melodrama; Hollywood
woman's film directors 86–87
A Woman's View: How Hollywood Spoke to Women 19, 86, 159*ch*1*n*3, 159*ch*1*n*4, 161*ch*2*n*3, 163*ch*4*n*20
Women Without Class: Girls, Race, and Identity 80, 163*ch*4*n*12
Wonder Woman (character) 4, 41, 78, 159*n*1, 163*ch*3*n*6
Wonder Woman '77 Meets the Bionic Woman (comic) 159*n*1
Wosk, Janice 103, 164*ch*5*n*2
www.bionicblonde.com 92, 95, 164*ch*4*n*29, 164*ch*4*n*30
Wyler, William: *The Heiress* (film) 21, 87

Young, Terence: *Wait Until Dark* (film) 58

Žižek, Slavoj 74, 163*ch*4*n*4

www.ingramcontent.com/pod-product-compliance
Lightning Source LLC
Chambersburg PA
CBHW032047300426
44117CB00009B/1219